IMMIGRATION,

Henry Flegenheim Esq
54 Leonard Str

AND THE

COMMISSIONERS OF EMIGRATION

OF THE

State of New York.

BY

FRIEDRICH KAPP,

ONE OF THE SAID COMMISSIONERS.

NEW YORK:
THE NATION PRESS, 27 ROSE STREET.

1870.

G. C. Verplanck

President.

Appointed Commissioner of Emigration May 5th 1847.
Elected President of the Board March 1st 1848.

IMMIGRATION,

AND THE

COMMISSIONERS OF EMIGRATION

OF THE

State of New York.

BY

FRIEDRICH KAPP,

ONE OF THE SAID COMMISSIONERS.

NEW YORK:
THE NATION PRESS, 27 ROSE STREET.

1870.

TO LEOPOLD BIERWIRTH, ESQ.

In public and private life, you have, for more than forty years in this your adopted country, labored to promote the welfare of this community, and to benefit humanity at large.

It was your good fortune to assist in suggesting and initiating the reforms which are treated of in the following pages. It was your privilege to be instrumental in inaugurating the new era, signalled by the formation of the Board of the Commissioners of Emigration. Of this body you were a highly honored member during the first two years of its existence, setting as such an example worthy of emulation by your successors. Although you withdrew a long time ago from active participation in their official duties, you have continued to work with undiminished zeal and energy in furtherance of the interests of which they are the custodians.

In view of this, and as an expression of my respect and friendship, I dedicate to you this essay.

FRIEDRICH KAPP.

New York, February, 1870.

PREFACE.

Having resided for the past twenty years at the greatest immigrant port in the world, and having been led by my official duties during a portion of this time to pay particular attention to the subject of emigration, I have been induced to enter into a somewhat extended study of this important question. The result of my researches is now laid before the public.

A great deal has been written about emigration, its causes, aims, and results, but, with a very few exceptions, the writers on this subject have dwelt more upon their own theories and conjectures than upon facts and events. In the physical world, it is manifestly impossible to build a house without having laid a foundation; yet, in the intellectual world, people too often reason and philosophize upon political and social questions without having made that careful investigation of facts which is the only sure foundation of accurate reasoning.

The present essay on immigration is chiefly confined to the narration of facts, and it is only here and there that I have given the conclusions which have seemed to me to be their natural result. Parts of it have already been laid before the public in a paper read in this city, on the 27th of October, 1869, before the American Social Science Association.

The emigration of European masses to this country is still in its infancy, and yet it is very difficult, if not impossible, to collect and preserve the materials relating to it. If I have succeeded in saving any which without my researches might, perhaps, have perished, I have accomplished my purpose. I trust that they may facilitate for the future historian the study and appreciation of this interesting subject.

Strange as it may seem, the youngest nation that has made its appearance on the historical stage is singularly deficient in that historical spirit which characterizes true civilization. Germany, France, England, and Italy are laboring more earnestly for the preservation of the records of their barbarism than the United States for the illustration of its unbroken record of civilization. How can this lack of interest be explained? Is it that the task of the hour makes Americans blind to all things else? Is it that so much is still to be done that no time is left for the consideration of what has been done? Be it as it may, it is a melancholy fact and seriously detrimental to the most vital interests of the nation. People look with indifference at this colossal immigration of the European masses, whose presence alone will exercise a powerful influence on the destinies of the Western World; National and State legislators care little or nothing for the direction which is given to this foreign element, and forget that their own welfare and the welfare of their children is indissolubly interwoven with the condition of the new-comers. In short, they are not yet aroused to the great importance of emigration, of its laws and its development, but consider it rather with an incredulous curiosity than with an earnest desire to fathom its resources and foresee its results.

My principal sources of information have been the minutes and the annual reports of the Commissioners of Emigration, which, wherever it was possible, I have quoted in their own language; the proceedings of the Common Council of New York City, the reports of the Comptrollers of this city, and the papers and official acts of the United States Senate and of the State Legislature at Albany. I have not given my authorities, as I cannot suppose that they are accessible to any of my readers, but the correctness of the statements is susceptible of verification, and may be implicitly relied upon.

I gratefully acknowledge the important services rendered me by Mr. Bernard Casserly, the efficient General Agent of the Commissioners of Emigration, who is familiar with all the minutiæ of the service, and the history of the Board for which he has labored ever since its creation with intelligence and zeal. I am also under special obligations to Mr. Andrew Carrigan and Mr. Thurlow Weed for the very interesting information contained in Chapter V. Mr. Weed, although confined to his chamber by illness, assisted me with his valuable advice, and gave me important information concerning the origin of the Commission.

I am likewise indebted to my friends, Mr. Henry Villard, of Boston, the able Secretary of the American Social Science Association, and Mr. Thomas Burke, of this city, for the revision of my manuscript; to Mr. Charles Goepp for the greater part of Chapter IX., and to several officers of the Commissioners of Emigration, among whom I would name Mr. George W. Wheeler, Col. L. Cantador, Mr. A. H. Hicks, and Dr. A. Reimer, for the readiness with which they have supplied me with copies of important tables and other necessary documents.

FRIEDRICH KAPP.

6 MANSFIELD PLACE, NEW YORK,
February 24, 1870.

CONTENTS.

IMMIGRATION TO NEW YORK.

CHAPTER I.

HISTORICAL INTRODUCTION — LAW OF EMIGRATION — THE UNITED STATES THE FAVORITE LAND OF THE EMIGRANT.

Causes of Emigration.

FROM the remotest ages down to the present day, from the first Phœnician and Greek colonies down to the settlement of the North Pacific coast, two principal causes have always induced emigration and led to the establishment of new states and empires, viz., political or religious oppression and persecution, and social evils, such as want of prosperity or insecurity, lack of employment, famine, and high prices of living in general. In modern times, either of these causes has proved powerful enough to produce emigration on a large scale from certain countries. People who are happy and comfortable at home do not emigrate; the poor and oppressed only, who cannot find a fair reward for their labor in the land of their birth, or who feel themselves obstructed and thwarted in their religious or political aspirations, seek to better their condition by a change of country.

Development of the United States due to Emigration.

The territory which constitutes the present United States owes its wonderful development mainly to the conflux of the poor and outcast of Europe within it. The adventurers who discovered and first settled it belonged to the feudal aristocracy of Europe. Being neither able nor willing to work, they failed and perished, and gave way to the so-called lower classes of society—to the sturdy farmer and the industrious mechanic. Feeble as their efforts were in the beginning, the toils and sufferings, the patience and perseverance of these voluntary and involuntary exiles have, in a comparatively short time, built up a powerful commonwealth, the proud structure of this Republic, which in itself is the glorification, the epopee of free and intelligent labor.

Scanty immigration previous to 19th century

The immigration of Europeans in large masses into America, however, is of a more recent date, an outgrowth of the nineteenth century. It is true, in earlier periods, immigrants also found their way to the European possessions in the New World, but their number at any given time was comparatively small. There arrived during the whole year, in all the American colonies, hardly as many as land now on one summer day in the city of New York alone. During the first century of the settlement of the country by the English and the Dutch, a few hundred new immigrants attracted the public attention of the whole colony, and towards the end of the last century the arrival of two ships laden with Germans, on one day, created quite a sensation in New York.

Reasons therefor.

The reasons for this numerical difference are obvious. Communication between Europe and America was in its infancy. During the favorable season of the year, a vessel now and then sailed from an English, Dutch, or French port for America. No Continental country had any intercourse with the then English colonies except by way of England. The trips required seldom less than eight weeks. Their regular time was from three to four months, but very often the passage occupied six months and more. On the other hand, the horizon of the European masses did not extend beyond their native village and its immediate neighborhood. The great majority of the people were too poor, too degraded even to conceive the idea of throwing off their shackles, of trying, at least, to run away from their misery to the New World. The two countries, which were then, as they are now, the principal sources of emigration, viz., Germany and Ireland, furnished a small number only. In South-western Germany, emigration on a large scale commenced in the beginning of the eighteenth century, in consequence of wars, famine, and religious persecutions; but, during the whole century, only from 80,000 to 100,000 Germans settled in America. Ireland did not send forth as many tens as it does now thousands.

This essay will be confined to the port of New York, and, when the contrary is not expressly stated, it treats of immigration in connection with New York only.

Commercial pre-eminence of New York, and its origin.

The present metropolis of American commerce, although one of the oldest cities built by European emigrants, had become more than two hundred years old before she assumed the leading part in the trade of the country. According to the first census, taken in 1790, the State of New York was the fifth in population, and ranked even after Massachusetts and North Carolina. In 1800, it rose to the third; 1810, to the second, and only in 1820 to the first position, which it has since maintained. The city of New York kept even pace with the State. During the first ten years of the present century, she was inferior to Philadelphia, the then largest city in the United States, in population and commerce. In 1820, she numbered, for the first time, a few thousand inhabitants more than the Quaker City; but, in the decade of 1820 to 1830, she established her superiority beyond any doubt.

The Erie Canal.

The noble work of her great statesman, De Witt Clinton, viz., the connection of the Atlantic with the great lakes by a canal, carried out between 1817 and 1825, proved the firm basis on which New York City built her all-controlling influence and power, always steadily advancing and never receding, and to-day mightier than ever before. Had there been no De Witt Clinton, had there been no Erie Canal, in vain would have been the central position and commercial advantages of this city. She was not the first city of America until her great men gave artificial extension and development to those advantages, and thereby fixed on her, for centuries, the honored advantage of being the emporium of the Western World. If she is to maintain this position, she will do it because she will have great men continually able to keep her in advance. As she has seized the canal, telegraph, and railroad and pressed them into her services, so she must be ready, as new inventions are presented, to seize them and turn them to her advantage. Prior to the completion of the Erie Canal, New York had but a small number, if any, of staple articles which she could export. Even ten years expired after that event before she could compete with the other harbors of the Eastern coast. Charleston had her cotton, rice, and indigo, for which European vessels preferred her port; Baltimore was the centre of the tobacco trade for Maryland, Virginia, and Ohio; Philadelphia monopolized the greater portion of the coasting business; but New York had first to build up her export trade. The interior was not sufficiently developed to offer commodities for European markets; even wheat, which forms in our days one of the most important export staples, was imported from the Baltic and Portugal as late as the years 1836 to 1838. About 1830, New York commenced with the export of whale oil, which the whalers brought to New Bedford, Sag Harbor, and smaller ports, where it was purchased by New York merchants for shipment to Europe. Tobacco soon followed, which was sent to New York from the interior, and, in consequence of the Tobacco Inspection established in 1834, could be assorted and purchased here just as well as in Baltimore and Richmond. Every subsequent year added a new article of export. Philadelphia, once paramount to New York, did not follow the latter in the path of progress, and European merchants became every year more satisfied that they would find at all times ready return freights from New York, and for this reason they preferred it before all other Atlantic ports. Thus, with her daily growing commerce, with her better facilities for shipping and freighting, and with her better inland communications, she naturally attracted more emigrants than any other port of the Union, and entered upon the second third of the present century as the great receiving depot of European immigration.

Exports.

Immigration in 17th and 18th centuries, under Dutch and English rule.

The facts connected with the immigration of the seventeenth and eighteenth centuries are only imperfectly known to us, and have almost exclusively an historical interest for the present generation. They can be explained in a few short paragraphs.

Under the Dutch rule (1625–1664) emigrants were attracted by land grants and other substantial inducements. At times they obtained a free passage; at other times they had to pay the small charge of one shilling per day. A ship or two per year carried all the reinforcements and supplies to the colony. During that whole period immigration did not exceed a few thousand.

The English Colonial Government did little or nothing for the encouragement of European immigration to New York.

The first and only attempt it ever made at settling emigrants was carried out in 1709 and 1710, when, out of about 15,000 Protestant Swabians and Palatines, it sent at its own expense about 3,000 to New York. These poor people, as stated above, were driven from their homes by war, famine, and religious persecution, and now threw themselves in endless numbers upon the sympathies of England. While others of these exiles were sent to Ireland and North Carolina, Governor Hunter settled the above 3,000 on the Hudson River, where he proposed to employ them in making naval stores. But the experiment failed in consequence of the narrow-mindedness of the colonial officers, the sharp practices of a Scotch speculator, and of the misapprehension of the conditions of an emigrant's success—first among which is freedom of action and of movement. The English Government wanted subjects and servants; the emigrants wanted to become free and independent. Hence first the irrepressible conflict, and finally the victory of the immigrants.

Colonization of 3,000 Palatine exiles on Hudson River.

All who thenceforth emigrated came on their own account. Thus the Scotch, under Captain Campbell, who settled near Lake George (1740); the Baden farmers, who, in the middle of the eighteenth century, founded New Durlach, the present Sharon in Schoharie County; thus the Germans, who settled in the Mohawk Valley, and the immigrants who were imported in 1793 and 1794 by the Genesee Association. During the whole of the last century, the immigration of from eighty to one hundred families, in a body, was an event of great and general interest. The ships, which arrived at intervals, seldom had more than a hundred or one hundred and fifty passengers on board. New York had only a secondary importance, and attracted fewer immigrants than Pennsylvania, because they were better treated in the Quaker State. For this reason, Philadelphia had regular communications with Holland and England, and, as an immigrant port, ranked far above New York.

Scotch and German immigrants to Central New York

But in Philadelphia, as well as in New York, the great majority of immigrants were very poor people, so poor that they could not pay their passage, and in order to meet the obligations incurred by them for passage-money and other advances, they were sold, after their arrival, into temporary servitude. During all the

Sale of Immigrants for passage money.

last century, the prepayment of the passage was the exception, and its subsequent discharge by compulsory labor the rule. The ship owners and ship merchants derived enormous profits from the sale of the bodies of emigrants, as they charged very high rates for the passage, to which they added a heavy percentage—often more than a hundred per cent.—for their risks. But the emigrants suffered bitterly from this traffic in human flesh. Old people, widows, and cripples would not sell well, while healthy parents with healthy children, and young people of both sexes, always found a ready market. If the parents were too old to work, their children had to serve so much longer to make up the difference. When one or both parents died on the voyage, their children had to serve for them. The expenses for the whole family were summed up and charged upon the survivor or survivors. Adults had to serve from three to six years, children from ten to fifteen years, till they became of age; smaller children were, without charge, surrendered to masters, who had to raise and board them. As all servants signed in-

"Indented servants."

dentures, they were called "indented servants." Whenever a vessel arrived at Philadelphia or New York, its passengers were offered at public sale. The ship was the market-place, and the servants were struck off to the highest bidder. The country people either came themselves or sent agents or friends to procure what they wanted, be it a girl or a "likely" boy, or an old housekeeper, or a whole family. Among the records of this traffic there is a characteristic anecdote about the wife of Sir

Sir William Johnson and his German wife.

William Johnson, the Indian agent, and most prominent man of Western New York, in the middle of the eighteenth century. Catharine Weisenberg had arrived in New York a poor German orphan girl, and had been sold as an indented servant to two brothers, Alexander and Herman Philipps, farmers in the Mohawk Valley. Catharine soon became the belle of the settlement, and was courted by a great many swains; but none of them was rich enough to buy her. Johnson, when passing by, saw her, and at once resolved to make her his wife. He offered one of the Philippses five pounds, threatening at the same time to give him a sound thrashing if he did not voluntarily part with the girl. Philipps knew that Johnson was the man to make good his word, took the five pounds, and sold Catharine to Johnson, who married her at once. The match turned out excellent.

"Robust farmers and sturdy mechanics," says D. von Buelow, the celebrated military writer, who first visited the United States in 1791, "find a very easy market. At times, however, an unsalable article creeps in which remains for a long time on the shelf. The worst of these articles are military officers and scholars. The captain who imports that kind of goods does not know the market. I have seen a Russian captain for more than a week on board of a vessel, heavy as ballast, without being able to obtain a purchaser. He was, in fact, unsalable. The captain of the vessel entreated him to try, at least, to find a purchaser, and, in order to get rid of him, he offered to sell him at a discount of fifty per cent. He sent the captain on shore to make the people take a fancy to him; but it was of no avail, nobody had a mind to buy him. The Russian always spoke of stabbing with bayonets, which, he said, he had often practised against the Turks and Poles. Strictly speaking, the use of the bayonet was the only art he had mastered. Finally, the captain and consignee released him upon his promise to pay his passage after six months, and flattered him with the hope of obtaining a schoolmastership in the country. He really obtained it. What he will teach the boys and girls I do not know, unless it be the bayonet exercise."

D. von Buelow on the Emigrant Market.

The unsalable Russian.

Peasants and mechanics generally got along tolerably well. Much, of course, depended on the character of the master. There are instances of immigrants having been treated worse than cattle, and driven to work with blows and kicks, so that the colonial authorities had to interfere. The better educated a man was, the more he had learned at home, the worse it was for him. Hard drinking and suicide were often the fate of the unfortunates of this class. Parents sold their children, in order to remain free themselves. When a young man or a girl had an opportunity to get married, they had to pay their master five or six pounds for each year they had still to serve. Yet a steerage passage never cost more than ten pounds. Run-away servants had to serve one week for each day, one month for each

Hardships of early immigrants.

week, and six months for each month of absence. If the master did not want to keep his servant, he could sell him for the unexpired time of his term of servitude. It was a daily occurrence that whole families were separated for ever. In short, the whole system was utterly vicious and little better than slavery. It was only slavery for a term of years, but in all other respects just as cruel and iniquitous as that form of bondage.

Immigrant slavery abolished in 1819.

This mode of making the immigrant pay his passage died out in the beginning of the nineteenth century. The last sales of passengers are reported in 1818 and 1819 in Philadelphia. We do not hear of indented servants after 1819, when immigration began to consist of a much better and well-to-do class of people, and the United States first intervened in behalf of this important economic interest.

Estimated immigration from 1775 to 1815.

From 1775 till 1815 immigration had been very slim, partly on account of the American Revolution, and partly on account of the wars ending with the overthrow of Napoleon I. In 1818, Dr. Adam Seybert, member of the House of Representatives from Pennsylvania, in his valuable "Statistical Annals of the United States" (pp. 28 and 29), wrote to the following effect: "Though we admit that ten thousand foreigners may have arrived in the United States in 1794, we cannot allow that an equal number arrived in any preceding or subsequent year, until 1817." Samuel Blodget, a very accurate statistician, wrote, in 1806, that, from the best records and estimates then attainable, the immigrants arriving between 1784 and 1794 did not average more than 4,000 per annum. Seybert assumes that 6,000 persons arrived in the United States from foreign countries in each year from 1790 to 1810. Both averages, however, seem to be too large; 3,000 for the first, 4,000 for the second period named is a very liberal estimate.

Immigration after Napoleonic wars.

The difficulty experienced in disposing of property at satisfactory prices prevented many from leaving the Old World immediately after the close of the Napoleonic wars. But the great famine of 1816 and 1817 drove several thousands over the ocean. Here it may be stated that, from that time forward, the material and moral causes of immigration, above alluded to, regularly governed the numerical proportions of the influx of Europeans into the

United States in successive years. To prove the controlling influence exercised over immigration by material misery, on the one hand, and political oppression, on the other, a few statistical data will suffice.

Social and political causes influencing Irish and German immigration.

While, in 1826, of 10,837 immigrants 7,709 came from the United Kingdom, in 1827 their number increased to 11,952 out of 18,875, and in 1828 to 17,840 of a total of 27,283; but in 1829 their number fell to 10,594 of 22,530, and in 1830 to 3,874 of 23,322 souls. These fluctuations were due to the great commercial panic of 1826, and the distress in the manufacturing districts of England, as well as the famine in Ireland, which drove thousands from their homes who, under ordinary circumstances, would never have thought of emigration.

Again, in Germany, where the abortive revolutionary movement of 1830–1833, the brutal political persecutions by the several state governments, and the reactionary policy of the federal diet, as well as a general distrust of the future, produced an unusually large emigration: In 1831, only 2,395 Germans had arrived in the United States; in 1832, 10,168; in 1833, 6,823; and in 1834 to 1837, the years of the greatest political depression, 17,654, 8,245, 20,139, and 23,036 respectively.

Greatest Irish immigration.

The emigration from Ireland, which from 1844 rose much beyond its former proportions, reached its culminating point after the great famine of 1846. During the decade of 1845 to 1854, inclusive, in which period the highest figures ever known in the history of emigration to the United States were reached, 1,512,100 Irish left the United Kingdom. In the first half of that decade, viz., from January 1, 1845, to December 31, 1849, 607,241 went to the United States, and in the last half, viz., from January 1, 1850, to December 31, 1854, as many as 904,859 arrived in this country. With this unprecedentedly large emigration Ireland had exhausted herself. Since 1855 her quota has fallen off to less than one-half of the average of the preceding ten years.

Almost coincident, in point of time, with this mighty exodus from Ireland was the colossal emigration from Germany which followed the failure of the political revolutions attempted in 1848 and 1849. Already in 1845 and the following years the

German contingent of emigrants to the United States showed an average twice as large as in the same space of time previous to the year named. But a voluntary expatriation on a much larger scale resulted from the final triumph of political reaction. The *coup d'état* of Louis Napoleon closed for all Europe the revolutionary era opened in 1848. In the three years preceding that event, the issue of the struggle of the people against political oppression had remained doubtful. But the 2d of December, 1851, having decided the success of the oppressors for a long time to come, the majority of those who felt dissatisfied with the reactionary *régime* left their homes. The fact that the largest number of Germans ever landed in one year in the United States came in 1854 showed the complete darkening of the political horizon at that time. The apprehension of a new Continental war, which actually broke out a year later in the Crimea, also hastened the steps of those who sought refuge in this country. People of the well-to-do classes, who had months and years to wait before they could sell their property, helped to swell the tide to its extraordinary proportions. From January 1, 1845, till December 31, 1854, there arrived 1,226,392 Germans in the United States, 452,943 of whom came in the first five years of this period, and 773,449 in the last five.

Greatest German immigration.

Domestic causes influencing immigration.

But the numerical strength of immigration to this country is not governed by material and moral disturbances in Europe only. While bad crops, commercial and industrial crises, and unfavorable turns in political affairs in the Old World tend to increase immigration, the appearance of the same phenomena in the United States as certainly tends to decrease it. Thus, in 1838 the total of immigration decreased to 38,914, while in the previous year it had amounted to 79,340, and in 1839 and 1840 it increased again to 68,069 and 84,066 respectively. The reason of this extraordinary decrease was the great financial crisis of 1837, which shook the foundation of the whole industrial and agricultural life of the United States. Again, the influx of aliens into New York was smaller in 1858 and 1859 than in any previous year since 1842, for the only reason that the commercial crisis of 1857 had frightened those who wanted to make a living by the labor of their hands. Thus, the total emigration from the

United Kingdom, which in 1857 had reached the number of 213,415, in 1858 fell off to 113,972, and in 1859 to 120,431. In 1858 and 1859 only 78,589 and 79,322 emigrants, respectively, arrived in New York, while in 1856 their number amounted to 142,342, and in 1857 to 186,733. In 1860 it rose to 105,162, but, in consequence of the breaking out of the civil war, it fell again in 1861 to 65,539, and in 1862 to 76,306. In 1867 the German immigration in New York increased over that of 1866 by more than 10,000, in which last-mentioned year it had already reached the large number of 106,716 souls. Its ranks were swelled in 1867 in consequence of the emigration of men liable to military service from the new provinces annexed to Prussia in 1866, and of families dissatisfied with the new order of things. Hanover contributed the largest share to this kind of emigration. In 1868 and 1869 the tide subsided again as people began to become reconciled to the sudden change.

In short, bad times in Europe regularly increase, and bad times in America invariably diminish, immigration.

Superior attractiveness of the United States.

There are many countries which, by the fertility of their soil, the geniality of their climate, and other natural advantages, are among the brightest spots on earth, but yet never have attracted immigration to any considerable extent. Thus, the Crimea, the lower parts of European Russia, and the Danubian principalities in Europe, Algiers in Africa, and, on our continent, parts of Mexico, as well as hundred thousands of square miles in South America, are, in regard to natural resources, equal, if not superior, to any part of the United States; and yet the latter attracts the masses of European immigration, and it is preeminently the country of the immigrant. Canada lies at the door of the Union; it offers about the same advantages as the North-western States, and yet the majority of European immigrants pass through this English colony to become citizens of the Republic.

Reasons: high wages, cheap land, social and political freedom.

Why is this, and how can we explain this apparent anomaly? However equal such inducements to emigrants as fertility of soil, salubrity of climate, security of property, and facility of communication may be in different countries, the emigrant prefers the country where labor is best remunerated, where land is cheap, where government does not interfere with him, where no class privileges exist, and where, from the day of his landing, he stands on a footing of absolute equality with the natives. Thus we find that, in this respect also, moral as well as physical causes control emigration. The first are as powerful, if not more powerful than the latter. In the United States, both are at work in attracting emigrants, and hence why there is a larger European immigration to this country than to any other on the face of the globe.

Requirements of the successful colonist.

The secret of the unparalleled growth, and of the daily increasing power of the United States, is that the Government, in its practical working, is confined to the narrowest limits, that it is the agent, not the master of the people, and that the latter initiate all changes in its political and social life. And similarly, it is the condition of the success of a colony or a settlement that the immigrant relies on his own strength, acts on his own responsibility, and seeks by his own efforts the prosperity which he is sure to find, if undisturbed. All mistakes which he may make, all errors of judgment which he may commit, are of no consequence, if his self-relying spirit is not interfered with. In spite of obstacles and disappointments, he will make his way, and ultimately attain his object. After abandoning the laws, the traditions, and the family ties of his old home, he does not wish to be unduly restrained in his aspirations, or owe responsibility to any one except himself. He will willingly undergo all the hardships and danger incidental to settlement in a new country, provided he finds a free government and no improper interference with his self-adopted mode of life. A colonist, in brief, must be his own master, in order fully to develop his mental and physical resources, and to become a useful agent in building up a free commonwealth.

Self-government the vitalizing principle of colonization, represented by Teutonic races

All modern colonies which were inaugurated by governments have failed; self-government, in the broadest sense, is the power which sustains colonies and instils into them life and independence. In the history of colonization, the Teutonic races represent the principle of self-government, which leads to the success of the immigrant, while the Latin nations represent that of state dependence and protection, which inevitably results in failure. Look at the Spanish republics, from Mexico down to Peru; at the French colonies, the youngest of which, Algiers, has ever since its first days been weak, and is almost dying from the effects of government care; and at the efforts of the Belgian Government to regulate the work of their colonists in Central America by military discipline, and compare them with the flourishing, thriving, and prosperous condition of the English colonies in America and Australia. The difference in the results of the two systems is too striking to require any further demonstration. In this country we had both systems working side by side in New France and New England. French rule, which, with its great captains, brave warriors, and indefatigable priests, tried to seize upon and fetter a continent, is a memory of the past; but New England, the growth of which—to use the eloquent language of Francis Parkman—was the result of the aggregate efforts of a busy multitude, each in his narrow circle toiling for himself, to gather competence and wealth—New England influences the destinies of a whole continent, and is one of the civilizing factors of the world.

Germans on the Hudson, and in the Mohawk and Schoharie valleys

I have shown, in a book on German immigration to this State, the third German edition of which is just published by Mr. E. Steiger, of this city, how the above-mentioned Germans, who were settled on the upper Hudson by the English Government, were a motley set of shiftless adventurers and vagabonds so long as they depended on the colonial authorities; but these same men, when left to themselves as settlers in the Schoharie and Mohawk valleys, soon became brave and daring pioneers, well-to-do farmers, and good citizens, who formed a living barrier against the inroads of the French and Indians, and conquered the finest parts of our noble State for civilization.

Slavery a bar to immigration.

Again, it was from no whim of the immigrant that he avoided the Southern States while they were cursed with slavery; for a land can have no civil liberty in which freedom of labor and the dignity wherewith respectable employment is invested do not exist. In natural advantages the North-west is much inferior to the northern States of the South. Middle and South Virginia, for instance, are gardens of Eden, which cannot be excelled by any State of the Union, and yet they are partly in a primeval state. Henceforth the North and Europe will send their peaceably conquering armies of farmers and mechanics to take possession of these rich grounds, and raise them to the importance which they would have reached fifty years ago, had it not been for the ban of slavery. So it will be in Tennessee, in Carolina, in Kentucky, and Texas. Foreign immigration, which, before the late war, almost exclusively settled in the free North, will henceforth pour into the South as well. The United States, by the successful termination of the war against rebellion, have indeed increased the attraction of this country for the immigrant, and there is not the least reason to doubt that the great Republic will in the future become more than ever the favorite land of the immigrant. And New York City is the main gateway through which the vast tide of emigration enters, and New York State the great thoroughfare over which it pours to be diffused over the Union.

CHAPTER II.

THE SEA VOYAGE.

Mode of carrying steerage passengers in 18th and part of 19th centuries.

During the whole of the last and the greater part of the present century, the ship-owners chartered the lower decks of their vessels to agents, for the payment of a certain sum for each ton or the whole space disposed of. The agents made the needful temporary arrangements for the accommodation of the passengers, and underlet the steerage, either to associations of emigrants, or parcelled it out to sub-agents or to single passengers.

Indifference of Ship-owners to comfort of emigrants.

Thus the owner of the vessel had not the least concern or interest in the welfare or good treatment of the passengers; all he looked for was the payment of the stipulated price for that part of the ship which he had let. The steerage passengers were simply additional and unwelcome freight; they had to follow the directions of the owner, and were subordinate to what he considered his more important interests. They had to wait for their departure as long as it pleased him, and had no other right than to occupy the ten or twelve square feet which were allotted to them. To the owner, they were less than a box of goods, and handled with less care, as they did not break, nor, if injured, require to be paid for. The agents, in order to make the business lucrative, sent on board as many passengers as they could get hold of, without the smallest reference to the conveniences of the steerage, the number of berths, the separation of the sexes, or anything except their own immediate profit. Besides assigning a space, however small, to the emigrants, they had no responsibility, and ran no risk whatever. There was no check to the overloading of the vessel. Even if it had more than double the number of passengers that it could accommodate, there was no authority to which the emigrants could apply for protection. The agents did just as they pleased. A vessel which was not good and safe enough to be used as a transport for goods and merchandise was, nevertheless, employed for the conveyance of place two or three times a day." Indians took care of Jungmann, and nursed him and his father till May, 1732, when they sailed for Philadelphia, where they arrived on the 16th day of that month, having been more than a year on their way there.

Reverend Dr. Kunze, in an oration delivered, in 1788, before the German Society of Philadelphia, stated that of 900 passengers shipped in one vessel in that year at Amsterdam for Philadelphia, 400 had died on the way. Henry T. Vierhaus, Secretary of the same Society, in a report, dated January 22, 1818, thus describes the cause of the mortality on board the ship *April*, Captain de Groot, just arrived in the Delaware:

Voyage of the ship *April* 1818.

"When the passengers came on board at Amsterdam," he says, "there were 233 *full freights*. The ship was ordered a few miles below Amsterdam to wait for more passengers, but no more came; whereupon the house of Kress & Rodenbrock, the ship-brokers, foreseeing a loss if they did not ship more passengers, proceeded to engage passengers from other vessels which were in the same situation, waiting for freight. These vessels had lain there for a considerable time, and, owing to bad food and poor attendance, those on board were, more or less, sick and full of vermin. These passengers were put on board the ship *April*, making the whole number near 1,200 souls. The sickness brought on board by those shipped in the manner described spread rapidly through the vessel. When the whole number was crammed into the ship, there were among them about 120 sick. Captain de Groot was ordered by Kress & Rodenbrock to put to sea, against which the captain protested, giving as a reason that he would not undertake the voyage with so many sick; that 115 dead persons had already been sent on shore; and that he did not think there was a sufficiency of provisions for such a large number. In consequence of this protest, the Amsterdam police sent four doctors on board, to examine into the state of the passengers and of the vessel. They found the ship in such a shocking condition that it was ordered into Quarantine at the Island of Wieringen. Here all the sick were put into the hospital, and the healthy separated from them. They remained there 19 weeks, and about 300 died, besides the 115 who were sent on shore dead."

We shall see hereafter that this shocking mortality is not confined to remote times, and that the living generation has witnessed thousands of deaths from the same causes. To give an adequate idea of recent losses of human life on board of ill-provided, ill-ventilated vessels, it may be stated here that out of 98,105 poor Irish emigrants shipped to Canada by their landlords after the great famine of 1846, during the summer of 1847 there died 5,293 at sea, 8,072 at Gross Isle (Quarantine) and Quebec, and 7,000 in and above Montreal, making 20,365, besides those who afterwards perished whose number will never be ascertained. Thus the *Lark*, reported at Quebec on August 12, 1847, from Sligo, sailed with 440 passengers, of whom 108 died on the passage and 150 were sick, almost all of whom died a short time after landing. The *Virginius* sailed with 496; 158 died on the passage, 186 were sick, and the remainder landed feeble and tottering; the captain, mates, and crew were all down. At that period, the ratio of the sick per one thousand was 30 on board British, $9\frac{2}{5}$ on American, and $8\frac{3}{5}$ on German vessels. Ship-fever and want of food were almost unheard of on board of vessels from Northern Europe, and particularly those from Hamburg and Bremen.

Mortality on recent voyages.

The *Lark*.

The *Virginius*.

It has been estimated by medical statisticians that not less than 20,000 emigrants perished by ship-fever, and in the various emigrant hospitals in American ports, during the year 1847. Compared with these losses, the mortality on board the Hamburg ship *Leibnitz* of the notorious Sloman line was quite small, for out of 544 passengers (children and infants included), 108 fell victims to the bad ventilation and insufficient provisions. The fever-ship *Leibnitz* arrived at New York on January 11, 1868.

Estimated No. of deaths of Emigrants in 1847.

The *Leibnitz*.

The first law which prescribed the space to be allotted to each steerage passenger was that passed by Congress on March 2, 1819, according to which a ship was forbidden to carry more than two passengers for every five tons, Custom House measure. This law, however benevolent its purpose, proved insufficient; for it did not prohibit the orlop-deck, nor provide for proper ventilation or side-lights, nor deduct the freight-room and accommodations for the officers and first-class passengers from the computation of the total amount of tonnage. Thus a ship which

First law regulating steerage accommodations—Act of March 2, 1819.

measured 1,000 tons and had a steerage of only 500 tons, could nevertheless take steerage passengers for the whole tonnage, that is, 400 instead of 200. Nothing was said about the height of the steerage. It must always be borne in mind that the construction of ships for the express purpose of carrying passengers only began about the year 1830; that up to that time all space which could not be used for shipping merchandise was temporarily arranged for steerage passengers; that often at the last moment, a few days before going to sea, the superfluous room was sold to an agent, and that in those days a steerage five feet high was considered fully sufficient for making two tiers of beds along their sides. And the hole beneath this hole was called orlop-deck, and likewise used for the transport of passengers.

Atmosphere of the steerage.

From this the nature of the atmosphere in the steerage of an emigrant ship can readily be imagined without a minute description. We have only to consider that the room was rarely more than six feet high, had no other aperture for the admission of fresh air than the hatches, which, during the night and bad weather, were generally closed, was crowded with passengers, of whom the greater portion were strangers to the virtue of cleanliness, and many of them down with sea-sickness or other equally loathsome diseases. What with the miasma of a damp hold, the excretions and exhalations from the bodies of the individuals thus confined, and the emanations from other and more offensive matter, an atmosphere was created which acted like poison on those who had to breathe it, and engendered ship-fever in a more or less violent degree.

Evil of requiring emigrants to provide and cook their food.

The health of the passengers was further impaired by another evil which prevailed on board of all emigrant ships up to a comparatively recent time—the emigrants were expected to provide themselves with food, and to cook it as best they could. The Bremen authorities were the first which, about 1830, required masters of ships to furnish cooked provisions for their passengers. It was at the furthest only a few years before the passage of the so-called Passenger Act of March 3, 1855, by Congress, that the Havre and Liverpool vessels included the fare and cooking in the prices of their passage.

Passenger Act of March 3, 1855.

The consequences of this vicious arrangement to those poor

and improvident people were self-evident. Many of them embarked without any provisions at all, and very few, if any, with a sufficient supply; many had not the means to buy food, and others had deceived themselves as to the duration of the voyage; hence it is doubtless true that not one of all the emigrant ships from British and Irish ports had a sufficient supply of proper food for all on board. But, supposing there were some among the cargo of passengers well provisioned for the voyage, there were no means at their disposal for having their food properly cooked. For, as the arrangements of which they could avail themselves for that purpose were insufficient even on board of the very largest and best of ships engaged in the conveyance of emigrant passengers, it can readily be imagined what they must have been on board of the fleet of vessels of an inferior class.

Cooking appliances.

On the upper deck of the ship, there were two small rooms for cooking, about five feet deep and four feet wide, called the steerage galley. Within was a grate corresponding to the width of the room, over which grate was fastened an iron bar, and on this there were two iron hooks, to which the emigrant hung his pot or kettle (if he had one) when he wanted to cook. These were all the arrangements for preparing meals for several hundred passengers. The result was that, except when they had nothing to cook or were sick, there was constant fighting for room near the caboose, and not one of the passengers could be sure of getting his food well cooked. The sufferings which they endured in this way embittered the emigrants one against another, and their quarrels ended when in the evening the fires were extinguished, but only to revive in the morning.

From these causes resulted not only want of sufficient and wholesome food, but also the impossibility of properly preparing what little there was. In view of this, it cannot surprise us that thousands of emigrants, greatly enfeebled already when going on board, either died on the passage or arrived with scarcely a spark of life in them.

Three chief diseases of emigrant ships.

An experience of fifty years, comprising an immigration of more than five millions, teaches us that the three diseases by which passenger-ships have been chiefly scourged are typhus or ship-fever, as it is called when it takes place at sea, cholera, and small-pox. "Of these three"—says John H. Griscom, M.D., and former Superintendent of the Commissioners of Emigration of New York, in a communication addressed on January 14, 1854, to a special committee of the United States Senate—"that to which the emigrant is most prone is ship-fever. The extraordinary prevalence of this disease at the present time, and for the past half-century, but especially for the past seven or eight years, is an astounding phenomenon, particularly when it is remembered that we live in the midst of all the light necessary for its prevention.

Dr. Griscom on Ship-Fever, or Typhus.

"My first practical cognizance of the horrible condition in which emigrants are frequently found on shipboard was in 1847, when, as a member of a committee of the New York Academy of Medicine, I visited the Quarantine establishment to enquire into the medical history of the typhus fever then extensively prevailing, and crowding that institution with patients. On that occasion we visited the ship *Ceylon*, from Liverpool, which had come to anchor a few hours before, with a large cargo of passengers. A considerable number had died upon the voyage, and one hundred and fifteen were then ill with the fever, and were preparing for a removal to the hospital. Before any had yet left the ship, we passed through the steerage, making a more or less minute examination of the place and its occupants; but the indescribable filth, the emaciated, half-nude figures, many with the *petechial* eruption disfiguring their faces, crouching in the bunks, or strewed over the decks, and cumbering the gangways; broken utensils and *débris* of food spread recklessly about, presented a picture of which neither pen nor pencil can convey a full idea. Some were just rising from their berths for the first time since leaving Liverpool, having been suffered to lie there all the voyage, wallowing in their own filth. It was no wonder to us that, with such total neglect of sanitary supervision, and an entire absence of ventilation, so many of such wretched beings had perished or were then ill of fever; it was only surprising that so many had escaped.

The *Ceylon*, 1847.

"Shocking as this case was, it has been frequently surpassed, at least as far as figures are concerned. In 1842, the ship *Eutaw* gave one hundred and twenty to the hospital on arrival; in 1837,

The *Eutaw*, 1842.

the *Ann Hall* sent in one hundred and fifty-eight; while, as far back as the year 1802, one hundred and eighty-eight were taken from the *Flora*, two hundred and twenty from the *Nancy*, and two hundred and fifty-nine from the *Penelope*. In 1851, the number of deaths at sea between Liverpool and New York rose to the astounding number of 1,879, almost wholly the result of ship-fever.

The *Ann Hall* 1837.

The *Flora*, *Nancy*, and *Penelope*, 1802.

"In addition to this, the poisonous influence which becomes infused into those who have escaped death or sickness on shipboard lies dormant for a few days or weeks after debarkation, and sooner or later develops itself and brings many of them to the hospital, where from fifteen to twenty per cent. more are added to the list of dead. Thus there were treated in the Marine Hospital, on Staten Island, in 1852, 3,040 cases of ship-fever, of whom seventeen per cent. died. These were all emigrants; and we must add to these the cases of the same disease, of the same people, which were treated in the large hospitals at Flatbush, Ward's Island, and Bellevue, at the City Hospital, and at other places throughout this State and the States immediately adjoining, nearly all of whom arrived at the port of New York alone.

"In considering the hygienic aspect of emigration, we start, then, with the remarkable fact that, of those who embark upon an Atlantic voyage on any of a certain class of ships, out of every twelve one falls a victim; that is, nearly nine per cent. either never reach the promised land or die soon after.

Rate of mortality in ship-fever

"The general causes, as well as the means of prevention, of this disease are so plain as not to require a medical education for their comprehension, but may be made clear to ordinary intelligence; and the vast importance of the subject will justify an allusion to both in this essay.

Its origin.

"Ship-fever, as it is termed, from the place of its greatest prevalence, is the product of a *miasma* as distinct as that of marshes, which causes intermittent fever. This ship-miasma is itself as inevitable a result of certain conditions, as the other miasma is the product of marshes. And further, the means for its prevention are as clear and controllable in the one case as in the other. Thus, if an offensive marsh be thoroughly drained and dried, its peculiar miasma, and the disease which it causes, will disappear, and so by preventing the formation of ship-miasma (as easy of accomplishment as the other) ship-fever will in like manner be prevented.

"What, then, are the circumstances which give rise to this typhus-breeding miasma? There are certain conditions essential to its creation, which I will enumerate in the order of their importance, beginning with the least:

"I. The confinement of people in apartments disproportioned in size to the requirements of wholesome respiration.

"II. The retention in the same apartment of the excretions from the bodies of the individuals thus confined; such as the matter of perspiration and other more offensive excretions. These, acted on by the artificial heat of the apartment, or even by the natural heat of the bodies alone, will become decomposed, and produce an effluvium which will react poisonously on the persons exposed to it.

"III. The exclusion of pure air.

"As to the first of these causes, the number of persons and the size of the apartment necessary to produce the miasma are merely relative. An apartment may be crowded without danger from this source, provided that from the first ventilation and cleanliness be thoroughly and constantly maintained.

Explanation of its virulence in steerage.

"With this brief explanation of the general causes of typhus, the reasons for its prevalence in the steerages of passenger-ships are very apparent. In great numbers of them, *all* the conditions enumerated above, as necessary for the creation of this disorder, are found to exist, and it is reasonable to infer the existence of some *specific* cause in addition to the general ones which have been mentioned.

Specific cause.

"We find ship-fever, within a few years, to have prevailed most frequently and extensively in those vessels which ply between several ports of Great Britain and this country, and this fact, together with an examination of the passengers, points unerringly to the *famine* which desolated a large section of that kingdom as the additional cause alluded to.

Famine.

"This is a direct, and at the same time an indirect cause. The infection is carried to the ship by the emigrants from a country where hunger typhus prevails; besides, the previous exhaustion predisposes to be attacked by miasma. In connection with this branch of the subject, another source of the development of ship-fever demands notice. In the cabins and hovels—the homes of these famine-stricken people—typhus fever raged a long time, and doubtless prevails extensively yet, produced by the same general and specific causes as have been described. The emigrants leave for the seaboard, and straightway enter the ships, unpurified and unwashed, reeking with the fever miasma of their habitations. Into the crowded and confined steerage they hasten for rest and escape from starvation and death. But unconsciously they bring the enemy with them; the fatal seeds are but sown in a fresh soil, and, as though from a hot-bed, they sprout even more vigorously. One such case on board a crowded and badly ventilated ship may cause the death of numbers.

"The food with which these people are supplied on shipboard, even if sufficient in quantity (which it is not always), is very often so badly cooked as to operate injuriously upon them. So great is often the difficulty, among from 300 to 1,000 people, of finding a proper time and opportunity for cooking, that it is a common occurrence for them to swallow their flour or meal only half cooked, or even mixed simply with warm water, if indeed *warm* water can be had. The effect of this kind of diet is but to add other evils, such as dysentery and diarrhœa, to the typhus miasma with which the steerage becomes infected, the debility of the inmates rendering them more susceptible to its influence than they would be if well fed. Improper food

"For the prevention as well as the cure of typhus, it is necessary that the physical stamina be well maintained by appropriate food, in sufficient quantity. With ordinary strength of body and elasticity of spirit, few persons can be induced to remain below deck for many hours together, and, while the pure air of the ocean directly increases animal vigor, it is also the surest preventive of typhus. Even the half-starved emigrant would find his energy and spirits revive, if compelled by a rigid sanitary police to make frequent visits to the ship's deck. Prevention and cure of Typhus

"Famine, therefore, though a frequent precedent and a powerful adjunct, is only an indirect cause of the fever as we find it on shipboard and in our hospitals; but we must continue to be burdened with it so long as poverty-stricken emigrants are admitted into the transport-ships in such great numbers, with food so insufficient in quantity and quality, and with such a total absence of sanitary police during the voyage.

Value of pure air as a curative.

"From what has been said, it will be readily inferred that in the prevention of typhus fever pure air possesses great value. Too much reliance cannot be placed upon it, either for this purpose or for subduing the intensity or arresting the progress of the disease. Of its efficacy as a remedial agent, a striking instance among many others that might be mentioned occurred at the New York Quarantine Hospital, under my immediate notice, during my connection with the State Emigrant Commission. A new building was erected on the summit of a hill within the enclosure, into which some forty patients were conveyed from the other overcrowded buildings. These had been kept in as good condition as possible as respects both cleanliness and ventilation. Though there were no specific provisions for the latter, yet the influence of the fresh atmosphere of the new building upon the patients was most decided and immediate; a load seemed to be lifted off them, and several, who, it was feared, would die, began at once to improve and rapidly recover.

Passengers of the *Phœbe* landed at Perth Amboy.

"In the month of August, 1837, a number of ships with emigrant passengers arrived at Perth Amboy, from Liverpool and other ports, on board of some of which ship-fever prevailed. There was no hospital or other accommodations in the town in which the sick could be placed, and no person would admit them into private dwellings, fearing infection; at the same time, they could not be left on board the ships. An arrangement was made to land the sick passengers and place them in an open wood, adjacent to a large spring of water, about a mile and a half from town. Rough shanties, floored with boards and covered with sails, were erected, and thirty-six patients were landed in boats, as near the spring as possible, and carried in wagons to the encampment (as it was called), under the influence of a hot August sun. Of the thirty-six, twelve were insensible, in the last stage of fever, and not expected to live twenty-four hours. The day after landing there was a heavy rain, and, the shanties affording no protection with their 'sail' roofs, the sick were found the next morning wet, and their bedding, such as it was, drenched with the rain. It was replaced with such articles as could be collected from the charity of the inhabitants. Their number was increased by new patients to eighty-two in all. On board the ship, which was cleansed after landing the passengers, *four* of the crew were taken with ship-fever, and two of them died. Some of the nurses at the encampment were taken sick, but recovered. Of the whole number of eighty-two passengers removed from the ship, not one died. Pure air, good water, and, perhaps, the rain (though only the first thirty-six were affected by it) seemed to have effected the cure.

"The ship was the *Phœbe*, with between three and four hundred passengers, a number of whom (twenty-seven) had died on the passage. The shanties spoken of were two in number, thirty feet long, twenty feet wide, boarded on three sides four feet up, with old sails stretched over them. The twelve who were removed from the ship in a state of insensibility were apparently in so hopeless a condition that the overseer, who was a carpenter, observed, 'Well, Doctor, I think I shall have some boxes to make before many hours.' 'The night after their arrival at the encampment,' says Dr. Smith, 'we had a violent thunder-gust, accompanied by torrents of rain. On visiting them the following morning, the clothes of all were saturated with water; in other words, they had had a thorough ablution; this, doubtless, was a most fortunate circumstance. The medical treatment was exceedingly simple, consisting, in the main, of an occasional laxative or enema, vegetable acids, and bitters; wine was liberally administered, together with the free use of cold water, buttermilk, and animal broths.' The four sailors who sickened after the arrival of the vessel were removed to the room of an ordinary dwelling-house. The medical treatment in their case was precisely similar, yet two of them died, and the others suffered from carbuncles while convalescing. The doctor adds, 'My opinion is, that had the eighty-two treated at the encampment been placed in a common hospital, many of them would also have fallen victims. I do not attribute their recovery so much to the remedies administered as to the circumstances in which they were placed; in other words, a good washing to begin with, and n abundance of fresh air.'

Typhus more fatal in cold weather.

"It has puzzled some to understand why it is that typhus fever and many other infectious disorders are more frequent and fatal in cold than in warm weather. This fact is attributed by some to the low temperature; but the true reason undoubtedly is, that in winter the external atmosphere is more completely excluded from our dwellings and hospitals by closing of doors and windows, which in warm weather are open and freely permit the ingress and egress of air. Hence, in winter, the greater necessity of artificial ventilation. The same reasoning applies to passenger-ships in cold or stormy weather, when the hatches are kept closed. Artificial ventilation, necessary at all times, is then more urgently demanded.

Reason.

Tenacity of the miasma.

"There is another fact connected with ships, as well as with hospitals and dwellings, which has a very important bearing on this subject. The miasma which has been spoken of has the property of attaching itself to clothing, bedding, furniture, and to the walls, ceilings, and floors of apartments. It is absorbed by them, and adheres with considerable tenacity, whence it is ever ready, unless thoroughly destroyed and removed by cleansing and the use of disinfectants, to issue forth, and to pregnate the atmosphere again with its poisonous influence. Into a room in which a case of typhus fever has once existed, even for a short time, it is unsafe to enter, unless the room and everything in it has been first subjected to a thorough airing and purification. Here, then, is a constant source of danger, which will probably account for many instances of devastation on shipboard by this disease. A vessel in which it has once occurred will have the miasmatic poison clinging to its sides, ceilings, and floors, from which it cannot possibly be eradicated without the most thorough airing, cleansing, and disinfecting, such as, I presume, no vessel engaged in the European passenger trade has ever received. In hospitals and dwellings, with hard-finished walls and painted wood-work, this fact is often demonstrated. In the peculiar structure of a vessel's inner walls, without plaster, paint, or whitewash, with thousands of crevices and cracks inaccessible to the scrubbing-brush or any other purifying implement, without windows for the free circulation of air, we see the perfection of a place for the long retention of the poison, and for its propagation for months afterwards, when the steerage shall be again crowded with sure victims.

"Moreover, the bunks or berths on these vessels are generally constructed of the cheapest kind of boards, often in the rough state, and put together without any nicety—the whole arrangement being of the flimsiest character. Nothing of the kind could be better adapted to harboring the fever miasma. At the end of the voyage, the bunks are sometimes taken down without disinfection or even washing, and, with all the filth and miasma adhering to them, stowed away, either as dunnage, amid the return cargo, or in bulk, to be appropriated to their original purpose on the next hitherward voyage. Now, it is evident that the next cargo of emigrants of such a vessel, though it may be composed of ever so healthy and cleanly people, and though the ship may be well supplied with stores, bedding, and other requisites, is yet liable to suffer from the latent seeds of disease, night and day, as the passengers are in contact with the fever-charged bunks. There is more than probability that more or less will be attacked. The pestilence once started, there is no telling where it will stop. Bunks repositories of pestilence.

"But even supposing this source of danger to be stopped by the destruction of the old bunks and the substitution of new ones after each voyage, the permanent timber of the vessel, if not disinfected, will still form a repository for the poison, whence its ravages may be renewed.

"The second of the diseases by which passenger-ships have been infested is cholera. The open air generally puts an end to typhus or ship fever, whereas cholera is controlled by no such corrective. Although this fearful disorder confines itself to no precise localities, there appear to be circumstances under which it is peculiarly apt to make its appearance. These circumstances have been ascertained to be in a great degree similar to those which give rise to typhus fever. The poor and vicious, whose vital powers are enfeebled by want of wholesome nutritious food and close confinement or criminal excess, are found to be much Cholera on shipboard.

more liable to become the prey of cholera than persons who have good nourishing food in abundance, take regular exercise, and abstain from indulgences that weaken the general tone of the system, whilst they add to the nervous excitability of the body. Cholera, it is true, often appears and disappears without any apparent cause, a fact the reason of which is still hidden from the eye of science, and can only be explained by time and experience. It is sufficient to know that, if the body is kept in a healthy, well-balanced condition, and its functions are not interrupted by any disturbing causes, it may, in the generality of cases, bid defiance to the assaults of the disease. The theory is entertained by some that cholera on shipboard arises from the virus of the disease having been imbibed by the persons or clothing of passengers previous to embarkation, or that it is met with in certain zones through which the ships pass in reaching the Western Continent. Concerning this it is proper to remark, that all that can be done by the owners of passenger-ships is to prevent the existence of any exciting cause of sickness on board of them, and of any state of things by which it may be nourished and sustained if contracted elsewhere. If there be anything in the atmosphere of particular zones or belts, it must be encountered alike by ships sailing probably within a few miles of each other, propelled by the same winds, and standing on the same courses. Such, however, is not the case. While passengers on Liverpool vessels died by hundreds from the cholera, those from Germany, who had left Hamburg and Bremen at the same time, and arrived in New York about the same period with those from Liverpool, had no sickness on board; for the reason that they were not so crowded, that they were cleaner and healthier when they embarked, and better provided for during the voyage. The German port regulations, which compel the ships to distribute cooked provisions among the emigrants, account for their superiority in respect to health and cleanliness."

Comparison of German and British ships.

Among twelve vessels, which arrived at Quebec on or about August 10, 1847, there were two German ships, the bark *Amy*, from Bremen, with 289 passengers, and the brig *Watchful*, from Hamburg, with 145 passengers, and one Irish brig, the *Trinity*, from Limerick, with 86 passengers, upon which there occurred

The *Amy*. The *Watchful*. The *Trinity*.

neither sickness nor death during the voyage. The other vessels, consisting of two from Limerick, one from Sligo, three from Dublin, two from Liverpool, and one from Greenock, with 2,386 passengers, had together 198 deaths and 286 sick on their passage.

But even ships which leave the same port simultaneously show a very remarkable difference in the respective health of their passengers. This must be ascribed to the better condition of the ship and of the passengers in the one case, and to the previous poverty and insufficient nourishment in the other. Thus, the ship *Lucy Thompson*, after a passage of twenty-nine days, arrived at New York, from Liverpool, on the 11th of September, 1853, with a loss of forty out of 835 passengers by cholera. The *William Stetson* arrived on the same day, after a passage of thirty-one days, with 355 passengers, having lost none on the passage. The *Great Western* arrived on the day previous, September 10, after a passage of thirty-one days, 832 passengers, no death having occurred on board. On the 19th of September, 1853, the *Isaac Webb* arrived at New York, from Liverpool, with 773 passengers, after a passage of twenty-nine days, seventy-seven having died of cholera. On the next day, the *Roscius* arrived from the same port, with 495 passengers, after a passage of thirty-five days, six days longer than that of the *Isaac Webb*, and yet without a single death. On the 15th of October, 1853, the *Montezuma* arrived at New York, from Liverpool, in forty-one days, with 404 passengers, and a loss of two; while the *Marmion* arrived on the same day, after a passage of twenty-five days, with 295 passengers, and a loss of thirty-six by cholera. The *Washington* arrived at New York on the 23d of October, 1853, after a passage of forty-one days, with 952 passengers, and a loss of eighty-one; while the *Guy Mannering* arrived on the 25th of the same month, after a passage of thirty-seven days, with 781 passengers, and without loss.

Difference in health of vessels leaving same port at same time.

The *Lucy Thompson*.

The *William Stetson*.

The *Great Western*.

The *Isaac Webb*.

The *Roscius*.

The *Montezuma*.

The *Marmion*

The *Washington*.

The *Guy Mannering*.

These examples might be multiplied almost at pleasure, showing that vessels which left the same port almost at the same time, and reached the same point of destination about the same time, and consequently would be supposed to have been in the same latitudes and subject to the same winds at the same time, suffered in very different degrees. The cases presented show conclusively that the disease on board of these vessels must be attributed to some exciting cause pre-existing within them, which could not be connected with the condition of the atmosphere or the prevalence of certain winds on the ocean.

Small-pox.

With regard to small-pox, the third in rank of the diseases which have affected emigrants, its nature and its means of prevention are too well known to require anything more than a single remark, viz., that the rules which apply to the prevention of typhus or ship fever and cholera are, in the main, also applicable in the case of small-pox.

Greater mortality on New York bound vessels.

The percentage of mortality among the passengers on board of New York vessels has been considerably greater than those of vessels trading to Boston, Philadelphia, and other ports. This is to be accounted for by a variety of reasons. New York being the great commercial emporium of the Union, passengers from every country in Europe have been induced to regard it as the point to which they should direct their courses. Hence the huge structures furnished by the enterprise of that great metropolis for the transportation of passengers have been crowded to excess, and, as a necessary consequence, the causes of disease have existed on board of those vessels to a greater extent than on any other. In general, the percentage of deaths is in direct proportion to the number of passengers, that is, it has been found that where passengers have been distributed in smaller numbers disease and death have been less prevalent. The smallest percentage of deaths has occurred on vessels from ports of Europe other than those of Liverpool, London, Bremen, Hamburg, and Havre, which, being off the great thoroughfares of commerce, have presented fewer attractions to the great mass of emigrants. The vessels from these ports, being less crowded, are more easily ventilated and kept clean, and present greater facilities for the proper preparation of the food of the passengers, and for their exercise in good weather.

Comparison of health of vessels from different ports.

During the four last months of 1853, 312 vessels arrived at New York from European ports, with 96,950 passengers. Of these vessels, forty-seven were visited by cholera, and 1,933 passengers died at sea, while 457 were sent to the hospitals on landing—there, in all probability, to terminate in a short time their miserable existence—making nearly two per cent. of deaths among the whole number of persons who had embarked for the New World, and nearly two and a half per cent. when including those who were landed sick. On board of the forty-seven vessels attacked by cholera, the number of passengers was 21,857, of whom 1,821 (being 8·48 per cent.) died on the passage, and 284 were landed sick, making 9·68 per cent. of dead and diseased, in an average passage of thirty-nine days.

Of the arrivals above mentioned, 112 were from Liverpool, with an average of 435 passengers on each. Twenty-four of these vessels, with an average of 577 passengers, or an average excess of 142 passengers each over the general average of the whole number of vessels, had cholera on board.

Of twenty vessels which arrived from London, five had cholera on board. The average number of passengers on board the vessels attacked by cholera was 411 each, while that of the whole number was but 326.

Of fifty-two vessels which arrived from Bremen, three had cholera on board. The average of passengers on board of each vessel, out of the whole number, was 201, while the average on board of those attacked by cholera was 259.

Of twenty-two vessels that arrived from Hamburg, six had cholera. Of forty-two vessels which arrived from Havre, six had cholera. The average on board of the whole number of ships was 409, while on board of the six cholera ships the average was 561.

Of sixty-four vessels which arrived from other ports of Europe, three had cholera on board. The average of passengers on board of the whole number of these ships was 148, while that on board of the ships attacked by cholera was 185.

The average on board of the whole number of vessels (312) that arrived from Europe during the four months was 311, while the average on board of the forty-seven that had cholera was 465. The average on board of the vessels which arrived, exclusive of those with cholera, was 283, showing that the cholera vessels carried an average excess of 182 each over those that were comparatively healthy.

Of the vessels which escaped from cholera, there were thirty-three, carrying on an average 335 passengers each, on board of which deaths occurred. On these vessels, the number of deaths was 112, out of 11,044 passengers.

It appears from the above statement of facts, that the ships on board of which cholera broke out were those which were most crowded with passengers, and that the vessels on board of which deaths from other diseases occurred were the next most crowded, whilst the remainder, which were healthy, had the lowest average of passengers.

Improvement in condition of emigrants on shipboard.

Much has been done since to alleviate the hardships connected with sea voyages. The liberal legislation of Congress, which, by the Act of March 3, 1855, first concedes and endeavors to secure the rights of the emigrants by giving to each of them two tons of space, and by providing for the proper ventilation of the ship, as well as for a sufficient amount of substantial and cooked provisions, has contributed much towards preventing the almost daily occurrence of sickness and privations on board of emigrant ships. The construction of sailing-vessels is better, but beyond this the steamers have taken the place of the former, and have begun to monopolize the transport of emigrants, of whom at present about eighty-nine per cent. arrive in steamers, while in 1856, for instance, only three per cent. of their number had availed themselves of this faster and healthier mode of conveyance. While in 1859 the average number brought by steamers was 230, against 184 in sailing-vessels; in 1868, it was 489 to 204; and, in 1869, 517 to 183; showing an average difference in favor of steamers of 285 and 334 respectively. The comparative mortality of passengers on board sailing-vessels and steamers shows, in 1868, a very large proportional disparity in favor of the steamers. Out of 180,449 passengers in 451 steamers, 200 died; while from among 31,953 in 200 sailing-vessels, the deaths were 393. In 1869, out of 229,190 passengers in 504 steamers, 210 died; of 28,333 passengers in 209 sailing-vessels, 138 died; being about one death in 1000 of the former, and 200 of the latter. There is every reason for the realization of the hope that in less than ten years the sailing-vessels, as transports of emigrants, will disappear from the ocean. There has seldom, if ever, been a complaint brought against the steamers, which make the average of their trips in less than a fortnight, and on account of the short voyage, the plenty

Comparative mortality on steamers and sailing vessels.

of good water, provisions, and fresh air, prevent their passengers from falling sick. Humanity has thus succeeded in making the exception now what was formerly the rule, and a mortality of one-fourth of one per cent. of the total number of passengers is now-adays considered a very large loss.

Much, however, as has been done, there is still ample room for greater improvement.

Act of 1868 of Legislature of State of New York.

To remove the most pressing evils, the author of this essay, in the winter of 1868, submitted a bill to the Legislature of the State of New York, "For the more effectual protection of emigrants arriving at the port of New York." By this bill, which on June 5, 1868, became a law, the Commissioners are severally invested with the power (subject to certain conditions) of examining under oath any witness respecting complaints made by any person relative to the ship in which any emigrant may have arrived, his treatment on shipboard, and the quality of the provisions furnished; or to take testimony in reference to any death that may have occurred during the voyage; and such testimony, if made in presence of the persons complained of, may be used as evidence in any subsequent action between any of the passengers and the owner, master, or charterer of the ship. Thus offending persons will be deprived to a great extent of the chance of escaping punishment, while the emigrant will be exposed in consequence to less risk of unjust treatment, or, if aggrieved, will have a speedier and more accessible mode of redress than has hitherto existed.

The *James Foster, Jr.*

The necessity of such a provision was almost immediately after its passage shown in the case of the *James Foster, Jr.*, a Liverpool emigrant ship, as without it the atrocious misconduct and brutality of her officers could not have been adequately punished.

Proposed Convention with European States.

It is to be hoped, however, that our General Government, as well as the governments of Europe, will themselves initiate the necessary reforms, and follow the just example set to them by the North German Confederation. The draft of a Convention between the United States and the several European governments, for the better protection of steerage passengers while at sea, prepared by Secretary Hamilton Fish, is a noble proof of the earnest desire of the United States to do their utmost in behalf of the emigrants.

It is in the interest of humanity that in future the Emigrant Courts, proposed by Secretary Fish, shall have exclusive control and power in all matters connected with the well-being of the emigrants.

CHAPTER III.

BONDING AND COMMUTING—PRIVATE HOSPITALS FOR IMMIGRANTS.

A NEW era in emigration began after the great Napoleonic wars. It may be said to have formally opened with the year 1819, which witnessed the passage of the first United States law on the subject.

Up to that time no precise and connected information concerning any phase of immigration was obtainable in this country. No systematic effort had been made where to gather reliable facts and figures, and the scanty data anterior to the year named that have descended to us are obtained from a variety of sources. With the law of 1819 a regular supply of statistics on the subject was assured.

Immigration after 1819.

The history of immigration after 1819 may be divided into two periods: the first opening in the year named and ending in 1847, the year of the creation of the Board of the Commissioners of Emigration of the State of New York; the second beginning with 1847 and coming down to our days. The former period will be first considered.

Sale of two shiploads of emigrants in 1817.

In 1817, no less than 22,240 persons, including Americans from abroad, arrived at ports of the United States from foreign countries. In no previous year had one-half as many foreign passengers reached this country. In December, 1817, two shiploads, bound for Philadelphia, were sold into the slave State Delaware. The transaction was shocking in the extreme, and created a painful sensation all over the country; but there were no laws of the United States either limiting the number of persons which a passenger ship or vessel was allowed to carry, or providing in any way for the health or comfort of the passengers. The subject attracted the immediate attention of Congress. On March 10, 1818, Louis McLane, of Delaware, reported to the House of Representatives a bill "regulating passenger ships and vessels," which was read twice and referred. In December of the following session, it was called up by Thomas Newton, of Virginia, who explained the necessity of its passage. It was read a third time, and passed the House. After receiving amendments from both the Senate and House, it was finally passed and approved March 2, 1819.

Act of March 2, 1819.

This act fixed the space allotted to the emigrants to five tons, Custom House measurement, for every two passengers, and in case of contravention punished the captain with a fine of $150 for each passenger. It declared the ship to be forfeited to the United States, if the number of passengers carried exceeded the said proportion of two to every five tons. It further specified the amount of water and provisions to be taken on board by emigrant vessels, and exacted a fine of three dollars for every day that any passenger was put on short allowance. Finally, it required the collectors of customs to report quarterly to the Secretary of State the number of passengers arriving in their collection districts, by sea, from foreign countries; also the sex, age, and occupation of such passengers, and the country in which they were born. Annual reports embracing that information have, in conformity with this act, been made to Congress by the Secretary of State ever since. Although, in some parts, incorrect and meagre, they form the only reliable statistical basis of the history of emigration during the period from 1819 to 1847.

Meagreness of immigration statistics.

In all other respects, our sources of information are rather imperfect and superficial. The emigrant is not a subject, but an object—not an active, but a passive, force in this international movement. We would probably never have heard of his history, and of his sufferings, except in legendary tales and indistinct family traditions, had not the rapacity of agents and ship-owners compelled the several governments to interfere in his behalf, and to protect him against the grossest imposition. Even as it is, emigrants are considered as an aggregate of human beings only, with no characteristic distinction except that of nationalities.

Emigrants regarded as numerical quantities.

They appear simply as a numerical quantity; they seem to have no individual existence, and the student of contemporary history does not take the trouble to study their individual motives, misfortunes, and aspirations. He contemplates the emigration of large bodies only from the stand-point of wholesale changes in the condition of nations, of social and political short-comings and disturbances. The poor peasant of the inland village who seeks to be an independent land-owner across the ocean, and the noble patriot who valiantly but unsuccessfully fought for human rights; the mechanic and the scholar; the rich and the destitute; the reckless swindler and the honest man—all represent but so many figures. They are looked upon as mere quantities added to the total wealth and strength of the land. And all this, although, as a whole, they emigrate with an intelligent and firm purpose to take up anew the battle of life, and to fight it through valiantly and honorably. Although the most lucrative article of import, emigrants were treated with the least possible care, with the utmost disregard of decency and humanity. With rare exceptions, they were robbed and plundered, from the day of their departure to the moment of their arrival in their new homes, by almost every one with whom they came in contact. They received less consideration on the voyage than even trees in course of transplantation. They were treated worse than beasts, and less cared for than slaves, who, whatever their condition may be in other respects, represent more or less capital, and, as valuable chattels, are sure to receive protection and assistance in case of danger or sickness. There seemed to be a secret league, a tacit conspiracy, on the part of all concerned in dealing with emigrants, to fleece and pluck them without mercy, and pass them from hand to hand as long as anything could be made out of them. The poor foreigners were virtually helpless against any sort of imposition and fraud. The thousands who died, or were killed, on the voyage, were thrown into the ocean with as little ceremony as old sacks or broken tools. If crosses and tombstones could be erected on the water as on the Western deserts, where they indicate the resting-places of white men killed by savages or by the elements, the whole route of the emigrant vessel from Europe to America would long since have assumed the appearance of crowded cemeteries. And, what is still worse, the sufferings of the emigrants seem destined to last for ever. The experience of one does not help the other, for the emigrants, after their arrival in America, disperse into all parts of the great continent. They seldom bring charges or make complaints, being satisfied that they will not be heard, or being eager to reach their new homes. Only here and there some victims tell of their ill-treatment, and it is almost exclusively upon their recitals, and upon the meagre official data, that we have to rely for a history of later emigration.

Immigration to New York, 1819-29.

During the ten years after the passage of the Act of 1819, the immigration to New York was very small. In the first five years, viz., from 1819 to 1824, it amounted to a little more than 4,000 per annum; while from 1825 to 1829, it rose to an average of 12,328 per year.

Poverty of emigrants.

A large majority were very poor. While their influx contributed to the general prosperity of the country, it injured the domestic poor, as it necessarily imposed heavier expenses on the city government in providing for those who from any cause became sick or destitute.

Comptroller Ewen relative to provision for support of foreign poor.

"Prior to 1817," says Comptroller John Ewen, in his report for 1846, "when the foreign poor did not amount to one-fourth of the present number, the Corporation (of the city of New York) received from the State one-third of the auction duties collected in this city on the sale of foreign goods, as an indemnity for their support. This provision, amounting annually to upwards of $70,000, was subsequently withdrawn, and an annual payment of $10,000 substituted instead; since then the State has received over six millions of dollars from auctions in this city, and only $53,000 from other parts of the State. This annual payment, however, proved insufficient, in consequence of the arrival of foreign paupers, who, in some instances, within a day or two after landing, where taken from the wharves in large numbers, in a state of destitution, and sent to the Almshouse. To protect the city against such extraordinary expenditures, the Legislature of the State, on February 11, 1824, passed an act 'Concerning passengers in vessels coming to the port of New York.' This act, commonly called the 'Passenger Act,' required every master or commander of any ship, or other vessel, arriving at the port of New York, from any country out of the United States, or from any other of the United States than the State of New York, to make, within twenty-four hours after the arrival of such ship or vessel, 'a report in writing, on oath or affirmation, to the

Passenger Act of 1824, New York.

Mayor of the city of New York, or, in case of his sickness or absence, to the Recorder of the said city, of the name, place of birth, and last legal settlement, age, and occupation, of every person who shall have been brought as a passenger in such ship or vessel on her last voyage.' Said act also authorized the Mayor 'to require, by a short endorsement on the aforesaid report, every such master or commander of any ship or vessel to be bound with two sufficient sureties (to be approved of by the said Mayor or Recorder) to the Mayor, Aldermen, and Commonalty of the city of New York, in such sum as the Mayor or Recorder might think proper, not exceeding three hundred dollars for each passenger, not being a citizen of the United States, to indemnify and keep harmless the said Mayor, Aldermen, and Commonalty and the Overseers of the Poor of the said city, and their successors, from all and every expense or charge which shall or may be incurred by them, for the maintenance and support of every such person, and for the maintenance and support of the child or children of any such person, which may be born after such importation, in case such person or any such child or children shall, at any time within two years from the date of such bond, become chargeable to the said city.'"

Insufficiency of the act.

This act worked tolerably well so long as emigration was small, and the bondsmen, and the passengers landed by them, could be controlled. Consequently, we do not hear of any serious complaints during the first ten years of its operation; but, as soon as emigration assumed greater proportions, the law became susceptible of the most flagrant abuses, which were actually practised under it, and it did not afford the slightest indemnity for the maintenance of those who became chargeable to the city. As the brokers engaged in the bond business were only expected to pay for the bonded passengers in case of their sickness or destitution, a large field for the exercise of fraud and deception was opened to these shrewd speculators. The ship-owners preferred the system of bonding to any other, as by the payment of a trifle it exonerated them from all liability, and as they, of course, received from each passenger one dollar, which was included in the price of the passage, while the brokers assumed their liability at prices varying from one dollar to ten cents for each passenger, or still cheaper, as, for instance, between the years 1828 and 1836, when the sum paid for bonding was only two dollars per vessel, whether the number of passengers was great or small. In some cases, however, it was found to be very convenient to the passenger-carriers, and advantageous to the city, to commute for alien passengers instead of requiring bonds, or, in other words, to accept a specific sum of no less than one and no more than ten dollars for each, and to waive the execution of bonds. For this reason, the Corporation of the city of New York, in 1839, passed an amendment to the Passenger Act, which authorized the Mayor to commute. Consequently, when the agent or master desired to commute, the Commissioners of the Almshouse directed an examination of the passengers, and reported their condition, when the Mayor fixed and received the commutation, and the master was discharged from all liability. While the State law required that bonds should be given, the Corporation ordinance merely conferred authority on the Mayor to commute in such cases, and in such manner, as might be mutually agreed upon, the right of bonding being reserved specially to the master.

Amendment to Passenger act by city of New York, 1839, authorizing commutation.

Abuses practised.

Thus the city did not gain much, and the old abuses were continued with the same impunity. In fact, the entire business became a private traffic between a set of low and subordinate city officials, on the one hand, and a band of greedy and unscrupulous brokers, on the other. It was a sort of legalized robbery, the headquarters of which was at the City Hall.

An ordinance of the city prescribed that the Clerk of the Common Council should receive all sums paid for commutation by alien passengers, account monthly for them, and thereupon pay over the money received by him to the Chamberlain of the city. But there never has been any check upon, or system of examination of, the accounts of the Clerk of the Common Council, and of receipts of such moneys, either to detect dishonest practices or to correct unintentional error.

Irresponsibility of clerks to whom commutation money was paid.

It seems that, from the first day of the application of the Passenger Act of 1824 down to 1842, all the moneys for commuted alien passengers were received by a certain John Ahern, a defaulter to the city in a very large amount, who first was private clerk to General Morton, the Clerk of the Common Council, or a subordinate in his office. Said Ahern kept no regular books of account, or vouchers, but made entries, or omitted to make them, as he saw fit. In 1834, the Common Council created the office of Clerk to the Mayor, and appointed this man, Ahern, to that office, General Morton still remaining Clerk to the Common Council. Ahern continued under him to perform the same services as when a private clerk, or subordinate, in Morton's office, and attended to the returns of captains of vessels, the receipt of commutation moneys, and other fees receivable by the Clerk of the Common Council. The moneys were paid by Ahern to the Clerk of the Common Council, and by that officer, under his own name, returned to the Comptroller. John Ahern.

Under the successors of General Morton, who died in 1836, Ahern continued to perform the same duties, made similar returns, which, without being first examined, were made a part of the County Clerk's returns to the Comptroller. During all these different clerkships, until December, 1842, the returns of captains of vessels, and the bonds taken, were sent to the office of the Commissioners of the Almshouse, to enable them to ascertain, when persons applied to them at that office for assistance, whether such persons had been bonded, so that the sureties might be called upon for their support; or whether they had been commuted for, and were to be supported at the expense of the city. No account or memorandum has been kept in the office of the Clerk of the Common Council of the number of passengers commuted for, or the amount of moneys received for the commutation of passengers.

This utter neglect of supervision or control existed for about eighteen years, without even exciting any suspicion. At last, in 1842, the impropriety of this course became so apparent that Mr. Underwood, Alderman of the Third Ward, at the meeting of September 12, offered a resolution appointing a committee of three, to examine into and report upon the subjects of reporting, bonding, and commuting of passengers, and the course pursued in relation to aliens and others who had made application to the Commissioners of the Almshouse for relief. Investigation by Committee of Board of Aldermen, 1842.

This committee, consisting of Messrs. John A. Underwood, H. W. Bonnel, and Hobert Jones, thoroughly performed their arduous duties, and, after carefully comparing the books and returns of the shipping merchants, the health officer, and the Custom House with the statements kept in the City Hall, on March 11, 1843, reported to the Board of Aldermen. It would lead us beyond the limits of this essay to enter into the particulars of their investigation, but a few of the facts, corroborated by the fullest evidence, will show how business was managed in the County Clerk's Office.

Report of same.

"All the accounts," says the report just mentioned, "from December, 1836, to July, 1842, contain the names of vessels in which passengers arrived, whether commuted for or bonded; but the whole business previous to June, 1837, was conducted without regard to detail, perspicuity, or regularity in the Mayor's Office, the office of the Clerk of the Common Council, and the Comptroller's Office, and it was impossible to ascertain what amount of money was or should have been paid previous to the dates last mentioned. It has, however, been discovered that moneys were received for commuting and bonding passengers previous to June, 1837, which were never paid into the city treasury, but it would be useless to ascertain what amount of such moneys was withheld, or by whom they were misapplied.

"From June 1, 1837, to July 2, 1842, the deficiencies for bonds and commutations, in accounts rendered to the Comptroller, amounted to $8,019 25. The number of passengers who were reported to the Comptroller as having been commuted for sums less than were recommended by the agent of the Commissioners of the Almshouse, but in relation to which neither receipts nor accounts had been obtained, was 8,965; and the passengers who had arrived from foreign countries, in vessels bringing ten or more passengers, none of whom had been accounted for, were 1,846."

Result of investigation and report.

The investigations of this committee, and the changes proposed by them in the supervision of the subordinate officers, effected a reform in the execution of the acts bearing upon immigration, but, nevertheless, the city was not greatly benefited by the change. With the daily increasing immigration, the profits growing out of the bonding system to the brokers became larger, and, with keen attention to pecuniary gain, these unscrupulous men appropriated to themselves what, of right, belonged to the city. They received, as before stated, from the ship-owners the sum of one dollar for each bonded passenger.

"These persons," says Comptroller John Ewen, in his report for 1845, "although worth the amount for which they may become liable for passengers in each particular case, afford but little indemnity to the Corporation for any considerable number of the bonded passengers, should they from any unforeseen calamity be thrown upon the city for support, several individuals being bondsmen for over $1,000,000 each. The aggregate of the bonds taken for the average number annually bonded during the last three years amounted to $16,149,600, and for the number bonded last year to $21,320,400. Some of those bonded are so disguised in the description rendered as scarcely to be identified six months after landing, and become inmates of the Almshouse, or are committed by the magistrates as vagrants, and in some shape maintained by the city. A bonded passenger, over fifty years of age, applied at the Mayor's Office some time since for relief, whose age was set down in the list of passengers at twenty years. Comptroller Ewen on worthlessness of bonds.

"The Mayor is authorized, by an ordinance of the Corporation, to receive not less than one nor more than ten dollars for each passenger as a commutation of such bonds; but, as this is entirely optional with the party, the greater number are bonded. The number of foreign passengers arriving annually at this port, within the last three years, has averaged 60,539; the number annually bonded within the same period, 53,832; and the number annually commuted in the same time, 6,707, or about one-ninth of the whole number.

"It would be more advantageous to the city to receive the sum of one dollar for each passenger, now paid to individuals, than to take the bonds. A large amount would then be annually received by the Corporation towards the support of foreign poor; and in case any of the passengers arriving at this port should, upon examination, prove to be paupers sent here from the parishes of Europe, they could, with the avails of this fund, be sent back to the places from whence they were brought; which would have a strong tendency to discourage a repetition of such practices.

"The number of passengers arriving at this port during the last three years amounted to 181,615, of which 20,119 were commuted $21,452 17

Received on account of passengers bonded the sum of 19,939 28

Making a total receipt from these passengers of . $41,391 45

The whole number of passengers which arrived, at one dollar each, would have amounted to . 181,615 00

Whereby the city would have received in addition the sum of $140,223 55

or $46,744 51 per annum paid to individuals, as before stated."

During all that time, those who became chargeable were sent to the Almshouse, and the bondsmen paid the expenses of their board to the city authorities.

Private hospitals for emigrant sick.

Even this arrangement, though pecuniarily advantageous, only excited cupidity, and the bondsmen concluded to support the sick and indigent at private poor-houses and hospitals, where they could sustain them at rates lower than those charged by the Almshouse department. Experience having proved the plan feasible and profitable, these establishments soon became numerous, some being conducted by the passenger-shippers and others maintained by individuals, whose profits and business were confined alone to the medical care or temporary maintenance of the pauper or unfortunate emigrant. To this latter class of establishments, on account of their cheapness, many merchants and passenger agents transferred the destitute; but this system was associated with many grave and flagrant abuses. These evils gradually attracted public attention, and the various emigrant societies urged the necessity of a prompt and radical change.

Their abuses.

On February 2, 1846, the Board of Assistant Aldermen of the city of New York appointed a committee, consisting of Messrs. Purser, Gilbert, and Candee, relative to the treatment of certain emigrants in a place designated "Tapscott Poor-House and Hospital." This institution was established by the firm of W. & J. T. Tapscott, passenger-brokers in South Street, New York, and situated in North Sixth Street, in the then town of Williamsburg.

Investigation of "Tapscott Poor-House and Hospital" by Committee of Board of Assistant Aldermen.

The preamble and resolution read as follows:

"*Whereas*, The affidavits of William Long and others, relative to the unwholesome food furnished to destitute and unfortunate emigrants at a place denominated 'Tapscott's Poor-House and Hospital,' reveal a system of flagrant outrage and cupidity, and demand the instant investigation of the Common Council;

"*And whereas*, The present mode of landing alien passengers has pastured a class of unprincipled brokers, who, apparently irresponsible to any authority, continue to realize fortunes by inflicting inhuman wrongs upon the alien stranger; therefore,

"*Resolved*, That a special committee be appointed to investigate the case of the unfortunate emigrants, and that the committee be requested to report at the next meeting."

The affidavits referred to above of William Long, Thomas Farrell, Daniel Kelleher, John Egan, Thomas Judge, Owny Hogan, and Henry Mulholland, sworn to on January 30, 1846, say, that the deponents were induced to emigrate to this country upon the representations of ship-brokers and their runners; that upon arriving in this country they found it impossible to obtain work, and applied to the agents of these ships, and offered to work for their board; that these agents sent them to Tapscott's Poor-House and Hospital, where they were obliged to do laboring work, digging, and wheeling.

"And we further depose and say that the bread furnished us was totally unfit for use, and that the black biscuit shown the Mayor is a fair sample of the bread which we were compelled to eat; that the breakfast furnished us was composed of a species of meal so black as to be unfit for use, and to that was added molasses and made into a pottage; that our dinner was at times salt fish and the before-mentioned bread, and at other times of refuse grease with other mixtures collected from the ships during their trips across the Atlantic: 'the crumbs that fell from the rich men's table.'

"And we do further depose and say that tnere are inmates of the above establishment who are lying sick and in the most pitiful and wretched condition of suffering, quite unable to help themselves, and compelled to eat the food above described; that from the effects of eating such food we have been reduced to such a state of health as to be unable to work, and in consequence orders were given *to stop our supplies, and we have been without food since yesterday morning*."

Visit of Committee of citizens of Williamsburg to Tapscott's Hospital, and their report.

In consequence of these statements, the citizens of Williamsburg, on February 2, 1846, called a public meeting, and appointed a committee, consisting of Messrs. H. Fitzgerald, A. P. Moon, and Michael McCaffrey, for the purpose of enquiring as to the mode of treatment carried out in the establishment of Messrs. Tapscott & Co. On February 3, at the request and solicitation of the same Messrs. Tapscott, they visited the said establishment, which visit they describe as follows: "To our utter astonishment, even horror, we found it, if possible, even worse than represented, exhibiting a state of misery and wretchedness not to be borne or countenanced by any civilized community; the situation, fare, etc., of the occupants being worse, infinitely worse, if we may be allowed the term, than that of those in similar institutions (by name) attached to or connected with our common prisons. We have, therefore, come to the conclusion, and hesitate not to say, that we firmly believe the statements made in the affidavits of William Long and others in every particular literally true; and that the deplorable condition of the unfortunate (women particularly) dupes of the Messrs. Tapscott in this same establishment demands and requires the earliest possible attention from the friends of suffering humanity. Since we have visited this 'poor house' the committee procured comfortable situations and homes for those of the female residents of this modern but altogether novel prison-house. We now boldly—yes, publicly—challenge and defy the Messrs. Tapscott, or any of their friends, to an investigation, proof, or conviction. Dare they accept?"

Visit of Committee of Board of Assistant Aldermen.

A few days later, the Committee of the New York Board of Assistant Aldermen likewise personally inspected the premises in question, when every reasonable facility of examination was afforded by Mr. and Mrs. Miller, the superintendents. Though the visit must have been anticipated, the condition of the building appeared very unsatisfactory, both as regarded cleanliness and comfort. The number of persons in the institution appeared to to be from twenty-five to thirty, but it occasionally contained a larger number. The superintendent spoke favorably of the diet and treatment, in which opinion some of the inmates concurred, though in a manner evidently constrained. A female witness, indeed, who was examined at this interview, acknowledged to the Chairman of the Committee, who had an opportunity of speaking to her privately, "that, if she had told the truth, she would have seen the road mighty soon." The Committee of the citizens of Williamsburg, above referred to, obtained from the inmates a direct acknowledgment of the facts sworn to in the affidavits of Long and others. These gentlemen, from personal and prompt inspection, convinced of the treatment and suffering of the inmates, forwarded them articles of food.

Quality of food furnished.

The comprehensive testimony fully confirmed the complaints. In relation to the food, some twenty witnesses distinctly swore that the biscuit was generally "blue moulded," and offensive to "taste and smell;" and the samples, though sworn to be of the best description distributed, were dark and hard, and unsuited for the support of the females and children at the "Poor-House and Hospital."

It appeared, under oath, that the biscuit was frequently given to the hogs—the inmates preferring to go hungry and supperless to bed. The fish was represented to have been bad, and to have fallen to pieces when put into water to boil; and all affirmed, who were beyond the influence of the establishment, that the food supplied was equally deficient in quantity and quality. The soup was usually innutritious, and manufactured from grease or mutton tallow, which was kept in the superintendent's store-room to be employed for that purpose. The meat used is stated to have been musty and dark, and the bread "distributed twice a week in slices (to use the language of a witness) as big as your hand, and not enough for a child."

These statements were corroborated partly by the admissions of Tapscott and his employees, as well as by about fifty affidavits, the most important of which may find place here.

Affidavits of inmates.

Margaret Bertram, an inmate for nearly twelve months in the institution, "recollects that two children died there. The mother of one died at sea; no particular nurse took charge of it; several of us had milk, perhaps four or five, and each took it by turns; it died of summer complaint. The other infant died five weeks since; it was brought here by a woman not its mother; it was a weakly child; we suckled it turn and turn about; no particular person attended to it; several now in the New York Almshouse nursed it."

Fannie Mitchell, an intelligent young married woman, now at Bellevue, stated under oath the following facts: "That the child referred to by Margaret Bertram was sent over from Tapscott's office, and lived about a fortnight afterwards; that it came on Saturday, and Mr. Tapscott called on the Sunday following, and, an objection being made to nurse the infant, declared that any one who refused should be turned right out of doors. Under such circumstances the women consented, and took it turn and turn about."

Ann Doyle: "While I was there, some of the women induced a man who was cutting up some meat to give them a few slices, one of the women alleging that she wanted it for a sick child. They obtained about a pound, and Miller (the superintendent) discovered it in the evening, and went and informed Tapscott, who came the next morning and turned the women out; one had the sick child before mentioned."

"Another transaction, sustained under oath, we introduce," says the Committee, "as a further illustration of the disregard manifested for the health of the inmates, and the sanitary usages observed even by uncivilized communities. It appears that, of *the pigs* during the summer, a sow became sick and nearly dead," and that in this condition the superintendent directed it to be killed by one Lavendel; that the sow was afterwards scalded, cut up, and on the following day served at table, but it was so "unpleasant to the taste that the witnesses were unable to eat it."

Said Lavendel, an emigrant from Ireland, and for some time after his arrival an inmate of the house, further states, on oath, that a quantity of mutton-hams were brought there (to the hospital), and served up for dinner, which stunk and were unfit for use; oatmeal porridge was also served up for breakfast, which was bitter to the taste, and smelled bad; also rice for dinner which was unfit for use, and smelled bad. Deponent was compelled to eat what was put on the table or go without food. He further states that the allowance of meat for one week, including bone, was about one pound; that he was sick, and kept his bed about five days before he received any medical attendance, although he requested it previously; and that the sleeping apartments were filthy, uncomfortable, and filled with vermin.

Testimony of attending physician.

Dr. E. L. Cooke, the attending physician, says: "The cleanliness there is not remarkable; have observed this, and required them to keep it cleaner; but the matron has answered that it was difficult to get the inmates to perform such labor. In other institutions of a public character, better discipline would prevail; but the inmates do not feel themselves under sufficient restriction. The general want of cleanliness observable, he presumes, might be attributed to this cause and the laziness of the inmates. Thinks the inmates are not examined when they enter, or aware that there are any specific regulations with regard to cleanliness. No wearing apparel has, to his knowledge, been distributed among the sick. With reference to diet, what he directed for the patients he believed was supplied. The matron informed him so; have never enquired of the patients; never observed any peculiar appearance of disease among those who had been long inmates. The institution, as regards diet, general comfort, and medical treatment, cannot be compared with similar public institutions."

Report of Committee—Impolicy of permitting private poor-houses.

"Your Committee conceive"—we give here again their own words—"that the evidence before them is sufficient to convince the Common Council and the Legislature that poor-houses and hospitals should not be continued by passenger carriers. The proprietors are certainly not likely to provide liberally for the necessities, much less the comforts, of a household which is a constant source of individual trouble and expense. The same selfishness that would induce them to evade relieving the applicants would dictate the reduction of their fare, when admitted to the work-house, to the lowest standard, both of quality and quantity. Neither the Common Council nor the Legislature could feel disposed to permit these irresponsible establishments to multiply, a result which must occur, however, unless the law is amended. The unwholesome nature of the food, and the treatment of the helpless infants, is in evidence before you. No wearing apparel appears to have been distributed among the sick or well, with some trifling unimportant exception; and Margaret Bertram, an inmate nearly a year, and very destitute, acknowledged that she never received, with the exception of an order for a pair of shoes, any clothing whatever. Even on the confinement of any of the women, the other women have to provide the requisite articles of clothing for the infants. No attention is paid to the education of children who become chargeable to these brokers, and the only boy at Tapscott's work-house, the superintendent, Mr. Miller, stated, was held back from school for want of clothing, and the proprietor himself acknowledged that he did not know whether he went to school or not.

Immorality of same.

"The accommodation and arrangements of the house preclude the proper separation of the sexes, and the moral habits of the unfortunate inmates must deteriorate. The sick and destitute, the vicious and the innocent, are gathered together promiscuously, without any of the ordinary restraints to which, perhaps, in a distant country, they have been subjected, while they are denied the salutary influence of even police regulations.

"These facts, which rest upon sworn testimony, must command attention. It cannot be disputed that the heavy responsibilities connected with a poor-house and hospital should be transferred to the municipal authorities. The health and character of our city, and humanity to the alien stranger, are involved in this measure.

Frauds practised to gain admission to City Hospitals.

"The great acknowledged inferiority of such an establishment to Bellevue is a strong incentive to the destitute to obtain admission to our Almshouse by deception. Aware that their reception and continuance in the Almshouse depends on suppressing the fact of being chargeable to any particular passenger broker, they manufacture facts to secure better fare and treatment. Indeed, it is not improbable, though no direct evidence exists before the Committee, that they have co-operated with the pauper in the practice of these frauds. It is unquestionably true that thousands are annually relieved from the city treasury, which are properly chargeable to the bondsmen. Intentional inaccuracies frequently appear on the passenger list regarding the ages, occupations, and names of the passengers, with the view of transferring legal responsibility from the carriers. In the event of establishing the system of commutation, the duty of examining the emigrant passengers will require the exercise of vigilance and honesty. To deceive the Quarantine officers, and obtain permission to proceed immediately to the city, the captains of vessels dress up their sick, and similar artifice will be employed to evade the provisions of the proposed law.

"The German and other emigrants not familiar with our language are liable to even more than ordinary imposition and suffering. To secure the assistance from the bondsmen, without which in the winter months they would perish, constantly requires the co-operation of the officers of their national benevolent institutions; and many remarkable instances of deception and cruelty have become known to your Committee.

"Agents are sent to the principal cities and ports of Germany with the view of securing passengers for some particular line of vessels, and from three to six Rix dollars is imposed as 'head' or commutation money, though, even if the law we recommend was adopted, $1 25 (25 cents for hospital fee) would be the actual outlay.

Bonds annulled by crime.

"It is maintained among some, if not all, of the passenger brokers that they are released from the obligation of sustaining the persons bonded whenever convicted of an offence and sentenced to imprisonment. Though we must dissent from this opinion, it appears to have been formerly acquiesced in by the authorities, or to have escaped their examination. The commission of crime, committals for misdemeanor or vagrancy, serve the selfish interests of passenger agents, though we are unwilling to believe that the practice is resorted to ordinarily. Occasionally, however, the inmates of these private work-houses and hospitals are unwarrantably consigned to the Penitentiary on Blackwell's Island. Hugh Graham, who was a sick man, was sent with eight others to be disgraced and contaminated in one of our worst prisons for insubordination. He, with his companions, purchased bread, and even ate it, without permission of the officials. He was taken before a magistrate, and committed without even being made acquainted with his crime or called upon for defence.

O'Connor's case.

"Another illustration of the feelings governing some of the passenger carriers is to be found in the following anecdote, communicated by the President of the Irish Emigrant Society: A man named O'Connor, with his wife and three children, arrived in this country, and, having contracted a fever on board the vessel, was detained in the city till his money was exhausted, and the bondsmen were applied to for relief. Recovering sooner than the other members of the family, he set out for St. Louis, where his father was comfortably settled, and, securing the necessary funds, returned with the fond expectation of accompanying his wife and children to their new home. He found, however, on reaching New York that his wife was dead and his children shipped to Liverpool, where they had neither friends nor relatives. One of the children died on the passage, and of the others no tidings have been obtained, though diligent enquiries have been instituted. Messrs. Tapscott were the agents and bondsmen in this case.

"With the gradual but certain increase of immigration, these evils must extend. The cupidity of the proprietors of these private establishments threatens even the health of our city, not only from uncleanliness, but the introduction of cases of ship-fever.

"With these views, your Committee respectfully submit the following resolution for adoption:

Resolution.

"*Resolved*, That the condition of Tapscott's Poor-House and Hospital, and the evidence relative to the general treatment of the inmates, strongly demand a change in the present system of bonding and commuting alien passengers."

Second Committee of Investigation of Board of Assistant Aldermen.

During the summer of 1846, another committee of investigation was appointed from the same Board, relative to the management of an emigrant hospital on Manhattan Island, which resulted in confirming the opinion that such irresponsible institutions were equally disastrous to the morals, health, and happiness of those compelled to seek a temporary asylum in them.

Report.

The report expressed strong disapprobation of the "want of comfort, cleanliness, and health prevailing," and the necessity of the employment of some means to remove the evils. After the interference of the committee, some improvement occurred in the treatment of patients, and the number of inmates in the two-story building, about 46 feet square, was reduced from 120 to 80.

The extreme heat of the summer, and the want of cleanliness, neglect of ventilation, and poor diet at this hospital, induced the Mayor to summon the Board of Health. A committee of that body examined the establishment, and reported strongly in favor of remedying the evils connected with these private hospitals and poor-houses, and, by a change in the law, urged the propriety of confiding in the city authorities the charge of the sick and destitute emigrants. Investigation by Board of Health.

"The system now existing," says the report of Alderman Purser, from which we have quoted the above, "is disgraceful to the city, and unparalleled in Europe. The municipal authorities are divested actually of the power of investigating and relieving cases of severe suffering and destitution. A ship arrives in our port with five hundred emigrants; a broker, irresponsible in every point of view, after examination, agrees to assume the responsibility of supporting those that may become chargeable within two years, at the rate of forty or fifty cents a head. Should any apply, as thousands do, annually, to the Almshouse Commissioners for relief, they are referred, however emergent and pitiable the case, to this broker, and his personal and pecuniary interest dictates refusal or delay. If compelled to provide for the unfortunate a temporary shelter, the treatment to which they are exposed is calculated to break their spirits and smooth the path of degradation and crime. Report of Alderman Purser, recommending a change in the system.

"A proper separation of the sexes is wholly neglected, and the young and innocent female is exposed to temptation, and her mind, at least, corrupted by infamous association. The destitution of the healthy emigrant is usually only temporary, and their future destiny governed, to a great extent, by the circumstances into which they are thrown at their arrival. With this view of the subject, your Committee are impressed with the conviction that legislative interference is imperatively demanded in justice to the tax-payer and humanity to the emigrant."

"Your Committee have before them a memorial in favor of the proposed alteration of the laws, signed by the acting Presidents of the Irish, German, British, Welsh, and Scotch emigrant societies, which states that the change would increase the revenue Memorial of Emigrant Societies in favor of same.

of the city and secure the emigrants from the frauds now practised upon them.

Paupers, care of refused by bondmen.

"Within the last month, nearly five hundred emigrants from Germany were sent directly from the ship to the Almshouse, where a large proportion now remain, being utterly destitute of means, and sent out at the expense of the property-owners in their immediate neighborhood.* The bondsmen refuse to pay the expenses in this instance, on some wholly insufficient pretence, and the city will be most probably compelled to commence suits for the recovery. It must have been known to the foreign agents shipping such passengers that they principally consisted of paupers. When compelled to leave the ship, they took refuge on the pier, where they continued until the city authorities removed them to Bellevue. Utterly destitute, and strangers to our language and country, sick from the effects of a long voyage and indifferent diet and accommodation, these people became an immediate charge upon the city, and yet the bondsmen refuse to indemnify the Corporation. A lighter was sent by the agents to take off the whole of these passengers, with the view of sending them to Albany; but, many of them being sick, and all being penniless and without means of supporting themselves for that journey, they refused.

"In the event of the bondsmen sustaining the decrepit or aged for the full period of two years required by law, on its expiration they are thrown upon the county for support. Such a class of persons for many reasons usually remain in our city; and, if a proper system of commutation prevailed, a fund would be raised adequate for their maintenance."

Establishment of Emigration Board.

The change so long desired by all disinterested parties was effected a year later by the establishment of the Board of the Commissioners of Emigration of the State of New York.

* The emigrants referred to were poor people from the Odenwald, who, however, had not been sent out by the property-owners in their immediate neighborhood, but at the expense of the grand ducal government of Baden. F. K.

CHAPTER IV.

ARRIVAL IN NEW YORK—RUNNERS—BOARDING-HOUSES—INLAND VOYAGE.

ALTHOUGH in point of time anterior to the period of which we are treating, the facts which constitute the basis of the narrative of this chapter refer to a state of things which, in a greater or lesser degree, had existed for the preceding twenty years, but which was fully exposed, for the first time, only by the careful official investigation, of which we shall speak in the following.

Attempts of Commissioners of Emigration to prevent frauds on arriving emigrants.

The kind of fraud and imposition on emigrants which is here described continued until the year 1855, that is, up to the time when, by an act of the Legislature, the Commissioners of Emigration secured the compulsory landing of emigrants at the Castle Garden depot, which gave them the control over them necessary for their protection. Not having sufficient means at their command, the Commissioners for years had tried in vain to protect the emigrants on their landing. They perceived the real source of the evil from the time of the creation of the Board, and did all in their power to do away with it. Complying with their urgent solicitations, the Legislature, in October 11, 1847, appointed a select committee to investigate the frauds and impositions alleged to be practised upon emigrant passengers arriving in this State.

Committee of Investigation of Legislature, 1847.

The Committee, consisting of Messrs. Thomas Smith, A. S. Upham, D. S. McNamara, A. E. Chandler, and James C. Rutherford, cheerfully assumed and most efficiently discharged their duties. It is due to the indefatigable and energetic efforts of these gentlemen that we have the documentary evidence of all sorts of frauds practised upon emigrants. In order to make a thorough investigation of the subject committed to their charge, they went to the city of New York, and made themselves acquainted with the various stages through which the emigrants passed after landing, till they got on board the steamboats to come up the river. It is their official report, with its accompanying documents, containing the examinations of the different parties and witnesses, which forms the basis of the following statements:

Report of same.—System of defrauding emigrants practised by boarding house keepers and runners.

"Your Committee must confess," the report says, "that they had no conception of, nor would they have believed, the extent to which these frauds and outrages have been practised, until they came to investigate them. As soon as a ship, loaded with these emigrants, reaches our shores, it is boarded by a class of men called runners, either in the employment of boarding-house keepers or forwarding establishments, soliciting custom for their employers. In order the more successfully to enable the latter to gain the confidence of the emigrant, they usually employ those who can speak the same language with the emigrant. If they cannot succeed in any other way in getting possession and control over the object of their prey, they proceed to take charge of their luggage, and take it to some boarding-house for safe-keeping, generally under the assurance that they will charge nothing for carriage-hire or storage. In this way they are induced to go to some emigrant boarding-house, of which there are a great many in the city, and then too often under a pretence that they will charge but a small sum for meals or board. The keepers of these houses induce these people to stay a few days, and, when they come to leave, usually charge them three or four times as much as they agreed or expected to pay, and exorbitant prices for storing their luggage; and, in case of their inability to pay, their luggage is detained as security. Some of these runners are employed by the month, and some work upon commission. Where they are in the employment of the forwarding establishments or passenger offices, and receive a commission for each passenger they bring in, they are, in many cases, allowed by their employers to charge all they can get over a certain sum for transporting the passenger to a particular place. This, it will be seen, stimulates the runners to great exertions, not only to get as many passengers as possible, but to get them at the highest possible prices. To enable them to carry out their designs, all sorts of falsehoods are resorted to to mislead and deceive the emigrant as to the prices of fare and mode of conveyance.

"Your Committee have been shocked to find that a large portion of the frauds committed upon these innocent and, in many cases, ignorant foreigners, are committed by their own countrymen who have come here before them; for we find the German preying upon the German, the Irish upon the Irish, the English upon the English, etc.; but at the same time we cannot hold our own countrymen entirely guiltless, for many of them, it is to be regretted, are engaged in this nefarious business."

State law relating to power of Health Officer at Quarantine.

It was then, and still is, the law of the State of New York that a vessel arriving at Quarantine is under the control of the health officer, and that consequently the ship-owners can exercise no control over their own vessels until they pass out of the hands of that officer.

Until 1844, the practice was for him to license small schooners or lighters, by which all the passengers discharged at the Quarantine were brought to the city. The suffering to which passengers were exposed by this mode of conveyance, from being frequently many hours on deck, exposed to sun and rain, and frequently arriving in the city at night, induced the larger shipping-houses to cause the emigrants to be brought up by steamboats, thus greatly increasing their comfort. The practice was for these houses to give their agents an order on the Custom House to receive permits to take the passengers from their ships, and thus to secure to them the exclusive privilege of bringing passengers from their ships. Other vessels, and especially those owned by smaller houses, proceeded at once directly to their piers in the city. The larger the immigration became, the more profitable it was for the runners to get hold of the ships; they spared no effort and resorted to all kinds of tricks and devices to obtain the exclusive control of the emigrant ships. They frequently went to the Custom House, and, under false pretences, took out permits without the knowledge or consent of the owners. Captains of vessels, which came directly to the city, were often paid several hundred dollars by the runners for the mere permission to board their ships at Quarantine, and proceed with them to their piers.

Devices of runners to evade same and board vessels.

"It is not uncommon," said the health officer, Dr. Henry Van Hovenburgh, in his examination, "after the vessel is cleared from Quarantine, for eight or ten boat-loads of runners to surround it; they are desperate men, and can be kept off only by an armed force."

This state of things must be borne in mind in order to properly understand the dangers to which the emigrants were exposed on their arrival in the port of New York.

Testimony of President of Netherland Emigrant Society.

The following affidavits will more fully show the mode of operations of these runners, and of the establishments in whose interest they worked. Thus, R. Schoyer, being duly sworn, says:

"I am a Director of the Netherland Emigrant Society. The first fraud practised upon the emigrant is this: the moment a vessel arrives it is boarded by runners, whose first object appears to be to get emigrants to their respective public-houses. Once there, they are considered sure prey. These runners represent the interests of all the various taverns and forwarding lines. Each party bringing with them their bullies to fight off their opponents, the emigrants become bewildered. As there is frequent bloodshed upon such occasions, the strongest party carry off the emigrants. Previously to going to the taverns, they are told that meals will be furnished for 6*d.* each, and 6*d.* for lodging, when, in fact, they are never charged less than 2*s.* and often $1, per meal; and their baggage is held until all is paid. The next ordeal through which the emigrant is obliged to pass is called 'booking,' by which is meant that the emigrant is taken to the forwarding office, and then induced to pay his money for the fare to the West. The emigrant is informed that that is the only office in which they can pay their money, the proprietors thereof being sole owners of the steamboats, railroads, and canal-boats throughout the entire route. After having thus gained the confidence of the emigrant, he unsuspectingly pays his money, upon the assurance that he will have no more to pay. The money received, the runner gets one dollar for every passenger booked, besides a salary varying from $30 to $100 per month, which is divided with the landlord."

"Booking.

P. H. Hodenpyle, being sworn, says: "I am agent of the Netherland Emigrant Society; have been since April last; I have been in danger frequently of personal violence from the runners; they are Hollanders, Germans, English, Irish, etc. There have gone, this fall, one Hollander and two German runners to Europe to establish agencies for forwarding passengers from New York to the Western States and Territories."

Charles H. Webb deposes under oath: "I am Superintendent of the British Protective Emigrant Society; have occupied the station three years. From my own knowledge, I have known frauds upon emigrants. One of the common frauds practised by the emigrant boarding-house keepers is that they generally have five or six persons about their establishments, who, if they cannot prevail on the emigrant to accompany them to the boarding-house they represent, when coming from the Quarantine to the city, on their arrival at the dock seize their baggage by force, and have it carried by cartmen, who are privy to their operations, to the boarding-houses. With the baggage once in the house, the emigrant, if dissatisfied with the accommodation and wishes his things removed to another place, is met by the landlord with a charge for either storage or one day's board, compelling him to put up with the accommodations offered him, or pay five or six dollars without an equivalent. These boarding-houses make it a rule, for instance, if emigrants arrive at 7 o'clock P.M. and leave the next day at 10 or 2 o'clock, to charge two days' board ar d lodging for what in fact constitutes only one day. The keepers of emigrant boarding-houses are invariably foreigners, the natives of each nation preying upon their own countrymen. The runners represent to the emigrant that his charges are sixpence sterling for each meal, and the same for lodging, and no charge for cartage of baggage to their houses or for storage while it remains there. When the emigrant is ready to leave, he calls for his bill, and is surprised to find that he is required to pay from $1 to $2 per day for his board, and often $2 to $3 cartage for his baggage. The keepers exercise their right of lien on the goods until the price is paid."

Testimony of Supt. of British Protective Emigrant Society.

Extortion of boarding-house keepers.

"I was in a boarding-house in Cherry Street," says Hiram Huested. "A man came up to settle his bill, which the landlord made out at $18. 'Why,' says the man, 'did you not agree to board me for 6*d*. a meal and 3*d*. for a bed?' 'Yes,' says the landlord, 'and that makes just 75 cents per day. You have been here just eight days, and that makes just $18.'"

Testimony of One-eyed Daley.

George W. Daley (the notorious One-eyed Daley), who had been engaged in forwarding passengers on the canal, and left business, as he alleged, from disgust with the imposition practised by his partners, and by the men in his employment, upon emigrants, said: "Mr. Roach (one of the former partners of Daley) spent his time in New York, and managed the business there. When a vessel was reported, he generally sent down three or four men to engage the passengers. If the vessel was a Dutch one (German), he would send down Dutchmen (Germans); if an English vessel, he would send Englishmen. He got the passengers at the best possible rates, sometimes at one price and sometimes at another. Men in our employ have frequently brought passengers to me, and stated that they had represented to the passengers that they were to go by railroad or packet; in such cases I have invariably told my men that I should not thus impose upon them, as we had no arrangement with the railroad and packets, and would not book them in that way, and that they must not promise them in that way. What I mean by 'booking' is, making bargains with passengers and giving them tickets. Our books are made in the form of a check-book; the ticket is cut out, like a bank-check, and a memorandum of it is left; the men who board the vessels carry a book with them and furnish the tickets.

'Booking."

"Frequently the 'night-watch' from the Custom House, when they board a vessel, extol some particular transportation line or emigrant forwarding-house; and, when they leave in the morning, manage to get the name of some one or more of the passengers, which they report to the emigrant forwarding-house. I do not know that they receive anything for their services, but I have no doubt they do; this is what is called 'stooling.' There is another way of 'stooling' frequently practised, which is for the runner to go on board and employ some one or more of the emigrants of influence to engage the passengers to go by his line, for which the emigrant is paid a bonus. The following case came to my knowledge two years ago this summer: A runner went on board an English vessel, at Quarantine, singled out a man of influence, and offered him a gold watch and chain if he would induce those on board to go by the line by which he was employed. The man agreed to it, on condi

'Stooling."

tion that he could have the watch in advance. The runner took it from his own pocket, threw the chain over the neck of the Englishman, and put the watch in his pocket. The man then went to work and got all the passengers booked according to agreement. They went up to the city in company. The luggage was taken to the boat. The runner and his friend went into an office, where they found a man, who seized the Englishman and exclaimed, 'Then you are the man that robbed the man of his watch, are you?' The runner made his escape precipitately, and the Englishman was compelled to give up the watch, and paid a handsome sum in addition."

Testimony of Police Captain Boudinot.

Tobias Boudinot, being duly sworn, says: "I am Captain of Police of the Third Ward. Many of the steamboats that land emigrants from Quarantine land at the docks in the Third Ward. There they are immediately visited by the runners from the emigrant boarding-houses, backed by bullies to assist in soliciting passengers to go to the different houses. As the emigrant attempts to take his luggage from on board the boat, the runner will endeavor to get it from him, and by force, unless there is a sufficient police to protect him, representing that they will keep them at sixpence sterling for each meal, and sixpence sterling for lodging, and no charge made for cartage or storage for luggage. When the emigrant comes to pay his bill, he is never able to get off at the contract price, but is compelled to pay from three shillings to fifty cents for each meal and lodging, one dollar and fifty cents for cartage, when, if it was paid at the time, it could not, under the law, be but thirty-one cents and fifty cents per day for storage for an ordinary-sized chest, and other things in proportion."

Forwarding Houses—Frauds of.

The greatest frauds, however, were committed by the forwarding-houses, to which some allusion has already been made in the foregoing affidavits. At that time, the only route West was *via* Albany, and thence by the canal, or, since 1846, by railroad to Buffalo, the Erie and Pennsylvania railroads not having been completed until 1852 or 1853. The trip from New York to Albany was made by steamer, and was comparatively the quickest part of the journey West, as it did not take more than ten hours to reach Albany. The emigrants generally bought tickets in

New York, with the understanding and assurance that they were to be forwarded on to their place of destination with their luggage without further charge; but, when they arrived at Albany, the person to whom they were consigned denied the authority of the persons of whom the tickets were bought. If the tickets were accepted, the emigrants were required to pay exorbitantly for the transportation of their luggage, and were often cheated in its weight. "Among the numerous frauds," says the Committee in their Report to the Assembly, "practised by these runners and forwarding-houses, there is, perhaps, none greater than that which exists in the sale of passage-tickets. The emigrant is shown a neatly printed ticket, with a picture of a steamboat, railroad-cars, and canal-packet, with three horses attached to it, and is given to understand that such a ticket will take him to a given place beyond Albany in a specified manner, and for a price to be agreed upon; and after disposing of the ticket for an exorbitant price, the emigrant is furnished with a steamboat ticket to take him to Albany, where he is to present this passage-ticket to some person or company upon which it is drawn, where it is often either protested, or objections taken to the mode of conveyance; and the passenger, instead of going upon the railroad or packet-boat as agreed upon, is thrust into the steerage or hold of a line boat, where he is often known to complain—when the only evidence he can furnish of the fraud committed upon him is to exhibit his ticket with a picture of three horses, while the line boats are only drawn by two.

"A pretence is also often set up for not honoring these tickets, that the freight is not paid, or, at least, that enough has not been paid upon the luggage, and the emigrant is either detained at Albany or compelled to pay additional charges

"It will be seen from the testimony taken that immense sums of money are drawn from these emigrants by overcharging, both for their fare and the freight of their luggage; and, not satisfied with this, some of the persons engaged in this forwarding business are in the habit of defrauding them in the weight of their luggage, by using false scales and giving false statements of the amounts forwarded."

"I have found in most cases (especially when they come in large bodies)," says David Neligan, an old citizen of Albany, and the official agent of the Commissioners of Emigration at that place, "that the emigrants were 'booked' in New York, meaning that they had agreed for their passage, and were consigned to some one of the forwarding-offices here. In such cases, they are generally furnished with a 'passage-ticket' purporting to be a receipt in full for the conveyance of themselves and luggage to their destination; but on their arrival here they find in many instances they must pay steamboat freight for their luggage, cartage to the office or canal-boat, and canal freight for their luggage again, which has all to be weighed; and here the poor strangers begin to discover that they have been imposed upon. In many cases, too, the emigrant discovers here, for the first time, that there is a balance due on his passage-money (which balance varies from one to twenty dollars), and is so endorsed on his ticket, and which he must pay on pain of detention and forfeiture of all he has previously paid. In other cases, the contract is to pay half the money in advance, and the other half at the end of the journey; but I have never known an instance of this kind in which the balance of the money was not exacted in Albany, although their destination may be in the far West or Canada. Remonstrance in such cases is utterly in vain, and the poor emigrant is compelled to submit, and frequently at a very great sacrifice of convenience, and even of physical requirements." Testimony of David Neligan, agent at Albany of Commissioners of Emigration.

We will now enter more closely into an examination of the three most flagrant modes of ill-treatment and fraud, namely, 1st, *False weighing*; 2d, *Overcharging the emigrant for transportation of himself and luggage*; 3d, *Brutal treatment on the part of agents and runners.* Three chief frauds

The ordinary prices from New York and Albany by steamer and canal were very low. The price paid by the forwarding-houses for passage on deck of the steamboats from New York to Albany and Troy was uniformly fifty cents for each passenger, including fifty pounds of luggage, and all extra luggage fifteen cents per hundred pounds; from Albany to Buffalo regularly fifty cents, and exceptionally only one dollar for steerage passage, forty pounds of luggage free, and extra luggage thirty-six and a half cents per hundred False weighing.

pounds. The emigrant, however, was never charged less than five dollars from New York to Buffalo, and one dollar for every one hundred pounds extra luggage; and the enormous difference between the prices paid by the forwarding-houses and charged to the emigrants were divided among the former and their soliciting agents or runners.

The prices of conveying passengers from Buffalo to the cities and villages on the upper and lower lakes varied between $1 and $5. Thus, for the fore part of the season of 1847, they were on the upper lakes, for the first two months, $3 each, and from $1 25 to $1 50 on the lower lakes; after that the forwarding-houses paid $2 on the upper and $1 on the lower lakes, and towards the close of the season the prices were raised to $5 on the upper and $2 on the lower lakes. The lowest prices charged to the emigrant were from New York to Cleveland, $5 50; Milwaukee and Chicago, $9 50 and $10; Cincinnati, $12; Louisville, $13; St. Louis, $14; and Galena, $16.

Testimony of Charles Cook, book-keeper in forwarding-house.

"From the opening of navigation in 1847 till 31st day of July," says Charles Cook (a book-keeper in an emigrant forwarding-house), "forwarding companies paid the transportation lines for steerage passengers by canal, river, and lake, from New York to Chicago, $3, including 65 lbs. luggage; they charged emigrants from $5 to $8; luggage costs from about 75 cents per 100 lbs., and is charged from $1 50 to $2 per 100 lbs. The actual cost for steerage passengers, in emigrant cars, from Albany to Buffalo, thence to Chicago, is $6 50, for which the emigrant pays $12; this includes 100 lbs. of luggage on the river and an indefinite amount on the railroad; the usual rate on the railroad is $1 25 per 100 lbs. A deduction of $3 is made to all passengers who stop at Detroit or any point this side, on the lower lakes; this costs the forwarding companies about $5 50 by railroad; if on the canal (steerage) the charge is $5, and it costs about $2. This is up to the 1st of August; on the lakes the rates have advanced since the 1st of August, $3, from Buffalo to Chicago, and $1 on the lower lakes."

Up to 1850 or 1855, only a very small percentage of emigrants went West by railroad, but the prices asked and obtained from them were none the less exorbitant, as will more fully appear from the following list:

Rates charged Western emigrants for railroad fares.

Price from New York.		Cost by Steamboat.	Railroad.	By Lake.	Total.	Profit.
To Buffalo.......	$6 00	$0 50	$4 00	$0 00	$4 50	$1 50
To Cleveland.....	9 00	0 50	4 00	1 00	4 50	3 65
To Detroit........	9 25	0 50	4 00	1 00	5 50	3 75
To Chicago.......	12 00	0 50	4 00	2 00	6 50	5 50
To Cincinnati.....	12 50	0 50	4 00	and canal 3 50	8 00	4 50
To Pittsburg......	10 50	0 50	4 00	3 00	7 50	3 00
To St. Louis......	14 50	0 50	4 00	5 00	9 50	5 00
To Louisville.....	13 50	0 50	4 00	4 50	9 00	4 50

In addition to the payment of the above prices to the agents of the railroad monopoly, the emigrants had to pay freight on their luggage from New York to Albany, and cartage from steamboat to railroad depot, and then cartage at Buffalo, from railroad to steamboat, and their freight on their baggage across the lakes, collected by one of these same contracting agents, located at Buffalo, although the prices charged for tickets include luggage fees.

All the above charges were, so to speak, legitimate, and, although yielding a very handsome profit to the forwarding-houses, they were not so exorbitant as to take more than a few dollars out of the pockets of the emigrants. The profits realized, however, by exacting these fares went exclusively into the pockets of the New York houses, for the emigrants on landing were cheated into the belief that it was to their interest to buy at once their tickets to their respective destinations (by which operation the runner secured to himself two or three dollars more). But the New York houses were not so cruel as to injure the interests of their Albany and Buffalo friends and correspondents. The emigrant was their common victim, whom they would despoil so long as he had anything left. The New York forwarders therefore, after having made their share out of him, handed the emigrant over to their friends West, with the expectation that he still had something out of which he could be defrauded.

False weighing at Albany and Buffalo.

When the passenger paid his fare in New York, it was the general rule to say nothing to him about the extra luggage.

Overcharging for and false weighing of the latter formed one of the chief sources of plunder of the Albany and Buffalo houses, and, if enough could not be made in this way, the repayment of the whole or part of the fare was exacted. The sworn testimony of some of the parties interested and of disinterested witnesses will more fully prove this.

Testimony of Geo. W. Daley.

1. *As to False Weighing.*—"I know," says the above-mentioned Geo. W. Daley, "that great frauds are practised in weighing luggage; a Mr. Weaver, in this city, did the weighing for Smethurst & Co.; I have known him to make luggage tally from 25 to 40 per cent. more than it weighed; his scales are generally wrong; he aimed to increase the weight about 33 per cent.; I have weighed on his scales 274 lbs., when my actual weight was about 170 lbs.; while I was with Smethurst as partner, I have fixed the scales, or had them fixed, four or five times."

Henry Bishop.

Henry Bishop sworn, and says: "I reside in the city of Albany, and am clerk for Malburn & Co.; I have seen at the emigrant forwarding-offices two separate tallies kept of the weight of the luggage; one for settling with the emigrant, and the other for settling with the owner of the boat. There was a difference between the tallies; it would vary about one-third; the tally that was kept for the boat was the true weight; that for the passengers was made to overrun the true weight 300 or 400 lbs. in 800 or 900 lbs. I have seen G. W. Daley do this at Smethurst's office, at No. 122 Pier, Albany, and also at 104 Pier, another of Smethurst's offices; this was a year ago. I have seen this done three or four times; have seen no one do it but Daley; was once in the employment of Smethurst; have weighed baggage there; have never kept two tallies."

Agent of Holland Emigration Society.

"I have known men in the employment of Smethurst," says Jonathan Brooks, Jr., agent of the Holland Emigration Society in Albany, "to take their scale on board the boat and weigh luggage there. I have seen them, in weighing luggage, put their foot upon the platform to increase the weight, and have spoken to them on the subject. I have lent them my scale, and had it returned out of order, invariably weighing more than it should."

Sergeant-at-arms of Assembly.

Benjamin D. Quigg, being duly sworn, says "that he is deputy sergeant-at-arms of the House of the Assembly. Some few days since he went, by direction of the Committee, to investigate frauds upon emigrants, to the office of H. D. Smethurst, Pier 122, Albany, who is engaged in forwarding emigrants, to serve a subpœna on said Smethurst and others, and saw a man weighing luggage. After he left the office, I stepped on the scales, and weighed myself, and weighed 163½ pounds by them. I then went to the store of Corning, Horner & Co., and was weighed upon their scales, and weighed 142½ pounds. I weighed a young man who was with me at the time on both scales, and found the same relative difference to exist."

Josiah Clarke.

"A few days ago," deposes Josiah Clarke, of Albany, in November, 1847, "I was weighed on H. D. Smethurst's scales, at his office, 122 Pier, Albany, and weighed more than 200 pounds. I had been weighed a week before, and weighed 169 pounds."

David Neligan.

"I have frequently attended," testifies David Neligan, the above-named agent of the Commissioners of Emigration, "to the weighing of luggage at the office of Smethurst, and on his boats; have detected and prevented frauds in the weight; in one instance, I saw a lot of luggage weighed and marked at 700 pounds at the above office; I thought the weight most extraordinary for so small a lot, and went to Mr. Roach, who, I believe, was a partner of Smethurst, and asked him to come and weigh a lot of baggage, not telling him that I knew the weight at which it had been set down; he came forward, and weighed it at 500 pounds. I saw on one occasion an emigrant pay, at that office, $16 for 400 pounds to Detroit, and on another $59 freight on 1,600 pounds to Milwaukee; have on many occasions known emigrants pay from $2 50 to $6 for 100 pounds to Milwaukee and Chicago, and in one instance, when the man objected to the price, he was told that most of it went to the Government."

"A lot of eighty-six Hollanders lay here waiting," writes an anonymous Buffalo philanthropist, on July 18, 1847, to the Mayor of Albany, "that had paid in Troy over $1,150 for fare, $680 for passage, and $433 for luggage. We weighed the luggage, and the overweight, at a fair price, will not come to $75. Shipped by P. O'Hern, New York, Emery Mathews, Troy."

Overcharging, etc.

2. *Relative to Overcharging, Repayment, and Extra Luggage.*—The New York runners always required pay in advance, giving a ticket on some person at Albany, generally on Roach & Smethurst. When the emigrants arrived at Albany, this ticket was often found to be a fraud, no one appearing there to pass them forward.

Testimony of Josiah Clarke.

Josiah Clarke, who had been most of the time for twenty years in the passenger and freight business at Albany, being sworn, said: "I know that the emigrant passenger business has been carried on fraudulently for three or four years in this city; frequently persons come on from New York with tickets which they suppose are to take them through to Buffalo by railroad, and find that they are to be provided with accommodation in the steerage of a canal-boat on their arrival at Albany. They frequently pay passage from here to Buffalo, and the man furnishing tickets, instead of entering payment in full, enters on the ticket $3 or some other sum '*on account*' of passage, and the man is compelled to pay over again as much as would have been sufficient to carry him through in the first instance. I have known a great number of instances of this kind."

George Thomas defrauded by Smethurst.

George Thomas, on October 13, 1847, agreed with a person in the city of New York to pay $20 for the passage of himself and family to Pittsburg, and to pay for freight not over $1 per 100 pounds; and he received a ticket and was directed to call upon Henry D. Smethurst, in this city. On arriving in this city, he went to Smethurst's office, who received the ticket, and then charged him $29 for extra luggage. Deponent told him of his contract in New York, and asked Smethurst for his ticket back; he refused to give it, telling deponent to help himself.

Wm. P. Pfaff, emigrant runner.

William P. Pfaff, one of the German runners of Smethurst at Albany, and one of the meanest of the whole gang, said: "I spend most of my time in transferring passengers from steamboats to the office and canal boats; Mr. Smethurst has no established price to charge passengers; most of the contracts are made in New York, and the passengers are consigned to him; luggage is not weighed in New York; he has no established price for luggage; sometimes the passengers contract in New York; if not, Smethurst charges what he pleases; passengers ordinarily think that the price paid in New York for passage included all their luggage; the runners in New York encourage them in that belief; Smethurst's agents, I presume, do the same; Smethurst employed runners in New York; I think in almost all cases passengers are displeased and disappointed when they are called upon to pay for their luggage; they say that they have already paid it, and insist upon it that they have done so; Smethurst exacts pay of them, and in some instances detains their luggage till he is paid; his charges are such as suit him, without reference to the convenience or will of the passenger; the exaction is arbitrary and must be paid, if the passenger has the means; when a passenger refuses to go on to his place of destination, Smethurst never refunds the money already paid; if a passenger who contracts for a passage to Chicago pays enough to go to Buffalo, and leaves the rest unpaid, he is never permitted to go beyond Albany till the balance is paid."

David Neligan citing various cases of extortion on citizens.

The most important evidence is that of Mr. Neligan. He says: "My attention has been called to many cases of fraud practised on American citizens, equally flagrant with those upon foreigners, some of which have already received the attention of your Committee. I will only mention a few more.

"Amasa Prescott, of Belfast, Me., paid $40 for two passengers from Boston to Milwaukee, by railroad to Buffalo, and cabin passage on the lakes. These tickets were refused at Albany, but an offer was made to convey him by canal and steerage on the lake, which would make a difference of $16. This statement was made by Prescott to Senator Beach. I do not know how he settled it, as I did not see him afterwards.

"Mrs. M. Frier, of Syracuse, paid $6 50 from New York to Syracuse by railroad, consigned to Smethurst in this city; but Smethurst refused to send her by that mode, and I had to procure a gratuitous pass from E. Corning, Esq., by railroad, Smethurst refusing to refund.

"I have seen many of the latter class who, upon discovering the fraud, destroyed their tickets and proceeded on their journey, rather than encounter the delay or trouble of seeking redress.

Same citing cases of emigrants defrauded.

"I will mention a few other cases of emigrants.

"James Heslop, a Scotchman, paid Smethurst & Co. thirty

sovereigns, or $145 25, for three persons to Port Washington, Ohio. The ordinary expense of the journey at that time (1st August) was $8 61. W. Reese, a Welshman, paid for two persons and two hundred and fifty pounds luggage from New York to Milwaukee, $27 36; but, on arriving at Buffalo, the ticket was repudiated by the agent, and Reese, I am informed, and several others in a like predicament, had to pay their fare over the lake. Reese returned to Albany to seek redress, but in vain.

"Mr. Carron and wife paid $21 to Milwaukee from New York. The steamboat tickets on the river were refused, and he had to pay one dollar and fifty cents for passage, and seventy-five cents for luggage (although he had less than a hundred pounds). He had to go twice to New York to prosecute Selover (the agent), who was indicted, and afterwards paid his fare by railroad, losing the whole sum which he paid originally for his passage, besides expenses of two trips to New York, detention, etc.

"Samuel Collis paid six sovereigns for five passengers from New York to Toronto. Smethurst demanded thirteen dollars more. On his stating his inability to pay it, he was told he could go no further. His Honor the Mayor, and Thurlow Weed, Esq., gave him twelve dollars, and I procured a passage to his destination for ten dollars. His affidavit, taken before his Honor the Recorder, is in my possession.

"James Clark paid nine dollars for three full passengers from New York to Cayuga Bridge by railroad from Albany. Smethurst refused to send him by railroad, and purchased his ticket back for one dollar and twenty-five cents.

"James Lind, a Scotchman, with five children, from New York to Hamilton, C. W., paid $26 50. At Rochester, the captain of the boat told him he could not send him to Canada, as he had received but ten dollars, and he must have three more for his trouble. Lind had no ticket or evidence whatever, as Smethurst said it was not necessary, and the captain was an honorable man. I was present at the making of this agreement myself, and supposed all was right, until I received a letter from Mr. Cook, editor of the Rochester *Democrat*, informing me that Lind and his family were in the Rochester Almshouse, and requested me to get the money back from Smethurst. This Smethurst refused to do, but he sent an order to his agent at Rochester to forward Lind immediately. I know nothing further of this case.

"I deem it unnecessary to increase this list, although I could do so to a much greater extent."

One of the most impudent frauds which are recorded in the Report of the Committee is that one perpetrated by two German runners, by the name of Pfaff and Schmidt, on two of their countrymen, a certain Christian Duensing and Wm. Heuer, both passengers per ship *Minna* from Bremen, and natives of Hanover. Each of them had a family, consisting of himself, wife, and four children, making in all four and one-half full passengers, and each paid in New York the sum of forty dollars and fifty cents for the transportation of himself and family and luggage to Chicago. On arriving at Albany, Pfaff snatched the tickets and receipts from them, saying; "These are papers which you should have delivered before, for they belong to me;" and Schmidt made Duensing as well as Heuer pay ninety dollars in addition to their fare, and forty-seven dollars for extra luggage. On this occasion, Schmidt said: "You must not imagine we can carry you so cheap; great deal of this money is to go to the government of the canal, which has laid out *upwards of eighteen millions of dollars;*" he said, if he took a cent more than was due, "may his wife and children become blind; you must take me for an honest man, for I am your countryman—I also am German." Fraud on two German emigrants.

3. *Relative to the Treatment of the Emigrants on the Way.*—It was extremely cruel and brutal. While they had room enough on the large Hudson River steamers, they were crowded like beasts in the canal-boats, and were frequently compelled to pay their passage over again, or to be thrown overboard by the captain. Says the notorious Smethurst, in his examination on November 15, 1847: Cruel treatment of emigrant passengers.

"The year before last, Captain Jacobs took a lot of Germans from Roach & Co., of this city, bound to Buffalo, received his Testimony of Smethurst.

Extortion and cruelty of canal-boat captains.

pay, and extorted payment again from them by threatening to put them ashore at Rome.

"During the present season, Sterling sent a lot of passengers by canal-boat *J. R. Jacobs* — Jacobs, Captain — to Buffalo or Rochester, and paid Captain Jacobs their passage; but on the way out the latter compelled them to pay it over again."

Josiah Clarke.

"Passengers are frequently crowded," says Josiah Clarke, "into the steerage of a boat half-full of merchandise and luggage, so that they have no accommodation, and are sometimes compelled to pay their passage over again by the captain. I have often thought something should be done to protect passengers against the outrageous frauds of crowding them into the hold of an old canal-boat at a large price, when there are a great many good and convenient boats ready and willing to take them forward at half the money."

Rev. J. N. Wyckoff.

Reverend Dr. J. N. Wyckoff writes: "I have seen a canal-boat, first so filled with luggage as to reach within four feet of the deck, and then more people required to be housed upon the luggage than could be laid down in two parallel rows from the stem to the stern of the boat."

Accommodations on Lake steamers.

The lake steamers did not offer any better accommodations. We quote, as an instance, the propeller *Phœnix*, which, on November, 1847, was destroyed by fire while it had two hundred and seventy emigrants on board, who almost all perished in the flames. "I went on board the *Phœnix* (before she left Buffalo on her last trip)," testifies Elic Van Valkenburgh, "and found her almost entirely filled with merchandise; so much so that passengers could have no accommodations below deck. There was a stateroom overhead, to which the emigrants had not access; and their only accommodations were such as could be found on deck, with a roof or deck overhead, supported by posts, with no side enclosings. There were plenty of steamers at Buffalo at the time, and of the first class, on board of which they could have been shipped at two dollars each. The propeller remained in port some ten days after the emigrants were put on board."

Testimony of James Roach, a runner.

"I left the emigrant business," deposes James Roach, one of the lowest runners, "because I was sick of it; the way business was done dissatisfied me; my partners were not such men as I like to do business with, particularly Daley; his treatment of passengers was uncivil and brutal; he has often been known to personally abuse and assault them, and otherwise impose upon them. Another reason of my leaving the business was, there was too much money collected from the emigrants. We were employing too many men at high wages to make the business profitable, unless extortion was resorted to."

Stools.

As stated above, it was one of the regular tricks of the runners to promise to one of a large party of emigrants, who had or was supposed to have influence with them, free passage and other considerations, if he procured their patronage for a certain line. The individual who thus made himself a tool of the runners against the interest of his friends, was called a *stool.* The following testimony of George W. Daley will explain this more fully:

Geo. W. Daley relative to same.

"The following," says he, "is a copy of a letter received by Mr Smethurst from Mr. Roach while I was a partner with them in the emigrant business, in Albany. There have been a number of similar letters written by different members of the firm; they are of frequent occurrence. Mr. Smethurst opened the letter and handed it to me, and I have kept it.

"'NEW YORK, May 20, 1847.

"'MR. SMETHURST:

'SIR: There is three hundred emigrants on the *Rochester*, to-night. There is three families on her that are booked by Brische; they are friends of Mr. Swarts, and their friends in Buffalo are people of standing, and you must put them on a boat where they will be comfortable, for Brische has been to see me about them, and also Mr. Swarts. You must be easy with them about their luggage, and weigh it straight. All that have my tickets, *put them through;* the head man is a "*stool;*" make him jump. Send down Van Toble's tickets. I shall not send you any money till I come up. I think that I shall make some arrangements with Noyes, so that he will not be opposition here. Run the O. P. line strong this week. Yours, JAMES ROACH.'

"'The *O. P. line'* meant, '*Rob* the passengers all you can, and divide the money with me.' The proceeds of the robbery were not divided among the members of the firm generally, but simply among those who personally participate in it.

"The '*stool*' above referred to was an individual who had influence with the passengers, and had procured their patronage for Smethurst's line, in consideration of a promise of his own passage and $100. The passage he had for himself and three members of his family, but the $100 he did not get. '*Stooling*' of a similar character is an everyday occurrence, but the '*stools*' seldom get off as well as this one. They are generally charged more than other passengers. They submit to it rather than be exposed to their companions as traitors to their interests.

Stools defrauded.

"The '*stools*' are not paid what they are promised one time in twenty. When they demand their pay, they are threatened with exposure to their companions, whose interests and rights they have so grossly violated, which is generally sufficient to silence them. The case of the watch is in point. The English '*stool*' in that case thought he was arrested by an officer of justice, and not only gave up the watch, but paid a handsome sum besides. The *officer* was in fact another runner, in the interest of the one who gave him the watch."

Profits of runners shared by shipping-houses, steamboats, and railroads.

All these nefarious operations were openly committed by the runners, but the shipping-houses, steamboats, and railroads shared the profits with them in a greater or lesser degree. Everybody was aware for what purpose these runners were kept; every newspaper reported almost daily their villainous transactions, but neither the public authorities nor the people dared to interfere with them. Now and then a complaint was made by one of the victims, but for a person unacquainted with the law and the language of the country it was difficult to obtain redress. In cases where it was probable that an exposure would be made, the matter was hushed up, the emigrant received his money back, and was by the quickest route sent West. Thus these runners for years infested the lower parts of the city, and by their means, recklessness, prodigality, and political influence, controlled the elections, and had a powerful voice in the State capital. Had it not been for their objections, the law creating the Commissioners

Power of runners.

of Emigration would have passed two or three years sooner. Even the Commissioners were unable to do away with these leeches so long as they had no landing-place from which the runners could be excluded. When, in 1855, they finally succeeded in obtaining a lease of Castle Garden, they at once put a stop to the operations of these creatures. It is said that on one day several hundreds of them sailed for California, where a large portion fell into the hands of the vigilance committee just then organized at San Francisco, while others tried to carry on the old business of defrauding and swindling, and some perished in the filibuster expeditions in Mexico and Central America. In the days of which we have been speaking, the runner business had culminated. These men were masters of the situation, and it was only by gradual efforts that the Commissioners of Emigration were enabled to take from them the sources of plunder. Even in their examination before the Committee of the Assembly, they found it unnecessary to conceal any of their frauds. They even openly and boldly avowed and testified to their own depravity. **Their boldness.**

"It is a fact," says Henry Vail, a New York runner, "that I and others engaged in the business get all we can from passengers, except that *I never shave a lady that is travelling alone;* it is bad enough to shave a man; I have all I get over a certain amount which is paid to the transportation companies." **Testimony of Vail and other runners.**

"I have been in Smethurst's office," continues Charles Cook, another New York employee in the emigrant passage business, "when Irish, Dutch (German), and English emigrants were there, and have heard Roach tell his men to promise them all they wanted, that is, they should have railroad passage and all of their luggage free; the same persons I saw afterwards with canal-boat tickets. Roach said he kept the party called the *Sixteen* at a great loss for the purpose of controlling the Dutch emigrants; the Irish were worth nothing; the English alone would not pay, but putting the Sixteen men, or fighting men, with them to help Brische, from whom he was obtaining Dutch passengers, he could make a good stake; *that there was no use of talking of being honest while in the passage business; all he wanted was to get hold of the cattle;* he did not care how or what they were promised; they would be compelled to *point* up in Albany while

Smethurst and a Dutchman were there. I have been in Albany and seen the luggage of emigrants weighed, and have seen the men that took the tally add to the weight called out by the weigher so as to average about fifty pounds to the passenger over the true weight; I have seen it done by men in the employ of Smethurst & Co., and the charge collected by them; I have also seen the same thing done in Malburn & Co.'s office in the absence of Malburn; I have seen Smethurst collect lake charges on luggage, and receipt only upon the canal ticket, compelling the emigrant to pay lake charges again at Buffalo; I have seen Daley, Smethurst, and Weaver, on two or three occasions, collect from passengers their passage, and freight on their luggage, and endorse on their tickets due upon this a balance in Buffalo.

The Sixteen.

"The men called the Sixteen party have their headquarters at 16 Front Street, headed by Huested, Hart, and others. I have heard several of the party say, after they had been booking emigrant passengers, that they had made a big thing of it, and at the same time they had skinned them of their money, and that they had skinned English and Scotch out of sovereigns. The English runners generally get the luggage of passengers in their office, then, if the passenger does not take passage with them; they make a heavy charge for storage.

"The notorious James Roach says that he considers those employed by Government *more valuable* as runners *in consequence of their official station* than others of equal capacity, and especially that a man connected with the Custom House as night-watch has an advantage over other men in booking passengers."

Prices paid to runners.

In Albany, the prices paid by the emigrant forwarding companies to runners varied from $40 to $100 per month. "I have been paid by Smethurst & Co. $150 per week," says George W. Daley, "from the 3d or 5th of August to the 20th of October last, for the purpose of keeping me from interfering with their business by establishing an opposition office. The New York runners averaged about $70 per month, and in Albany about $55 per month. There are about twenty runners in this city, and in New York Smethurst & Co., Malburn & Co., and E. Mathews employ and pay about sixty runners, and indirectly about one hundred; this includes runners, boarding-house keepers, and boarding-house runners"

"I have runners employed in New York," testifies Henry D. Smethurst, on November 15, 1847, "and the following are their names and salaries: Smethurst's statement of salaries to his runners.

George Cornell,	$30 00 per week.
Charles Gallagher,	25 00 " "
Richard Cornell,	25 00 " "
William F. Hart,	25 00 " "
Aaron Piersons,	20 00 " "
John O'Donnell,	15 00 " "
—— Brady,	15 00 " "
Jesse Olmstead,	25 00 " "
Hiram Ketchum,	18 00 " "
George Burns,	18 00 " "
Henry Shanfroid,	20 00 " "
—— Sullivan,	12 50 " "
George McDonald,	$600 for the season
—— Hamilton,	600 " "
Hiram Huested,	20 00 per week.
John Leonard,	18 00 " "
Chris. Penny,	10 00 " "
William Ford,	10 00 " "
Charles Andrews,	20 00 " "

"The following persons reside and transact business for me at Albany:

James Roach,	$2,000 00 for three months.
W. F. Sterling,	750 00 " " "
George W. Daley,	1,500 00 " " "
Adolphus Shoemaker,	60 00 " " "
Felix McCann,	100 00 " " "
Thomas Sales,	75 00 " " "
Charles Bartell,	50 00 " " "
Henry Snyder,	50 00 " " "
Sidney Goodrich,	50 00 " " "

Samuel Bryington, ...	40 00	for three months.
Peter Finnigan, ...	30 00	" " "
Henry Nichols, ...	45 00	" " "
William Kerney,.	40 00	" " "
Sylvester Trowbridge, ...	600 00	for the season.
J. L. Weaver, ...	75 00	per month.
William P. Pfaff, ...	50 00	" "
William Smith, ...	50 00	" "

"All these men have been in my employment during the present season. They have worked by the season, month, or week, most of the time; part of this time I paid them a commission."

"I have," continues James Roach, "looked over the list of persons mentioned by Mr. Smethurst as being employed by him, and it is correct as far it goes; the following names should be added:

O. B. Teal, New York, ...	$800 00	for the season.
Samuel Bennett, ...	75 00	per month.
Philip Caswell, ...	600 00	" season.
Hiram Johnson, ...	75 00	" month.
Robert Miller, ...	600 00	" season.
Stephen Gordon, ...	75 00	" month.
George Dunning, ...	75 00	" "
Charles Cook, ...	300 00	" "

And others to whom we paid small sums at various times during the season, among whom was Ralph Schoyer at $37 50 per week, etc."

The list of these frauds, continued, as before stated, until the year 1855, could be multiplied *ad infinitum*, but the instances which we have enumerated are sufficient to show the utter helplessness of the emigrants against the imposition and deception which were practised upon them. It is a reproach to humanity that these infamies continued so long.

CHAPTER V.

THE BOARD OF COMMISSIONERS OF EMIGRATION OF THE STATE OF NEW YORK.

Necessity of legislation for protection of emigrants made apparent.

THE extortions and frauds which, in all the forms that rapacity could invent or suggest, had been practised for many years, finally, in 1845 and 1846, assumed such fearful proportions, and became the object of such general abhorrence, that legislation for the protection of emigrants seemed the only possible remedy. The community finally began to understand that it had to suffer in the same if not in a greater proportion than the emigrants themselves, if the latter were not secured from the cupidity of the runners and mercenary attempts of the agents. Thus humanity and sound policy equally indicated the necessity for a thorough change of the old system, and a strong desire manifested itself among all political parties to reform the existing laws.

The problem to be solved was to protect the new-comer, to prevent him from being robbed, to facilitate his passage through the city to the interior, to aid him with good advice, and, in cases of most urgent necessity, to furnish him with a small amount of money; in short, not to treat him as a pauper, with the ultimate view of making him an inmate of the Almshouse, but as an independent citizen, whose future career would become interwoven with the best interests of the country.

Adverse interests seeking control of emigration.

There were two adverse interests at work desirous of controlling and regulating all measures relating to the emigrant. The city authorities, and especially the Almshouse Commissioners, endeavored to have concentrated in their own hands the right to provide remedies and suggest reforms. Their sphere of action did not extend beyond the city limits; all they cared for was an increase of their power by resuscitating and amending the existing laws. On the other hand, there were a number of leading and public-spirited citizens, journalists, merchants, influential members of the Chamber of Commerce, and philanthropists, who, being impressed with the necessity of a radical change and a more liberal legislation for the benefit of the emigrant, were opposed to the action of the city officials. Among the latter, Comptroller Ewen, Assistant Alderman Purser, and the Almshouse Commissioners were the most active, while, among the citizens at large, Messrs. Leopold Bierwirth, Robert B. Minturn, Thurlow Weed, Andrew Carrigan, and Archbishop Hughes labored with untiring zeal and energy.

Creation of Board of Commissioners of Emigration by Act of May 5, 1847, and causes thereof.

The efforts of both parties finally led to the Act of May 5, 1847, creating the Board of the Commissioners of Emigration of the State of New York. This result, however, was just the reverse of what had been intended at the beginning by the city authorities. In order to enable the reader to properly understand the operations of the conflicting interests, it is necessary to give a short statement of the means by which the Legislature was induced to pass the above act.

The Common Council, at the conclusion of their investigation of the frauds committed by the Clerk of the Mayor, became fully convinced of the pecuniary importance of the subject of emigration. Since 1842, not a year passed without some effort on their part to correct the most flagrant of the abuses practised on the emigrants, and to extend to them more effectual protection; but however well-meaning some members of the Common Council were, the influence of those who lived by fleecing the poor aliens was sufficient to, and did, control the majority, and thus repressed every attempt to effect the much-needed reform.

From 1845 to 1847, all the efforts of the city officials were exclusively directed towards having the Mayor vested with the power of bonding and commuting alien passengers.

Recommendations of Comptroller Ewen and Alderman Purser.

Thus, in his Report for 1845, the Comptroller, General John Ewen, recommended application to the Legislature for an amendment of the law, so as to authorize the Mayor to require the payment of one dollar for each of the alien steerage passengers in lieu of bonding them, in all cases where he should deem it for the public interest to do so. He prepared the draft of a law to effect this object, and submitted it to the Common Council, which advocated its adoption during the session of the Legislature in 1846.

On September 29, 1846, Mr. G. H. Purser, then an Alderman,

who took a lively interest in the subject, reported, as Chairman of a select Committee of the Common Council, among other things, as follows:

"To avoid the importation of persons utterly unable to maintain themselves, from infirmity of mind or body, and who must necessarily become a permanent charge, your Committee believe that discretionary power should be given to the Mayor to exact bonds in such cases, but distinctly divesting the bondsmen of any authority to maintain them at any private irresponsible establishment. Nearly two millions of dollars being now annually expended in the transportation of passengers to this port alone, it appears unreasonable that the tax-payer should be burdened in proportion to the benefits conferred on a particular class of the community. Voluntarily the passenger agents will never permit the commutation-money which they receive to pass into the city treasury.

"The unceasing hostility of these men towards any modification of the law was indicated in their unscrupulous exertions last winter (1846), at Albany, to postpone the action of the Legislature on the subject. The draft of a law submitted by the Comptroller, and approved unanimously by the Common Council, was permitted to fail without even defence or examination. The passenger-brokers even succeeded in getting through the Legislature a law exclusively for their own benefit, and under circumstances which we hope may be eventually exposed. An amount of fifty cents per head is levied upon every steerage, and two dollars upon every cabin passenger, and designated hospital-money; and for many years, instead of being applied to the support of the emigrant in sickness or destitution, has been appropriated to the building of churches and the maintenance of sailor boarding-houses. The law, lobbied through the Legislature, provides that the Marine Hospital at Staten Island shall receive the alien passengers, when sick, for the period of one year after arrival, though previously this burden devolved upon the bondsmen, who thus increase their profits to the extent of five thousand dollars annually. During the next session of our Legislature, we trust this fund may command the attention of our delegation, and that it

Law lobbied through Legislature for benefit of passenger-brokers may be applied to uses better calculated to lighten the taxation of our citizens.

"Your Committee feel convinced that as a financial measure the subject is important, and that some policy should be adopted of a permanent character. There is every reason to believe that emigration to this port will increase rather than diminish, and that legislation should equally regard the interest of the city and the emigrant. To repose the duty of alleviating the sufferings of the alien stranger to a class of men prompted by every selfish consideration to avoid the responsibility, is to legalize a system of outrage and oppression. The claims of the sick and destitute should be entertained and relieved by the authorities of our city, and not be decided by those interested in denial or delay.

"Your Committee have before them a memorial in favor of the proposed alteration of the law, signed by the acting presidents of the Irish, German, British, Scotch, and Welsh emigrant societies, which states that 'the change would increase the revenues of the city, and secure the emigrants from the frauds now practised upon them.' Resolutions adopted at a large public meeting evince that the subject is one of public interest.

"The sympathies of the adopted citizens have been enlisted especially in this question from the peculiar opportunity they enjoy of becoming familiar with the workings of the present system, and a natural desire which they entertain not only to secure the emigrant from the treatment to which he has been for years exposed, but gradually to establish a fund from commutation adequate to the maintenance of the alien poor.

"For these reasons, a law should be passed, authorizing the Mayor or Recorder to require the payment of a commutation fee of one dollar for each passenger, or bonds at his election. The law might be rendered still more advantageous by requiring that each surety to any bond taken under the act duly make oath at the time of becoming surety that he is a householder, resident in the city of New York, intending to reside there permanently, and worth the sum or sums in which he is bound, over and above all his debts, and over and above all liabilities, whether by bond or suretyship, or otherwise.

"The propriety of reserving to the Corporation the power of

requiring passengers to be bonded in certain cases appears obvious on examining the history of emigration, and the unscrupulous conduct of European governments and cities in transferring to our country aged and decrepit paupers, and occasionally even criminals. Without this provision to arrest abuses so obviously calculated to demoralize the community and increase the burden of taxation, any change in the law would be impolitic. The admission of such persons would bring odium, however unmerited, upon the industrious and intelligent emigrant, and, as far as your Committee had the opportunity of consulting the opinions of citizens by adoption, they appeared strongly in favor of the proposed restriction."

On January 18, 1847, the Comptroller recommended to the Common Council that a further application be made to the Legislature for the passage of a law, vesting in the Mayor the power of commuting or bonding alien passengers. "As the enactment of this law," says the Comptroller, "will afford partial indemnity to the city, without drawing a dollar from the treasury of the State or imposing any additional burden upon the immigrants, it is believed that a very moderate degree of interest on the part of the City Delegation in the Legislature will serve to secure its passage."

Public opinion aroused; efforts of Messrs. Minturn, Weed, Carrigan, and Archbishop Hughes

By this time, public opinion had become aroused to the importance of the proposed changes. The subject was discussed in the Chamber of Commerce of New York, and the opposition to the insufficient measures suggested by the Common Council took a definite form early in the session of 1847, in a letter written by Robert B. Minturn, a distinguished merchant of New York, to Mr. Thurlow Weed, the influential editor of the Albany *Evening Journal*. Mr. Weed for two or three years previously had been doing what he could individually, and through the columns of the *Journal*, for the protection of the immigrants, whose sufferings he had daily occasion to witness at Albany, where the canal boat-runners were, if possible, still more hungry and rapacious than the boarding-house scalpers in New York.

In consequence of Mr. Minturn's letter, which first took a comprehensive view of the subject, Mr. Weed went to New York to confer with Mr. Minturn, Mr. Andrew Carrigan, and the late Archbishop Hughes, in regard to the details of a law which should fully secure the emigrant. These preliminary steps alarmed the Almshouse Commissioners, to whom the power, both in a pecuniary and political sense, was of too much value to be surrendered. Those Commissioners induced the Common Council to press the immediate passage of a law to protect emigrants from fraud and imposition. That, however, was simply a flank movement. The provisions of their bill merely kept the word of promise to the ear of the emigrants. In the meantime, the real friends of reform prepared a substitute, which, when the Assembly bill came to the Senate, was offered by Senator F. F. Backus, from Monroe County. The various influences unfavorably affected by the substitute offered by Dr. Backus united and made desperate efforts to defeat it. An earnest but unsuccessful party appeal was made to senators by the late John Van Buren and other distinguished politicians.

Alarm of Almshouse Commissioners.

Resolutions of Common Council urging on Senate the adoption of a law to protect New York City and alien passengers.

Alarmed at the aspect of the question in the Senate, the New York Common Council, on March 15, 1847, took up this important subject, and passed a series of resolutions for the purpose of submitting them to a public meeting, to be called irrespective of party. The Mayor approved these resolutions on March 17, 1847:

"*Whereas*," they say in their proceedings, "The number of emigrant passengers annually arriving at this port has steadily advanced from 11,501 in 1829 to 114,000 in 1846; and

"*Whereas*, The Passenger Act adopted in 1824, by imposing the bonding system exclusively, has gradually enabled mercenary brokers and agents to assume the charge and custody of the sick and destitute stranger, and from various causes greatly increased the burdens of taxation; and

"*Whereas*, The annual expenses of the Almshouse Department have now reached the enormous sum of three hundred and fifty thousand dollars; during the month of January, five thousand three hundred and forty-three persons being sustained at the expense of the city, and out-door relief extended to nearly three thousand; and

" *Whereas*, A bill correcting these important evils, and protecting the interests of the city and the emigrant, has been recently passed with great unanimity by the Assembly of this State, with the concurrence of the Common Council, and various emigrant societies, irrespective of party, but has been arrested in the Senate, either from misunderstanding the nature and magnitude of the evil, or from the influence of those pecuniarily interested in its defeat, and whose profits are partially derived from the injustice and inhumanity connected with the present system; therefore,

" *Resolved*, That the Common Council earnestly and confidently urge on the Senate the prompt adoption of a law which may afford protection to the city and the alien passengers, and which, by providing a uniform commutation fee of one dollar for every industrious emigrant, and making it the duty of public authorities to retain them in the event of sickness and destitution, will effectually prevent the extortions now practised in Europe in relation to the rates of commutation, and secure them, on their arrival, from the treatment to which they are now exposed in private almshouses and hospitals.

" *Resolved*, That the bonding reserved under the proposed law is expressly for the 'infirm, decrepit, and those likely to become a permanent charge,' and is a distinct, plain, and reasonable provision, calculated to prevent the kingdoms of Europe indiscriminately introducing into our city persons from their respective poor-houses, physically and mentally incapacitated for labor, to become necessarily a permanent charge upon our public or private charities.

" *Resolved*, That his Honor the Mayor be requested to call a public meeting of the citizens, irrespective of party, to take this subject into consideration, and urge on the Legislature the necessity and justice of prompt action.

" *Resolved*, That a committee of five be appointed from both Boards to make arrangements for such public meeting, and prepare suitable memorials to the Legislature."

The meeting alluded to in the foregoing resolutions was called for March 22, 1847, to be held at the Tabernacle in Broadway.

Mass Meeting at Tabernacle to support views of Common Council.

Mr. Carrigan, on learning the names of two prominent Demo crats who had been spoken of to preside at the meeting, called on them, and frankly and fairly stated the merits of the whole question. Those gentlemen declined to serve; and, finally, Mr. Charles O'Conor was designated. Mr. O'Conor, before taking the chair, had made himself acquainted with the merits of the two bills, and unhesitatingly approved of that submitted by Dr. Backus. The speakers named for the occasion were Messrs. Charles O'Conor and John McKeon, each of whom was expected to sustain the views of the Almshouse Commissioners and the Common Council. These speakers also, in preparing themselves for the occasion, possessed themselves of information which entirely changed the programme.

Meeting controlled by independent citizens.

The Tabernacle was densely filled at an early hour. The question to be passed upon having in the meantime been extensively discussed, the independent citizens took the matter into their own hands, and the majority of those present, instead of responding to the principles of the bill urged by the Common Council, were in favor of a law which, while it looked to the protection of the city, had regard also for the welfare of emigrants. For this reason, the nomination first of Mr. Campbell, then of Alderman Purser, who were in favor of the Common Council's bill, for chairman, was rejected, and, on motion of Mr. Carrigan, Charles O'Conor was called to the chair by acclamation, and, on the same gentleman's motion, Charles H. Marshall, Moses H. Grinnell, James B. Nicholson, and G. W. Blunt were appointed Secretaries. James T. Brady and Alderman Purser addressed the meeting for the Common Council, the latter offering resolutions in support of the bill. John McKeon took a broader and more philanthropic view of the question, and submitted the following resolutions, which, after those offered by Alderman Purser had been rejected, were adopted by an emphatic majority:

Resolutions of Mr. John McKeon advising creation of a per capita tax and appointment of commissioners to administer the fund.

"*Whereas*, The law of this State relative to passengers arriving at the port of New York, as at present administered, has failed alike to afford indemnity to the city and protection to the emigrant, causing a traffic in their sufferings which is abhorrent to humanity, creating private hospitals and poor-houses, which give to the emigrant neither the food nor care proper to their situation, and deny to their dying hours even the consolation of religion; and, whereas, a bill has passed the House of Assembly, which tends in some measure to remedy these evils, and is now before the Senate of the State, awaiting its action;

"*Resolved*, That, in the opinion of this meeting, any and all legislation on this subject should be directed in that course which, while it but advances the interests of the emigrant, will have reference to the complete indemnity of the city and State from their support, and will not, at the same time, by imposing unnecessary burdens on the honest ship-owner, tend to enhance the price of passage and retard immigration from lands of starvation to lands of plenty.

"*Resolved*, That the enactment of a law requiring, from the master or consignee of any vessel arriving at this port with foreign emigrants, the sum of one dollar for each and every passenger, with the privilege of exacting instead thereof, in cases of mental or physical incapacity for self-support, where, from the total want of relatives and friends, such persons are liable to become charges to the city or State, bonds which will secure the city or State for their support, will create a fund which, properly administered, will not only relieve the city and State from a heavy burden, but will greatly benefit the emigrant.

"*Resolved*, That, in the opinion of this meeting, it would be advisable to separate the receipt and disbursement of the fund so to be created from the rest of the city revenue, and place the same in the hands of commissioners, whose high character and moral integrity would, apart from all political considerations, be the guarantee for the proper administration of their duties.

"*Resolved*, That a committee of five be appointed to proceed to Albany, and urge upon the Legislature the passage of a law conformable to the policy of the preceding resolutions."

On motion of Mr. McKeon, it was

"*Resolved*, That the chair proceed to appoint the Committee."

The Chairman then announced the following gentlemen as the Committee: James Lee, George Montgomery, Mortimer Livingston, Theodore Sedgwick, and Andrew Carrigan.

On motion,

"*Resolved*, That the proceedings of this meeting be authenticated, and transmitted to the Senate and Assembly of the State of New York."

Efforts of Mr. Carrigan to secure passage of bill.

Of the committee above named, Mr. Carrigan alone went to Albany, and in a great measure it is due to his indefatigable exertions that the Legislature finally passed the people's bill.

The Common Council likewise appointed a committee to proceed to Albany and oppose the passage of the bill. On that committee were two Whig aldermen, namely, Abraham Wakeman and Thomas McElrath. These two aldermen were the personal and political friends of Mr. Weed. The attention of neither had been previously directed to the enormous frauds to which emigrants were subjected. But as they were just and fair men, the facts, when presented to them, had the effect produced upon all impartial minds. Messrs. Wakeman and McElrath returned immediately to New York, and reported themselves in favor of the measure which they had been sent to Albany to oppose.

Bill passed by the casting vote of Lieut. Gov. Gardiner

The bill introduced by Dr. Backus and drafted by Senator Ira Harris had the support, with one exception, of all the Whig senators. That exception was the Hon. George Folsom, of New York. It required the votes of eight Democratic senators, of which number seven only could be obtained, and this occasioned a *tie* vote, so that the bill was finally passed by the casting vote of the Lieutenant-Governor. That Lieutenant-Governor was the Hon. Addison Gardiner, of Rochester. Judge Gardiner, though greatly and deservedly esteemed by his Democratic friends, was accused by the excited opponents of the bill with listening too readily to the representations of Mr. Weed, with whom the Lieutenant-Governor had been for many years on terms of warm personal friendship. The simple truth was that Judge Gardiner was too enlightened and philanthropic to allow any considerations but those of justice and duty to influence his action upon such a question. The same motives and feelings prompted Mr. John E. Develin, of the Assembly, to give his voice and vote for the bill. The bill was finally saved by the casting vote of Lieutenant-Governor Gardiner. The highest praise, however, for their indefatigable and successful services in the cause of humanity belongs to Messrs. Thurlow Weed and Andrew Carrigan. Both these gentlemen received, of course, more than their share of abuse from the politicians of New York for the stand they had taken.

"For an effort made to reform these great wrongs," said Mr. Weed on a later occasion, "I encountered the combined hostility of the 'scalpers;' was threatened with personal assault, and deluged with libel suits. On one occasion, I was required to appear, on the same day, before seven magistrates in seven different and distant towns."

The said bill became a law on May 5, 1847, and still remains the law of the State. The first Emigrant Commissioners were Gulian C. Verplanck, James Boorman, Jacob Harvey, Robert B. Minturn, William F. Havemeyer, and David C. Colden. In the bill as reported by the Committee, a blank was left for the names of the Commissioners. On the morning of the day that the bill was to come up as a special order, Mr. Carrigan and Mr. Weed met at the house of the Hon. Ira Harris, the Chairman of the committee that reported the bill, to designate Commissioners. It was understood between them that gentlemen of high intelligence, stern integrity, and proverbial benevolence only should be appointed Commissioners; and then, without indicating names, each privately wrote the number to be appointed on a slip of paper. On comparing names, all those found on Mr. Carrigan's slip, with one exception, were found also upon Mr. Weed's, who had named Mr. Carrigan instead of Mr. Harvey. Mr. Carrigan a year later succeeded Mr. Havemeyer in the Board, and, after five years' service, he was elected President of the Irish Emigrant Society, and thus continued his connection with the Commission as an *ex-officio* member for about twelve years. First Emigration Commissioners.

The principal features of the act creating the Board of the Commissioners of Emigration, which, since its passage on May 5, 1847, have been amended several times, in their present shape read as follows:

"§ 1. Within twenty-four hours after the landing of any passenger from any ship or vessel arriving at the port of New York, Emigration act. Report to be made of all passengers.

from any of the United States other than this State, or from any country out of the United States, the master or commander of the ship or vessel from which such passenger or passengers shall have been landed shall make a report in writing, on oath or affirmation, to the Mayor of the city of New York, or, in case of his absence, or other inability to serve, to the person discharging the duties of his office, which report shall state the name, place of birth, last legal residence, age, and occupation of every person or passenger who shall have landed from such ship or vessel on her last voyage to said port, not being a citizen of the United States, and who shall have, within the last twelve months, arrived from any country out of the United States, at any place within the United States, and who shall not have paid the commutation money, or been bonded according to the provisions of this act, or of the act hereby amended, or of the act of February eleventh, eighteen hundred and twenty-four, concerning passengers in vessels coming to the port of New York, nor paid commutation money under the provisions of this or any former act. The same report shall contain a like statement of all such persons or passengers aforesaid as shall have been landed, or been suffered to land, from any such ship or vessel at any place during such last voyage, or who shall have been put on board, or suffered to go on board, of any other ship, vessel, or boat, with the intention of proceeding to and landing at the said city of New York, or elsewhere within the limits of this State. The said report shall further specify whether any of the said passengers so reported are lunatic, idiot, deaf, dumb, blind, infirm, maimed, or above the age of sixty years, also designating all such passengers as shall be under the age of thirteen, or widows having families, or women without husbands having families, with the names and ages of their families, and shall further specify particularly the names, last place of residences, and ages of all passengers who may have died during the said last voyage of such vessel, also the names and residences of the owner or owners of such vessel. In case any such master or commander shall omit or neglect to report as aforesaid any such person or passenger, with the particulars aforesaid, or shall make any false report or statement in respect to any such person or passenger, or in respect to the owner or owners of any such vessel, or in respect to any of the particulars hereinbefore specified, such master or commander shall forfeit the sum of seventy-five dollars for every such passenger in regard to whom any such omission or neglect shall have occurred, or any such false report or statement shall be made, for which the owner or owners, consignee or consignees, of every such ship or vessel shall also be liable, jointly and severally, and which may be sued for and recovered as hereinafter provided.

Owner or consignee of ship or vessel to give a several bond for each person or passenger named in report.

"§ 2. It shall be the duty of the said Mayor, or other person discharging the duties of his office aforesaid, by an endorsement to be made on the said report, to require the owner or consignee of the ship or vessel from which such persons were landed, to give a several bond to the people of the State, in a penalty of three hundred dollars for each and every person or passenger included in such report, such bond being secured as hereinafter provided, and conditioned to indemnify and save harmless the Commissioners of Emigration and each and every city, town, or county in this State from any cost which said Commissioners or such city, town, or county shall incur for the relief or support of the person named in the bond, within five years from the date of such bond, and also to indemnify and refund to the said Commissioners of Emigration any expense or charge they may necessarily incur for the support or medical care of the persons named therein, if received into the Marine Hospital or any other institution under their charge. Each and every bond shall be secured by two or more sufficient securities, being residents of the State of New York, each of whom shall prove by oath or otherwise that he is owner of a freehold in the State of the value of three hundred dollars over and above all or any claim or lien thereon, or against him, including therein any contingent claim which may accrue from or upon any former bond given under the provisions of this act; or such bond may, at the option of the party, be secured by mortgage of real-estate, or by the pledge and transfer of public stock of the United States or of the State of New York, or of the city of New York, or by deposit of the amount of penalty in some bank or trust company; such security, real or personal, having been first approved by

Each bond to be secured by two or more sureties.

the said Mayor. It shall be lawful for any owner or consignee, at any time within twenty-four hours after the landing of such persons or passengers from any ship or vessel in the port of New York, except as in the section hereinafter provided, to commute for the bond or bonds so required, by paying (to the Health Commissioner of the city of New York) the sum of two dollars and fifty cents* for each and every passenger reported by him as by law required; the receipt of such sum (by said Health Commissioner) shall be deemed a full and sufficient discharge from the requirements of giving bonds as above provided. And fifty cents of the amount commuted for any passenger or passengers shall be set aside as a separate fund for the benefit of each and every county in this State, except the county of New York. The Commissioners of Emigration shall deposit the moneys of said fund, so set apart, in any bank that the said Commissioners may select, and the same, or as much of it as may be necessary, shall be distributed to the several counties, except the county of New York, once in every three months, and the balance that may be left after such three months' payment shall be paid over to the Commissioners of Emigration for general purposes.

Owner or consignee may commute for the bonds.

Commutation money.

Condition of passengers to be examined into.

"§ 3. It shall be the duty of the Commissioners of Emigration, hereafter named, to examine into the condition of passengers arriving at the port of New York in any ship or vessel, and for that purpose all or any of the said Commissioners, or such other person or persons as they shall appoint, shall be authorized to go on board and through any such ship or vessel; and if on such examination there shall be found among such passengers any lunatic, idiot, deaf, dumb, blind, maimed, or infirm persons, or persons

The original amount of the commutation money was one dollar (law of May 5, 1847). By the Act of July 11, 1851, § 7, it was increased to one dollar and fifty cents, and to be paid directly to the Chamberlain of the city of New York. By Act of April 13, 1853, § 13, it was further increased to two dollars; by Act of May 14, 1867, it was temporarily raised to two dollars and fifty cents; and by Act of May 10, 1869, it was unconditionally fixed at two dollars and fifty cents. As the commutation is paid in currency, while the shipping-merchants receive it in gold, it is evident that there is in fact no increase, and that the amount of $2 50 currency is actually less than the sum of $2, which, until the outbreak of the war, was paid in gold.

above the age of sixty years, or widow with a child or children, or any woman without a husband, and with child or children, or any person unable to take care of himself or herself without becoming a public charge, or who, from any attending circumstances, are likely to become a public charge, or who, from sickness or disease, existing at the time of departure from the foreign port, are, or are likely soon to become, a public charge, they shall report the same to the said Mayor particularly, and thereupon, and unless a bond, as required in the second section of this act, shall have been given, the said Mayor, or the person discharging the duties of his office, shall require in the endorsement to be made as aforesaid, or in any subsequent endorsement or endorsements thereon, and in addition to the commutation money, that the owner or consignee of such ship or vessel, with one or more sufficient sureties, shall execute a joint and several bond to the people of the State in a penalty of five hundred dollars for every such passenger, conditioned to indemnify and save harmless the Commissioners of Emigration, and each and every city, town, or county within the State, from any further cost or charge which said Commissioners, or any such city, town, or county, shall incur for the maintenance or support of the person or persons named in such bond, or any of them, within five years from the date of such bond. The sureties of the said bonds shall be required to justify before and to the satisfaction of the officer making such endorsement, and by their oath or affirmation shall satisfy such officer that they are respectively residents of the State of New York, and worth double the amount of the penalty of such bond, over and above all debts, liabilities, and all property exempt from execution. The subsequent endorsement authorized in this section may be made at any time within thirty days after such examination, or of the landing of any such person or passenger.

"§ 4. Gulian C. Verplanck, James Boorman, Jacob Harvey, Robert B. Minturn, William F. Havemeyer, and David C. Colden are hereby appointed Commissioners, for the purpose of carrying into effect the intent and provisions of this act; of whom the said Gulian C. Verplanck and James Boorman shall constitute the first class, and shall hold their office two years; and the said Jacob Harvey and Robert B. Minturn shall constitute the second

Commissioners of Emigration.

class, and hold their office four years; and the said William F. Havemeyer and David C. Colden shall constitute the third class, and hold their office for six years; and upon the expiration of their several terms of office their places shall be filled by appointments, to be made by the Governor, by and with advice and consent of the Senate, and the persons so appointed shall respectively hold their offices for the term of six years. The Mayor of the city of New York, the Mayor of the city of Brooklyn, the President of the German Society, and the President of the Irish Emigrant Society of New York, shall also severally, by virtue of their respective offices, be Commissioners as aforesaid. The said Commissioners shall be known as the 'Commissioners of Emigration,' and by that title shall be capable of suing and being sued. The money, so as aforesaid to be paid to the Chamberlain of the city of New York, shall be paid out on the warrant of the said Commissioners, or a majority of them. It shall be the duty of the said Commissioners to provide for the maintenance and support of such of the persons for whom commutation money shall have been paid as aforesaid, or on whose account bonds shall have been taken as aforesaid, as would otherwise become a charge upon any city, town, or county of this State; and the said Commissioners shall appropriate the moneys aforesaid, for that purpose, in such manner as to indemnify, so far as may be, the several cities, towns, and counties of the State, for any expense or charge which may be incurred for the maintenance and support of the persons aforesaid; such appropriation shall be in proportion to the expenses incurred by said cities, towns, and counties, severally, for such maintenance and support. And the more fully to effect the object contemplated by this act, the said Commissioners are authorized to apply in their discretion any part of the said money, to aid in removing any of said persons from any part of this State to another part of this or any other State, or from this State, or in assisting them to procure employment, and thus prevent them from becoming a public charge. The said Commissioners are also authorized in their discretion to apply any part of the said moneys to the purchase or lease of any property, or the erection of any building, which they may deem necessary for the purposes aforesaid. But any expense so incurred by the

Their powers.

Commissioners in any city, town, or county shall be charged to the share of such moneys which any such city, town, or county shall be entitled to receive thereof, for expense incurred in the support or maintenance of the persons for whom commutation money shall have been paid as aforesaid, or on whose account bonds shall have been taken as aforesaid.

"§ 5. In case any of the persons for whom commutation money has been paid as aforesaid, or for whom a bond has been given as aforesaid, shall, at any time within five years from the payment of such money or the execution of such bond, become chargeable upon any city, town, or county within this State, it shall be the duty of the said Commissioners to provide for the payment of any expense incurred by any such city, town, or county for the maintenance and support of any such person, out of the commutation money to be paid as aforesaid, and the moneys collected on such bonds, so far as the same will enable them to do so. The said Commissioners shall prescribe such rules and regulations as they shall deem proper for the purpose of ascertaining the right and the amount of the claim of any city, town, or county to indemnity under the provisions of this and the preceding section. The said Commissioners shall have power to provide for the support and maintenance of any persons for whom commutation money shall have been paid, or on whose account a bond shall have been given as hereinbefore provided, and who shall become chargeable upon any city, town, or county in such manner as they shall deem proper; and after such provision shall have been made by such Commissioners, such city, town, or county shall not be entitled to claim any further indemnity for the support and maintenance of such person.

Provision in case of persons becoming chargeable for whom bonds were given.

"§ 6. The said Commissioners are authorized to employ such agents, clerks, and servants as they shall deem necessary for the purposes aforesaid, and to pay a reasonable compensation for their services out of the moneys aforesaid.

Appointment of clerks and agents by the Commissioners.

"§ 7. It shall be the duty of the said Mayor, or other person discharging the duties of his office as aforesaid, by an endorsement to be made on the said report, to require the master or commander of such ship or vessel to pay to the Chamberlain of the city of New York the sum of two dollars and a half for

$2 50 to be paid by each passenger.

every person or passenger reported by said master or commander as aforesaid, which sum shall be paid as aforesaid within twenty-four hours after the landing of such person or passenger from any ship or vessel arriving at the port of New York.

Commissioners to report to Legislature.

"§ 8. The said Commissioners shall annually, on or before the first day of February in each year, report to the Legislature the amount of moneys received under the provisions of this act during the preceding year, and the manner in which the same has been appropriated particularly.

acancies how be supplied.

"§ 9. In case of a vacancy in the said Board of Commissioners, the same shall be filled by an appointment to be made by the Governor, by and with the advice and consent of the Senate. The person so appointed shall hold his office for the remainder of the term of the person in whose place he shall be appointed. The said Commissioners shall, in all cases, be residents of the city of New York or city of Brooklyn.

Action may be brought on bond.

"§ 10. If any person for whom a bond shall have been given as aforesaid shall, within the time specified in such bond, become chargeable upon any city, town, or county of this State, or upon the moneys under the control of the said Commissioners as aforesaid, the said Commissioners may bring an action on such bond in the name of the people of this State, and shall be entitled to recover on such bond from time to time so much money, not in the whole exceeding the penalty of such bond, exclusive of costs, as shall be sufficient to defray the expenses incurred by any such city, town, or county, or the said Commissioners, for the maintenance and support of the person for whom such bond was given as aforesaid, and shall be authorized to collect and apply such money from any of the real or other security mortgaged, pledged, or deposited therefor in conformity to this act.

Penalty in cases of neglect or refusal.

"§ 11. Any owner or consignee as aforesaid, who shall neglect or refuse to give any such bond or bonds and security therefor, as hereinbefore required, for each person or passenger landing from his ship or vessel, within twenty-four hours after the landing of such persons or passengers, in respect to bonds required by the second section of this act, or shall not within that time have paid the moneys authorized by said second section to be received in cases where such bonds are herein authorized to be commuted for, every such owner or consignee of such ship or vessel, severally and respectively, shall be subject to a penalty of five hundred dollars for each and every person or passenger on whose account such bond may have been required, or for whom such commutation money might have been paid under this act; such penalty to be sued for as provided for in the twelfth section of the said act hereby amended.

"§ 12. The penalties and forfeitures prescribed by this act may be sued for and recovered with costs of suit by, and in the name of, said Commissioners of Emigration, in any court having cognizance thereof, and, when recovered, shall be applied to the purposes specified in this act. It shall be lawful for the said Commissioners, before or after suit brought, to compound for any of the said penalties or forfeitures, upon such terms as they shall think proper. How recovered.

"§ 13. Any ship or vessel, whose master or commander, owner or owners, shall have incurred any penalty or forfeiture under this act, or under the Act of April 11, 1849, amending the same, entitled, 'An Act to amend certain acts concerning passengers coming to the city of New York,' shall be liable for such penalties or forfeitures which may be a lien upon such ship or vessel, and may be enforced and collected by warrant of attachment in the same manner as is provided in title eighth of chapter eighth of the third part of the Revised Statutes, all the provisions of which title shall apply to the forfeitures and penalties imposed by this act; and the said Commissioners of Emigration shall, for the purposes of such attachment, be deemed creditors of such ship or vessel, and of her master or commander and owner or owners respectively. Ships or vessels liable to penalties.

"§ 14. The said Commissioners of Emigration are, and each of them is, hereby vested with the same powers in regard to the administering oaths of office to employees, and to the binding out of children with consent of parents or next of kin, actually chargeable upon them, and also in regard to persons in the institutions, or any of them, under the charge of said Commissioners, for the prevention or punishment of an infraction or violation of the rules or orders and regulation of such Commissioners or their Powers of Commissioners.

officers in regard to such institutions as are possessed by the Commissioners of Public Charities and Correction in the city of New York, or any of them, for the same purposes.

Property of alien emigrants.

"§ 15. Whenever any alien emigrant, whose personal property shall not exceed the value of twenty-five dollars, shall die on the passage to the port of New York, or in the Marine Hospital, or in any other establishment under the charge of the Commissioners and in all cases in which minor children of alien passengers shall become orphans by their parents or last surviving parent dying, as aforesaid, the personal property which such alien emigrant or such parent or parents may have had with them, shall be taken in charge by the Commissioners of Emigration, to be by them appropriated for the sole benefit of the next of kin of such alien emigrant or of said orphan children; and said Commissioners shall give, in their annual report to the Legislature, a minute description of all cases in which property shall come into their possession by virtue of this section, and the disposition made of the same, unless it shall appear that there are other persons entitled by will or otherwise to such property or distributive share thereof. Whenever it shall so appear, the portion only to which the next of kin or said minor orphans would be legally entitled shall be transferred to them or applied to their use, and the remainder shall be received, held, and distributed to the parties severally entitled thereto, in the same manner and with the same authority as by law provided in respect to the Public Administrator of the city of New York, except that the said Commissioners are hereby authorized to distribute the same after a notice for creditors to appear and put in their claims within one week from the publication of the said notice. The said notice shall be published once in one of the daily papers of the city of New York."

CHAPTER VI.

CASTLE GARDEN.

THE Commissioners of Emigration organized on May 8, 1847, at the Mayor's Office in the City Hall, and on June 14 elected Mr. Wm. F. Havemeyer President, who resigned, however, in February, 1848, and was succeeded, on March 1, 1848, by Mr. G. C. Verplanck, who has ever since held that office. Organization of the Commissioners of Emigration.

The work of the Board was originally apportioned among several standing committees, four of which are still existing, namely, the *Ward's Island* Committee, consisting of six members, and the *Auditing*, *Finance*, and *Purchasing* Committees, of which the two former consisted each of three, and the latter of two members. In the course of years, owing to the increase of business, four other committees were added to the original four, namely, the *Castle Garden* (1855), consisting of six members; the *Railroad* (1867), of three; the *Agencies and Counties* (1867), of five; and the *Labor Exchange* (1868), Committees, of five members. The *Marine Hospital* Committee, the most important of the original four, consisting of three members, ceased to exist when, in 1859, the Commissioners gave up the Marine Hospital. Standing Committees.

The Commissioners had their first official quarters in the old Almshouse building (where the new Court-House stands at present). There they remained until January 19, 1854, when the building was destroyed by fire. They then found a temporary place in Franklin Street, between Broadway and Elm Street, for the meetings of the Board, where the offices of the Vice-President and Secretary, the examining physicians, and the receivers of applications for relief or admission to the hospitals, were also located. Another office was kept in Canal Street, for the reception of applications for employment, advice, or similar aid. But an alarm soon arose from the apprehended introduction of contagious diseases in the neighborhood of both locations, which was intensified by the fear of the owners of adjoining real-estate of a depreciation in the value of their property. Injunc- Quarters of the Commissioners.

tions were applied for and granted as to both offices; but, after an injurious interruption of more than two weeks, the injunction against the Canal Street office was dissolved. Before the other case could be brought to trial, the cholera made its appearance in the city, and the almost vacant Franklin Street office was taken possession of by the Board of Health as a cholera hospital. Towards the close of the year an opportunity occurred of hiring on lease a large and unoccupied building in Anthony Street—now Worth—opposite the hospital grounds, a few doors west of Broadway, erected and formerly used as a church edifice, a location where little or no danger could be apprehended to the neighborhood. Here the Commissioners remained till the spring of 1858, when all their offices were removed to Castle Garden.

It is not the purpose of this essay to give a detailed account of all the proceedings of the Board within the last twenty-three years; but its design is to point out only that part of their history which has at present a direct bearing on the protection of the emigrant. To this end we shall first describe Castle Garden and the offices connected with it, and next the institutions on Ward's Island. This chapter will be confined to Castle Garden.

Compulsory Landing Act of 1848.

The Commissioners were not long in discovering that the benevolent intentions of the law creating their Board could not be realized as long as they had not the absolute control of the emigrant, and as long as they were thus prevented from protecting him against the frauds practised on him by forwarders, boarding-house keepers, agents, and runners. They therefore, in the first year of their existence, applied to the Legislature for an act authorizing them to lease a dock or pier, where all the emigrant should be landed; where no outsiders would be allowed to enter without permission of the Commissioners; and where the emigrants could be cautioned and admonished against all the wiles of those who lay waiting for him on his arrival. The law of April 11, 1848, authorized the Commissioners to purchase or to lease such a pier or dock, and by virtue of this act, on May 8, 1848, they leased from the Common Council, for a term of five

Renting of Hubert Street Pier.

years, the large and commodious pier at the foot of Hubert Street, at an annual rent of $3,000.

It was anticipated that this pier would be in proper order for use by the middle of July; but, to the surprise of the Commissioners, they were, immediately after the execution of the lease, served with an injunction, obtained by some of the residents in the neighborhood. This injunction was granted and sustained against the appeal of the Commissioners on the ground that the landing of emigrants at the foot of Hubert Street, in the vicinity of St. John's Park, would bring into a quiet part of the city a noisy population, without cleanliness or sobriety; would endanger the health and good morals of the ward, and seriously affect the value of real-estate. Injunction against same.

The Commissioners now endeavored to get some other landing-place in the lower part of the city, where the nuisance, if such it could be called, already existed, and where the emigrants for a number of years had been landed. But, though the Common Council, whom they considered bound, in a measure, to furnish a pier, seemed favorably disposed, yet none could be procured and rendered suitable for the purpose. Consequently the Commissioners could not reach the emigrant before he fell into the hands of the plunderers who stood ready to deceive him; frauds which had formerly excited so much indignation and sympathy were practised with as much boldness and impunity as ever, and all the exertions of the Commissioners, though beneficial in many cases, were quite insufficient to put an end to these abuses. Difficulty o securing a suitable landing-place.

In spite of repeated petitions to the Legislature to provide efficient remedies by giving to the Commissioners exclusive possession and occupation of a pier for the landing of newly arrived emigrants, it took just eight years before that body, by the Act of April 13, 1855, complied with that wish. This act was as important as the one creating the Board of the Commissioners, for it first gave the power to afford really efficient protection to the emigrant. It required the transporting and conveying companies to deliver to the Mayors of New York, Troy, Albany, and Buffalo, in each and every year, a written or printed statement of the price or rates of fare and the price for the carriage of the baggage of the emigrant; it specified the penalty for violating the provisions of this act, and authorized the Commissioners of Act of 1855.

Emigration "to designate some one place in the city of New York, as they should deem proper, for the landing of emigrant passengers; providing further that "it should be lawful for such passengers to be landed at such place so designated; and likewise (meaning the Commissioners) to purchase, lease, construct, and occupy such wharves, piers, and other accommodations, in the city of New York, as may be necessary for the accommodation of emigrant passengers."

Lease of Castle Garden.

This important act finally enabled the Commissioners fully to carry out the benevolent objects of their trust. From that time only the Board could be said to be clothed with the necessary powers and to have become responsible for the well-being and protection of the emigrant. The Commissioners, on May 5, 1855, leased the old fort at the foot of Manhattan Island, known as Castle Garden, and immediately proceeded with the fitting up of the premises in a manner suitable to the designed purpose.

Obstructions.

"Owing, however," says the Commissioners' Report for 1855, "to the extensive repairs required, and the obstructions thrown in the way by those who, on different grounds, apprehended injury to their private interests, the place was not in readiness for use until the first of August, when it was formally opened as the *Emigrant Landing Depot.*

"It is not deemed necessary to allude to the efforts made to obstruct the execution of the law in this instance, further than to state that, where that effort was resorted to with the design of rendering nugatory the power conferred, and for the ejectment of the Commissioners from the occupancy of Castle Garden, the courts have sustained the law in its beneficent objects, and the Commissioners in the possession of the premises for the purpose of carrying the law into effect; and that, where violence threatened with a strong hand to lay waste and destroy, the police authority of the city, by prudent and decisive action, effectually checked the thoughtless and lawless in their course, and preserved a valuable property from destruction or damage, and the reputation of the State from disgrace.

Benefits of the Landing Depot.

"Two hundred and fifty vessels have landed their passengers at the Depot in the five months it has been in operation, bringing, in the aggregate, fifty-one thousand one hundred and fourteen

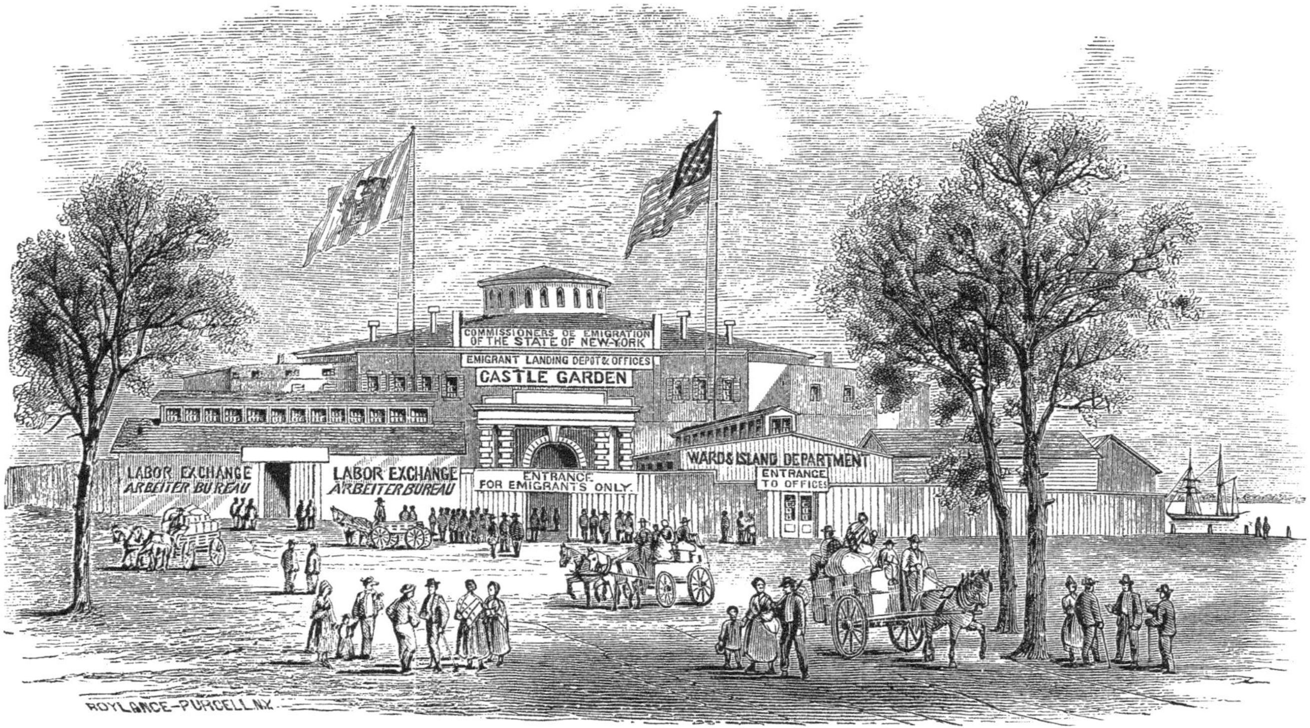

State Emigrant Landing Depot, Castle Garden, N. Y.

persons, during which period no accident of any kind has occurred. All have been landed safely, without accident to themselves or property. When landed, proper means have been used to secure their comfort and protection. They have been screened from the intrusion of that class of persons who have heretofore abused the confidence of the emigrants, and despoiled them of the means they had provided to convey them to their ultimate destination, and to sustain them after they had reached it—who have long been in the practice of taking possession of the person and property of confiding emigrants, and seldom permitting them to pass out of their hands without damage; in many cases reducing them from comparative affluence to destitution, and making them subjects for relief by the funds of the Commission; but in a larger proportion crippling their means to an extent which has affected their after life.

"Every facility is provided at the Depot, for those whose destination is to the interior, to proceed without unnecessary delay; and without need or pretext for intercourse with the class of persons in the city before mentioned. By this arrangement, much for the benefit of the emigrant, the shipper, the Commission, and the community at large, has been accomplished. Among these benefits may be mentioned:

"*First.*—To the emigrants. In a more safe and speedy landing of their person and effects: In the greater safety of their effects after having been put on shore, depredators being limited to fellow-passengers, and but slight opportunity existing for successful pillage by them. In relief from the importunities and deceptions of runners and bookers. In being enabled to continue their journey without delay from the same wharf where they had just landed. In relief from all charges and exactions for landing, 'baggage smashing,' and porterage; and, where they are proceeding to the interior, from cartages. In being enabled to obtain passage tickets at the lowest rates directly from the various transporting companies. In having their baggage accurately weighed; and in being relieved from excessive charges for that which is extra. In obtaining reliable information relative to the various routes of travel throughout the country. In being relieved from

To Emigrants.

the necessity of transporting their baggage to boarding-houses when exigencies require a temporary sojourn in the city of New York. And thus in being enabled to depart for their future homes without having their means impaired, their morals corrupted, and probably their persons diseased.

To Shippers.

"*Second.*—To the shipper. In the greater readiness with which passengers are discharged where freight and merchandise do not interrupt the process. In the ship being relieved of its passengers at once, and immediately on arrival. In the consignee being relieved from the supervision of the landing of the passengers.

To the commission.

"*Third.*—To the funds of the Commission. In the increased facility afforded for the discovery of cases liable to special bond. In the opportunity for ascertaining the means of passengers for support. In the reduction of sickness and distress among Emigrants. In the diminished proportional number that will become a charge to the Commissioners; and in the means to readily discover paupers and criminals transported hither.

To Statisticians.

"*Fourth.*—To the statistician. In furnishing reliable data of the fiscal means of emigrants on arrival; in developing the points of individual destination; thus exhibiting the number of persons who, at the time of arrival, are destined for each State, and the money-means with which they are provided.

To the Community.

"*Fifth.*—To the community in general. In the diminution of human suffering. In the reduction of calls on the benevolent throughout the country; and in the dispersion of a band of outlaws attracted to this port by plunder, from all parts of the earth."

Defeat of the Emigrant runners.

These predictions were verified by the experience of every subsequent year. The establishment at Castle Garden fully proved its efficiency and usefulness. The decisions of the courts in 1856 and 1857 upon deliberate argument and advisement having put an end to all legal obstacles attempted to be interposed to this establishment on the part of persons who on various grounds

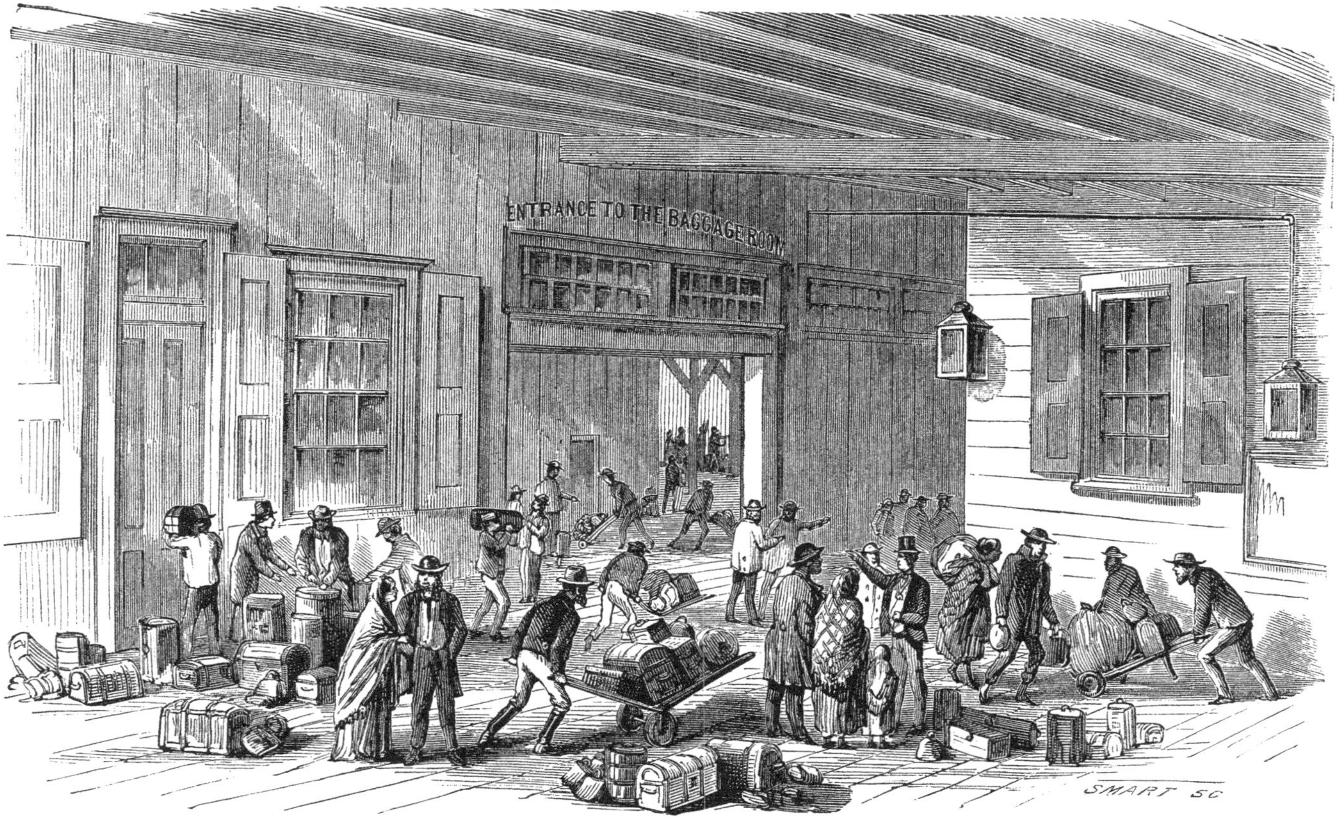

Castle Garden Baggage Room—I. Receiving and Storing Luggage of Arriving Emigrants.

feared or thought their pecuniary interests affected, the opposition did not since extend beyond acts of inferior but continued annoyance, originating with those who had formerly profited by taking advantage of the ignorance of the newly arrived and friendless strangers. As stated in a preceding chapter, during the first year of the working of the institution several hundred emigrant runners, unable to follow this business any longer in New York, left for California. When those who remained here discovered that by applying to the law or by threatening and abusing they could not undo what the Act of April 13, 1855, had brought about, they in the end either disappeared or submitted to the new state of things.

Superintendents of the Landing Depot.

A successful experience of fifteen years has now confirmed the utility of the establishment at Castle Garden. The able and efficient Superintendent, Mr. John A. Kennedy, who first organized that department, discharged the duties of his station until June, 1860, when he accepted the appointment of Superintendent of the Metropolitan Police. He was succeeded by the present Superintendent, Mr. Bernard Casserly, who has most efficiently performed the duties of his office. It has contributed largely to the success of Castle Garden that the services of two very able executive officers were secured, that during the whole time of its existence only one change has taken place in the highest executive office, and that consequently uniformity and regularity in the service could be maintained.

Departments of the Landing Depot.

A description of the several departments, among which the various duties are divided, will give an idea how business has been and is now carried on at Castle Garden.

Boarding Department.

I. *The Boarding Department.*—On arrival at the Quarantine Station (six miles below the city), every vessel bringing emigrant passengers is boarded by an officer of this department, stationed there for the purpose, who ascertains the number of passengers, the deaths, if any, during the voyage, and the amount and character of sickness, examines the condition of the vessel in respect to cleanliness, and receives complaints, of which he makes report to the General Agent and Superintendent at Castle Garden; he remains on board the ship during her passage up the Bay, to see that the law prohibiting communication between ship and shore before emigrant passengers are landed is enforced. On casting anchor in the stream, convenient to the Landing Depot, he is relieved by an officer of the Metropolitan Police force, detailed at the Castle Garden, and the passengers are transferred to the care of

Landing Department.

II. *The Landing Department*, under the supervision of which the Landing Agent proceeds with barges and tugs, accompanied by an Inspector of Customs, to the vessel. After an examination of the luggage, it is checked, and the passengers, with their luggage, are transferred to the barges and tugs, and landed at the Castle Garden pier. On landing, the passengers are examined by a Medical Officer, to discover if any sick have passed the Health authorities at Quarantine (who are thereupon transferred by steamer to the hospitals on Ward's or Blackwell's Island), and likewise to select all subject to special bonds under the law—as blind persons, cripples, lunatics, or any others who are likely to become a future charge. This examination being ended, the emigrants are directed into the Rotunda, a large-roofed circular space in the centre of the Depot, containing 50,000 square feet, and with a dome in the centre for ventilation, about 75 feet high, with separate compartments for English-speaking and other nationalities, to

Registering Department.

III. *The Registering Department*, where the names, nationality, former place of residence, and intended destination of the emigrants, with other particulars, are taken down, thus forming an interesting record for future reference. The passengers are then directed to

Railroad Agents.

IV. *The Agents of the Railroad Companies*, from whom they can procure tickets to all parts of the United States and Canada, without the risk of fraud or extortion to which they are subjected outside of the Depot. In the meanwhile, the baggage and luggage are stored east of the Rotunda in the baggage-room. The old accommodations being insufficient, a new baggage-room was built in 1869. The necessity for this improvement had long been felt, the old room not having anything like the proper capacity to contain

Castle Garden Baggage Room—II. Discharging Emigrant Luggage for City Delivery.

the immense quantity of baggage, which numbered at times 7,000 pieces. The new building, which was finished in October, 1869, at a cost of nearly $75,000, is 200 by 350 feet, and is amply sufficient to accommodate 15,000 pieces of baggage. The very perfect system by which the thousands of trunks and boxes are distinguished and delivered safely to their respective owners is well worthy of explanation. A brass ticket, with any letter of the alphabet from A to F inclusive, and a number from 1 to 600, is delivered to the emigrant on landing, and a duplicate fastened on his piece of baggage. The trunk or box is then placed in the baggage-room. This room has six bins, designated by the letters A, B, C, D, E, F, and each bin has six hundred numbers. Accordingly, when the emigrant produces his ticket, a baggageman at once goes to the bin indicated by the letter and number on the ticket, and delivers the baggage required. In case of necessity, all the letters of the alphabet can be used in a similar way. Baggage Room.

The emigrants destined inland, on delivery of their check, take their baggage to the weigher's scales. After having been weighed and paid for, it is sent free of charge to the depot of the railroad or dock of the steamboat by which he leaves. Such emigrants as design remaining in this city and vicinity are directed to

V. *The City Baggage Delivery*, which ascertains the address to which the emigrants may desire to have their luggage sent, and takes their orders, exchanging the brass check received from the Landing Agent, on shipboard, for a printed paper one. The luggage is then promptly delivered in any part of this city and vicinity at a moderate rate of charges, approved by the Commission. At the same time, those having gold or silver which they may wish to have exchanged for United States currency are directed to one of three City Baggage Delivery.

VI. *Exchange Brokers*, admitted into the Depot, who changes their specie for a small advance on the market rate, which is set forth in a conspicuous place under the observation of the emigrant, the daily fluctuations in rates being duly noted. Exchange Brokers.

These last three departments are conducted by responsible parties, who, while not officers, are nevertheless under the close and constant supervision of the Commission, and are required to keep a record of all transactions, subject to the inspection of any member of the Board.

Information Department.

VII. *The Information Department.*—When the foregoing operations are completed, the emigrants are assembled in the Rotunda, and an officer of the Commission calls out the names of those whose friends attend them in the waiting-room at the entrance of the Depot, and to whom they are directed. At the same time are called out the names of those for whom letters or funds are waiting, which are then delivered to the proper owners through the Forwarding Department. Emigrants who desire to communicate with friends at a distance are referred to

Letter-Writing Department.

VIII. *The Letter-Writing Department*, where clerks, understanding the various Continental languages, are in attendance to write; the emigrant, while waiting a reply, if destitute, finds a home in the institutions at Ward's Island.

Boarding-House Keepers.

IX. *Boarding-House Keepers*, licensed by the Mayor and properly certified as to character by responsible parties, are admitted to the Rotunda after the foregoing business has been completed, to solicit for their respective houses such emigrants as desire to remain in the city for any length of time. These boarding-house keepers are subjected to careful supervision and to certain regulations, which will be found in the Appendix, and every precaution is taken to guard the emigrant against the abuses and imposition to which he was formerly liable.

Forwarding Department.

X. *The Forwarding Department* receives, through the Treasurer, all communications and remittances from friends of emigrants, sent either before their arrival or in response to letters written by the Letter Department, and applies them to the purchase of tickets. The amount of money and orders for passage received and disbursed through it will be found under the head relating to the Treasurer's duties.

Ward's Island Department.

XI. *The Ward's Island Department* receives all applications for admission to the Institutions, and examines the records, to ascertain the right of the applicant to admission. It also keeps the records of all daily admissions to, and discharges from, Ward's Island, and examines the records in all cases of claims for indemnity from the several counties of the State for emigrants chargeable to the Commission who may have received aid or support in such counties. Attached to this Department are two physicians, whose duties are to examine all sick and destitute applicants for relief, and to visit all such at their residences in this city, and report to the General Agent.

XII. *The Labor Exchange.*—A Labor Exchange was first established in 1850. The increasing number of persons demanding the aid and advice of the Commissioners, and the widely extended knowledge of their arrangements for the disposal of laborers, made it necessary to hire, in December, 1850, a large double building, Nos. 25 and 27 Canal Street, at which place emigrants desiring work, and persons desiring laborers, found ample opportunity for meeting their wants; while, prior to that time, useful employment and means of self-support had been procured to over 8,000 emigrants. Proportionably a far greater amount of service was rendered to them with the additional facilities afforded by the Canal Street establishment. Thus, in 1851, not less than 18,204 emigrants were provided with opportunities for self-support in such kind of labor as their previous habits best qualified them to perform. In 1862, 14,973 persons were provided with places or employment; but in the course of years this institution dwindled down to a mere intelligence office for city servants. During the seven years from 1860 to 1866, the number of females who found employment as servants through the Castle Garden agency amounted to 40,222, that of males to only 10,224.

Labor Exchange.

In 1867, at the suggestion of Commissioner Philip Bissinger, the office was revived and re-established in its original condition. The present Labor Exchange is a spacious and well-arranged building, and was erected during the latter part of the year named. It is a one-story building, 80 by 52 feet, with a large ventilator in the roof, thus furnishing an ample supply of fresh air and light, and, being situated on the additional ground added to these premises in 1867 by permission of the public authorities, it is easily accessible without disturbing the arrangements of the landing depot.

In the centre of the floor, a sufficient space has been railed off, and reserved for officers and for use of employers. On one side are seated the male emigrants, and on the other side the females, thus securing a separation of the sexes. These again are subdivided, according to their several occupations and the length of time they have been here, and also into those with and without references. Each emigrant on entering is requested to enter his or her name, ship, date of arrival, and character of employment; while every employer is required to enter his or her name, residence, recommendations, references, and description of labor wanted.

This Labor Exchange furnishes an intelligence office, *without charge*, for emigrants desirous of finding employment or service in the city or at a distance; and undertakes to supply all sorts of skilled mechanical and agricultural labor to employers in any part of the United States, who come with a proper guarantee of character and other necessary qualifications.

The Labor Exchange, since its reorganization, has existed for a period of only two years; but the result obtained in this comparatively short time is sufficient to prove its usefulness. In 1868, it procured employment for 31,143 emigrants, namely, 18,114 males and 13,029 females; and, in the year 1869, for 34,955 emigrants, namely, 22,844 males and 12,111 females. In these two years, there were among the males 4,311 and 5,594 mechanics respectively; while the balance of 13,803 and 17,250 respectively were agricultural and common laborers. Of the females, there were 474 and 438 respectively skilled laborers (seamstresses, cooks, laundresses, etc.), but 12,555 and 11,673 respectively were common house-servants. In 1868, 351 families were engaged, consisting of 1,551 persons, and, in 1869, 452 families, consisting of 1,232 persons.

Those who were employed represented, in 1868, fifteen, and, in 1869, sixteen nationalities. Irish and Germans were predominant. Of the whole number, there were, in 1868, 9,269 male and

11,975 female, Irish, Scotch, or English; and, in 1869, 11,703 males and 11,340 females, of the same nationalities. We find in the Germans and Swiss there were, in 1868, 8,034 males and 921 females, and, in 1869, 10,021 and 659 respectively; of Scandinavians, 414 and 78 and 477 and 75 respectively; Dutch, 6 males in 1868 and 62 males and 11 females in 1869. France, Italy, and Belgium sent 274 males and 35 females in 1868 and 39 and 7 respectively in 1869. As a curiosity, it may be stated that, in 1868, 6, and, in 1869, 8 Moors were engaged; they entered their names in Arabic letters.

Of the emigrants employed by the instrumentality of the Labor Exchange in 1868, 7,397 could not read or write, namely, 3,096 males and 4,301 females; and, in 1869, 7,139, namely, 3,498 males and 3,641 females. Among the 9,269 Irish, Scotch, and English engaged in 1868, there were 2,714 who could neither read nor write; and among the 11,703 individuals of the same nationalities in 1869, there were 3,058 unable to read or write. Among the 8,034 and 10,020 Germans and Swiss in the two corresponding periods, we find 279 and 321 respectively who could not read or write. Of the 23,315 Irish, Scotch, and English female servants engaged in 1868 and 1869, 7,682 could neither read nor write, and of the 1,825 females of other nationalities 260 were equally ignorant.

The States of New York and New Jersey in both years furnished employment to more emigrants than the rest of the United States together. As long as no means will be found to neutralize or avoid the difficulty and risks attending the transportation of laborers to more distant regions, this state of affairs will remain unchanged. In both years, the demand was much greater than the supply. Not the tenth part of the large orders for railroad laborers could be filled; and only a small part of the orders for farmers (Germans) and common laborers (Irishmen) could be responded to. Of the immigrant farm-laborers, only a small number remained in New York, the majority, and especially the well-to-do class, proceeding spontaneously to the Western and North-western States. Only a few German servant-girls asked for employment through the Labor Exchange.

It is very difficult, and at present almost impossible, to direct the European mechanic and laborer to the South, which has thus far tried in vain to attract immigrants, and this for the reason that most of the immigrants look out first for the place where they are sure of employment. It is in vain to tell them that many tracts of land are to be had cheap or even for nothing. Work is more attractive for them than land, at least at first. For this reason, and in consequence of the large settlements of Europeans there, the immigrant is attracted to the West and especially the North-west, where the fertile soil enables farmers to give ready employment to all the laborers that may present themselves.

Explanation of Immigration to West and not to South.

This is the whole explanation of the continual flow of emigrant laborers into those regions. There is work there. It is to be found everywhere, work which they understand, work which they can perform, work sufficiently remunerative to warrant the expectation of a happy future. This advantage they are sure of finding only in the West and North-west. Once employed, they easily arrive at independence. By saving their monthly wages, they secure the means of attaining it, and when the proper moment comes they have learned by experience where to settle and what they must do to succeed. The matter is simple, and requires on the part of the Western States no exertion of thought or money. On examining the conditions offered by the South, we can easily detect the causes which put that section at a disadvantage as regards the supply of labor. A class of farmers ready to receive the laborers who may offer themselves is almost everywhere wanting, and nowhere more so than in the extreme Southern districts, where there are only great planters, whose modes of cultivation have no attractions for the immigrants. The European immigrant detests the work in gangs as much as the negroes like it. His individuality is overlooked, his self-respect impaired, and he is viewed as a mere unit in the mass. He seeks not the planter, but the farmer.

The great land-owners who hold large tracts of land wish to cultivate them as before without loss of time. To attain their object, they must always keep a sound stock of freed slaves, which daily becomes more difficult for them, as the number of laboring hands is continually decreasing.

What will happen under these circumstances may be inferred

from what has been said. The inability of these large planters to procure the needed labor will cause them to be superseded in the course of time by small farmers, who will work themselves, and who will be able and willing to employ the white immigrants like the Western farmers.

A modest culture is required with two or three hands, living, in a patriarchal way, with the farmer's family. Whenever that will be generally introduced, immigrants will come and remain, or, if they leave again, it will be to settle in the neighborhood. Farms should be laid out for the reception of European laborers, and it is upon the formation of these farms and the introduction of Europeans that the future of the South depends. Results more satisfactory to both the Southern people and the immigrants would no doubt be reached, if some such plan were pursued by other districts as that adopted by the district of Newberry, South Carolina.

Here an Immigration Society has been formed, under the auspices of Rev. T. S. Boinest, consisting of the most notable farmers and planters, who have raised a fund of $5,000 or $6,000 for the purpose of defraying the necessary travelling and other expenses of the European laborers they wish to employ. By this means, the society, though existing but two years, has induced about 400 immigrants to make the district (Newberry) their home, and according to the latest reports both the employers and employees are satisfied and content.

Immigration Society at Newberry, S. C.

The society has appointed as agent, a European, Mr. F. W. Bruggemann, who is familiar with the character and wants of the immigrant, and forms the connecting link between the latter and their native employers, and to this circumstance is due the happy result of its efforts.

North of the Rotunda and adjoining it are the offices of the Commissioners. They consist of three rooms, occupying nearly the entire front of the building on the second floor, and include the offices of the General Agent and Treasurer, the Meeting-Room of the Board, and the General Agent's private office.

Offices of the Commissioners.

XIII. *The General Agent's Office* is a large vaulted room, the central one and largest of the three, in shape a parallelogram, extending on its longest axis east and west, and containing about

General Agent's Office.

thirteen hundred square feet. Here is transacted all the executive business of the Commission, complaints are heard and investigated, grievances remedied, and the general correspondence, except that relating to the Treasury Department, conducted by a force of several clerks, under the direct supervision of the Deputy Superintendent. To this officer the chief clerks of the various departments make their reports, which are by him laid before the General Agent, who bases his instructions upon them. The General Agent, who unites with these functions the duties of Superintendent, is the chief executive officer of the Commission—the centre and focus of all its business. He controls the interior working machinery of the Commission, transacts its outside business, and conducts its correspondence. He receives all communications to be laid before the Board, and acts generally as secretary at its meetings. He also supervises the inland transportation of emigrants, and his vigilance is constantly exercised to prevent the extortions and impositions in the way of overcharges and delays to which they are subjected. It is his office, moreover, to regulate advances on the luggage of emigrants, which are made from time to time out of the funds of the Commission to enable the owners to proceed to their destination. The business of the Commission before the Legislature is likewise attended to by this officer, in securing such amendments to the emigration laws as the experience of the Commissioners from time to time may suggest.

Treasurer's Department.

XIV. *The Treasurer's Department* is conducted by the Treasurer, Mr. George W. Wheeler, who has most creditably occupied that position since the formation of the Board, and by two clerks under him. It is divided into various branches, having severally charge of correspondence, of the money affairs, and of the business with the various counties and institutions of the State.

Correspondence

A. *Correspondence.*—One of the clerks, under the authority of the Treasurer, receives daily from the New York General Post-Office *all* letters deposited in the box of the Commissioners of Emigration, comprising letters addressed to the Commissioners of Emigration; to the Treasurer, to the General Agent and other officers of the Commissioners of Emigration in Castle Garden;

to the Castle Garden Railroad Agency, and its employees; to the Superintendent of Ward's Island, and physicians, employees, and emigrant inmates of Ward's Island; and to recently arrived or expected emigrants at Castle Garden.

The total number of letters received during the year 1869, including express packages containing remittances for emigrants, was 23,917.

All letters and express packages addressed to the Commissioners of Emigration, to the Treasurer, or to emigrants not in the institution on Ward's Island, are opened and read or distributed, as may be necessary. Those containing money or other remittances for emigrants are retained in the "Forwarding Office," a branch of the Treasurer's Department. A daily record is made of all receipts under appropriate heads, as follows: Number of remittance; date; amount; from whom received; for whom; name of vessel; nature of remittance; destination, etc.

Many remittances are received for emigrants after they have landed and left Castle Garden. Such remittances in due time are applied for by the sender, and returned immediately on application. Emigrants very often neglect to apply for remittances on hand, although duly notified that such are awaiting their call. Such remittances are also returned on application to the senders, either by mail or express, or to the parties in person who have made deposits with this department.

Its correspondence is large. In addition to that incidental to the return of uncalled-for remittances, replies are made to impatient senders of remittances for emigrants, who either have not arrived or have found employment from the Labor Exchange in Castle Garden, or perhaps are in hospital at Ward's Island. The parties so employed and for whom remittances have been received are duly notified to call at Castle Garden for the purpose of being forwarded to destination. The sender is also notified of the whereabouts of his or her relative or friend, and of the time when it is probable he or she will proceed to destination. From August 27, 1860 (the date on which the business connected with this subject was transferred to the Treasurer's Department), to December 31, 1869, the total number of remittances received for emigrants was 35,227, of an aggregate value of $481,955 21. The average value of each remittance received was $13 68. The following statement shows the increase of business in this one branch of the Correspondence Department:

There was received in		1860,	$6,034 60
"	"	1861,	9,465 09
"	"	1862,	18,990 55
"	"	1863,	46,147 91
"	"	1864,	58,583 44
"	"	1865,	62,288 88
"	"	1866,	57,359 11
"	"	1867,	66,865 89
"	"	1868,	64,054 70
"	"	1869,	92,165 04
			$481,955 21

B. *Money Affairs.*—The commutation fund, created and deposited according to law with the Chamberlain of the city of New York, is under the control of the Commissioners of Emigration, and is drawn upon semi-monthly by the Board, to defray current and other expenses of the Commission.

Supplies are furnished to the institution at Ward's Island, on requisition of the steward, countersigned by the Superintendent of Ward's Island, and approved by the Ward's Island Committee.

The requisitions are filled by the authorized purchasers, who render original bills of all articles purchased.

Drugs and medicines are supplied on requisition of the apothecary, countersigned by the Physician-in-Chief, and approved by the Ward's Island Committee. The requisitions are filled in the same manner as those of the steward.

The Treasurer receives from the steward and apothecary statements of all articles received by them on their requisitions. The bills are examined and compared with the statements, and all charges for articles not included in the statement are deducted.

Many articles and necessary supplies are furnished to the institution at Ward's Island in addition to those called for on regular semi-monthly requisitions, such as flour, coal, meat, fish, etc., etc. All bills for these articles are sent to the Superintendent of Ward's Island, and, if correct, are certified by that officer and the steward, and approved by the Ward's Island Committee. These and all other bills for supplies, for work performed, and all claims on account of Ward's Island and Castle Garden, are, previous to each semi-monthly meeting of the Commissioners of Emigration, submitted to the Auditing Committee, consisting of three members of the Board, upon whose approval they are presented to the Board of Commissioners, and ordered to be paid in the following manner: All bills and claims are numbered and entered in a book kept for that purpose. A warrant is drawn and signed by six Commissioners (this number constituting a majority and quorum of the Board), setting aside to the credit of the Vice-President of the Commissioners of Emigration, from the commutation fund in the hands of the City Chamberlain, a sum equal to the aggregate amount of these bills and claims. A check is then drawn to the order of each claimant (for the amount respectively due to him), signed by the Vice-President, and countersigned by one of the Commissioners of Emigration. Receipts corresponding with the number of the checks are taken by the treasurer in a book kept for that purpose.

C. *Business with the Counties and Institutions.*—Claims against the commutation fund for indemnity for expenses of emigrants who have become chargeable to any of the several counties of this State are made as follows: **County Claims.**

The agents appointed by the Commissioners at Albany, Rochester, Suspension Bridge, Buffalo, and Dunkirk, or, where there are no such agents, the superintendent or overseer of the poor in the locality where a recently arrived emigrant asks relief or assistance, is required to render, under oath, to the Commissioners of Emigration, monthly bills, accompanied by an affidavit of the person who has received relief or assistance, in which the following facts have to be set forth, namely: Name and age of person; name of vessel in which such person arrived at New York; the name of the master of such vessel; last place of residence before coming to New York; and that he or she has no relations or friends in this country, able, at their own charge, to support him or her. This statement is compared with the record on file in the office of the Commissioners of Emigration, and, if correct, and the charge for relief reasonable and proper, the amount is allowed and paid to the superintendents or overseers in the same manner as other claims, except that payment for expenses of emigrants in the several cities, towns, and counties in this State is made but once during the year, namely, at the last regular meetings of the Commissioners of Emigration in the year.

Monthly bills for support and care of emigrants, accompanied by the necessary affidavits, are received (at present) from thirteen different charitable institutions and hospitals situated in the several cities of this State. These bills undergo the same examination and scrutiny as the county bills, and are paid quarterly. The total amount paid to the several counties in this State, including the city and county of New York, for care and support of emigrants, from the organization of this Commission, May 5, 1847, to December 31, 1869, was $994,279 92, and to institutions and hospital, the sum of $168,371 96; making the total amount reimbursed to counties, cities, towns, and institutions, $1,162,651 98, as will more fully appear from the table in the Appendix.

Castle Garden is open both day and night. The regular business hours are from 8 o'clock A.M. to 5 o'clock P.M.; but, in cases of necessity, the employees are obliged to remain till ten, and even later. There are seven private watchmen and seven policemen, whose duty it is to keep strict guard over the emigrants, and to preserve order and discipline.

The yearly rent of the Garden is $12,000. The buildings, furniture, and fixtures are insured at $50,000, and the baggage of the emigrants at $30,000.

The business of all the offices connected with the Staten Island Boarding Station and Castle Garden is performed by seventy-six officers and employees, from the General Agent to the night-watchmen. Together their yearly salaries amount to $82,894.

Front View of the State Emigrant Refuge and Hospital Institutions, Ward's Island.

CHAPTER VII.

WARD'S ISLAND.

PREVIOUS to the year 1847, the Quarantine law provided for the care of the sick emigrant. A general tax, levied under State authority on all passengers arriving at the port of New York, was applied to the support of the Marine Hospital at Quarantine. Aliens as well as others arriving here, suffering under contagious or infectious diseases, such as yellow-fever, ship-fever, etc., were there received and gratuitously treated for one year. But no further provision was made from that period for the relief of emigrants not afflicted with any contagious disease, and they had to apply to the Almshouse authorities for admission to their medical institutions.

Provision for sick emigrants under Quarantine law.

The whole government and property of the Quarantine hospitals was transferred to the Commissioners of Emigration immediately after the constitution of the Board. But, owing to the want of other buildings, they were at first obliged to send all their patients to Staten Island. In consequence of this, the hospitals there were filled to excess, while, in spite of every precaution, crowds of sick, suffering under milder or non-contagious diseases, or requiring only surgical aid, were exposed to ship-fever, small-pox, yellow-fever, or cholera. These difficulties continued until April 11, 1849, when the Marine Hospital was formally restricted to the reception of contagious diseases. After this step, the Commissioners considered it their first duty to provide for and furnish hospital accommodations for those who suffered from other than contagious diseases, and a refuge for those who were destitute.

Insufficiency of same.

In 1847, the pressure for increased accommodations became very great. Thousands of sick emigrants arrived in the summer of that year, the greater portion of whom were the victims of the Irish famine, and had to be provided for at once, and as well as possible. Several hundreds of them were sent to private hospitals, such as Dr. Williams's and Dr. Wilson's, others to the New

Pressure in 1847. Temporary accommodations.

York City hospitals, and still others to the Almshouse. The convalescent were nursed at the public-stores on Staten Island, the use of which had been granted by the United States Government for a limited period. Others, as, for instance, the passengers of the cholera-ship, the *New York*, from Havre, were, by permission of the Secretary of War, sent to Bedloe's Island, where temporary hospitals had been erected for their accommodation. These temporary measures, however, were wholly inadequate to the many wants and necessities of the emigrant; and the Commissioners speedily came to the conclusion that, in order to save expenses and provide sufficient accommodation for all their sick, they would have to build their own hospitals and places of refuge.

Choice of Ward's Island for emigrant institutions.

Ward's Island was the spot which they selected for the location of these establishments. A better choice could not have been made. This island, which consists of about 200 acres, and has the shape of an irregular square, is situated in the East River, north of Blackwell's and south of Randall's Islands, and extends opposite to the city from about One Hundredth Street to One Hundred and Sixteenth Street. Its proximity to the city, and its accessibility at all seasons of the year, its exemption from the inconveniences and annoyances of a thickly settled neighborhood, together with the facilities it afforded of acquiring land of sufficient extent to meet possible future needs at a much more reasonable rate than could be obtained elsewhere, under equally favorable conditions of location, these several advantages induced that selection. The Commissioners have not been disappointed in the result, now that the demands upon the island have reached to a magnitude much beyond their anticipation. As early as June 4, 1847, they tried to buy a tract of about 8 acres of land, with an old stone building originally built for a factory, for the accommodation of the increasing number of their sick, but they could only obtain a lease of the ground. On July 14, 1847, the Commissioners resolved to erect a two-story shed, 200 feet long and 22 feet wide, for the accommodation of those who could not find employment and had not the strength to work. Early in 1848, they determined to build a hospital, within a short distance of the building used as a refuge. On November 1, 1848, it was finished and occupied. The structure was of wood,

First hospital erected 1848.

filled in with brick, having a frontage of 119 feet, and two wings, running east and west, of 40 feet long by 25 feet wide. It contained, besides apartments for physicians, apothecary, and nurses, and the apothecary's shop, eleven large rooms for patients, each of the dimensions of 40 feet by 25, and affording accommodations for 250 beds.

While this hospital was in the course of construction, the Board became satisfied that still more ample accommodations would soon be needed, and that more especially a proper establishment for children was imperatively demanded. They, therefore, determined to erect a nursery building, to contain, besides dormitories and play-room, a school-room and chapel. By the end of 1848 this building was finished and partly occupied. Erection of Nursery building 1848.

As it became essential to have more ground than, under the lease, was in the possession of the Commissioners, and as several lots or parcels of land on Ward's Island happened to be for sale, it was resolved to take advantage of the opportunity. Accordingly, in the month of July, 1848, 12 acres and 22 perches were purchased for $12,289 38. These purchases were continued from time to time, so that by the end of 1849 the Commissioners owned 95 acres 3 roods and 6 perches, for which they had altogether paid the comparatively small sum of $63,818 83. In 1858, they held in fee simple 106 acres, with appurtenant water-rights and marsh. In 1864, they bought a piece of land for $7,200, containing 2 acres and 22 perches, lying on the eastern side of Ward's Island, quite separate from their other lands, but very desirable and even indispensable for a landing-place on the eastern or the Sound side of the island, and well adapted for hospital purposes when required. Finally, in 1868, the Commissioners purchased a tract of about 11 acres of land on the south side of the island for $50,000, so that they now hold more than one-half of the island, or about 121 acres, for which they have paid $140,930 62, including the whole of the water front which faces New York City. The remaining portion is chiefly owned by the Commissioners of Public Charities and Correction, a local board exercising the functions of the poor officers of the county. Purchases of land.

Much, of course, has been done during the last twenty-two years for the improvement of the island. Temporary and wooden Improvements.

buildings have been replaced by substantial brick structures, sewers have been built, walks laid out, sea-walls erected, and not a single year has passed in which the Commissioners have not spent thousands and hundreds of thousands of dollars for the benefit and succor of those who are entrusted to their care. It would be tedious and tiresome to narrate the history of each improvement suggested and carried out for the amelioration of their condition. It will be sufficient to give a description of the buildings and institutions at present comprised in the establishment on Ward's Island. Before doing so, however, it will be necessary to state, in a few words, the history of the connection of the Marine Hospital on Staten Island with the other establishments of the Commissioners, which connection existed for just sixteen years, that is, from May 5, 1847, to April 29, 1863.

Connection of Marine Hospital, Staten Island, with Ward's Island establishment.

When the Commission was organized in 1847, it had no lands, nor buildings, nor means. Hence it was a wise policy to commit to its charge the Quarantine grounds and hospitals, even saddled with the condition that the Commissioners of Emigration had to receive and gratuitously nurse non-emigrants, such as sailors and sick citizens. In this way, the indispensable means were at once provided for receiving and caring for arriving immigrants, who were affected with various contagious and infectious diseases, among which cholera, small-pox, and ship-fever were widely prevalent. The number of sick was appalling. In the first eight years of the Commission, nearly 50,000 were treated within these hospitals. Since that time, large hospitals on Ward's Island have been erected, owing to which the sanitary condition of the immigrants has greatly improved. Accommodations for all emigrants not affected with infectious diseases being afforded on Ward's Island, the reasons for placing the Marine Hospital in the charge of the Commissioners ceased to exist. There was, in addition, other strong and positive ground for a change; it was unjust to those from whom the emigrant fund is collected to make that fund to contribute towards the support of the Quarantine and the maintenance of the health laws. In years in which the means of the Commissioners were seriously diminished by a decrease of immigration, it was hardly possible for them to maintain those who paid the commutation money. Nevertheless, the Commissioners were expected to bear the cost of supporting all who suffered from infectious diseases. This injustice was only repaired by the act of April 29, 1863, which created a Board of Quarantine Commissioners. Since that time, the cases of contagious fever amongst emigrants have been sent to Ward's Island, where the former surgical and isolated wards are devoted to their reception, while the small-pox patients, chargeable to the Commissioners, by an arrangement with the Commissioners of Public Charities, have been received at the Small-pox Hospital on Blackwell's Island, and regularly paid for at a rate agreed upon between both Commissions.

State injustice to Commissioners.

Another injustice which the State perpetrated against the Commissioners of Emigration is the following: On September 1 and 2, 1858, a furious mob had violently attacked and destroyed all the buildings and hospitals on the Quarantine grounds. The loss of property amounted to several hundred thousands of dollars.

Award to Commissioners on account of Quarantine riots diverted to other purposes.

A committee was appointed to assess the damages, which awarded to the Commissioners of Emigration, for the destruction of their personal property at the Marine Hospital, the sum of fourteen thousand dollars, payable in bonds, and issued to them by the Supervisors of the county of Richmond. Of the sum thus raised, the whole was expended for strictly Quarantine purposes, except a small balance of about $500. An additional sum of $107,521 was also awarded to the Commissioners of Emigration for the destruction of their buildings, houses, and hospitals, but the Supervisors of Richmond County, claiming that the Commissioners of Emigration were merely trustees for the people of the State, refused to issue or deliver them to the Commissioners, and deposited them with the Treasurer of the State.

Application was made on the part of the Commissioners for a mandamus to compel the Supervisors of Richmond County to issue these bonds to them, in accordance with the award under the act. It was, however, held by the Court of Appeals that, inasmuch as the Commissioners of Emigration were trustees of the people of the State, a delivery of the bonds to the people was a substantial compliance with the law. In other words, the judgment of the Court of Appeals substantially made the State a present of more than $100,000 of the funds of the poor emigrant.

An application to the Legislature for the transfer of these bonds to the Commissioners proved equally futile. "If, however," says the Report of the Commissioners for 1864, "for any reason these bonds should be retained by the State, then it is most respectfully submitted that, as they are given as compensation for destruction of buildings, etc., erected at various periods from funds contributed by alien emigrants, for whom the Commissioners are the agents and trustees, or from moneys borrowed on mortgage for and applied to those buildings and improvements for which these bonds were given, they should be regarded as the proper fund to pay off the encumbrances on the property of the Commission, without demanding payment of any portion of it from the Emigrant Fund." Since that time these bonds have been applied to the payment of expenses incurred in the erection of the new Quarantine Station and buildings on the West Bank, and the Commissioners have in consequence received no advantage whatever from the award.

Another illustration of the arbitrary way in which the State of New York disposes of the emigrant funds is the following:

Unjust debt saddled on Commissioners for payment of interest on mortgage on Marine Hospital.

As above stated, the act was passed on April 29, 1863, establishing the new Quarantine Board, and directing the Commissioners of Emigration to convey to the State all the right, title, and interest which they had in the real estate on Staten Island. This property was subject to a mortgage of $200,000, covering the former Marine Hospital lands, with all the Ward's Island property held by the Commissioners. The debt was contracted at various times, and the mortgage given with the express consent of the Governor, Attorney-General, and Comptroller, as required by law, during the administration of Governors Fish, Hunt, and Morgan. The loan was obtained upon the credit of the estimated value of the Quarantine property. The Commissioners thought that, if they contributed $50,000 towards the payment of the mortgage, it would be fully as much as the relative value of the two pieces of property, the equity of the mode of raising, and the application of the fund from alien emigrants would justify. As this sum was recommended by the Comptroller in a report to the Legislature, and had been formerly approved in an act passed in 1867, the Commissioners assented to this division of the debt. In 1868, this property was sold, but the mortgage had not been

paid off, and the amount realized from the sale was directed to be applied towards the erection of the new Quarantine structure on the West Bank. Thus, since 1858, although the Commission has received no benefit from the lands on Staten Island, and although, since the appointment of the Quarantine Commission, the Commissioners of Emigration have been relieved of the duties which formerly devolved upon them, yet they have been called upon during the past eleven years to pay the interest on the whole $200,000, of which $150,000 was debt incurred in support of the Marine Hospital, and acknowledged as such by the Legislature. All applications to the latter for the refunding of the interest thus paid, amounting to $115,000, by the State to the Commissioners of Emigration, so that the emigrant money may be applied to its legitimate purpose, have thus far proved of no avail, and the Commissioners of Emigration, although desirous of getting rid of the debt unjustly saddled on them, are magnanimously allowed to continue to pay the yearly interest on $150,000, with money diverted from its original object for the benefit of American citizens.

Buildings on Ward's Island.

To return, however, to Ward's Island, where, since 1863, all the hospitals and refuges of the Commissioners are concentrated. We shall first give a brief description of the different buildings erected there in the course of years by the Commissioners for the use of the emigrants and the several employees. These buildings are:

Verplanck Hospital.

The New Hospital.—This is the chief building of interest on the island, it having been constructed upon the most approved plans for perfect ventilation and all necessary comforts for the sick. It consists of a long corridor, 450 feet in length and 2 stories in height, from which project 5 wings, each 130 feet long and 25 feet wide, and 2 stories high, except the centre wing, which has 3 stories. It is used exclusively for non-contagious diseases and surgical cases. The corridor affords ample room for exercise for convalescent patients, as well as a connection for the separate wings. The corners of each wing are flanked with towers, which have upon their tops tanks for water; below and attached to each ward are bath-rooms and water-closets. The rooms are heated by hot air, which is forced through registers by a large fan-wheel. The same power is used in the summer to secure a current of cool air through the wards. Projecting from the corridor in an opposite direction from the wings is a fire-proof building, which contains the boilers, three in number, the engines, etc. The cook-room, with 18 steam-kettles and ranges, where the cooking for the entire island is done, and above this the bakery, with 4 ovens, of a capacity each of 300 loaves of bread; also the washing-room, with machinery for washing and wringing the clothing, and 63 wash-tubs. On the upper floor are the drying and ironing rooms. The building also contains a basement-room for storing flour, vaults for coal, and dummies for hoisting purposes. The hospital proper has accommodation for about 350 patients. The rooms are ventilated by pipes connected with the main chimney, into which the steam is exhausted, thus forming a perfect and powerful draught. The basement is used for storage, and, in cases of emergency, as sleeping quarters for inmates of the Refuge.

Nursery.

The Nursery.—The home of the children, to the right of the new hospital, is a frame building, three stories and basement, with Mansard roof, 120×190 feet. The basement contains the dining-room, play-room, and bath-room; the first floor, the matron's rooms and sleeping-rooms; the second floor, sleeping-rooms, also the school-room and recitation-rooms; the third floor is mostly occupied by the Catholic Chapel and ante-rooms attached. This building was completed only in 1868, having been thoroughly renovated and a new roof put on. The school is conducted by teachers from the city, under the supervision of the Board of Education, and has every convenience for the comfort of the scholars. The chapel is a neat and commodious room, and will seat comfortably about 500 persons.

Refuge.

Refuge Building.—This is a brick building, three stories and basement, with three wings, total size 100 feet by 98 feet. It is used as follows: Basement, for wash and bath rooms, and storage for blankets, bedding, and heavy groceries; first floor, for steward's department, with store for island supplies, matron's rooms, cutting-rooms, also sleeping-rooms. The second and third floors

GROUND PLAN OF THE "VERPLANCK" STATE EMIGRANT HOSPITAL.

REFERENCES:

A—WARDS. B—DINING ROOMS.
C—NURSES' ROOMS. D—SCULLERIES.
E—LINEN ROOMS. F—HALLS.
G—SANATORIUMS. H—BATH AND SINK ROOMS.
I—WATER CLOSET ROOMS.

NOTE.—The lower floor of the right-hand Pavilion is appropriated for Committee Rooms, the Superintendent's and Distribution Offices, and a Fire-proof Vault for the Records of the Institutions.

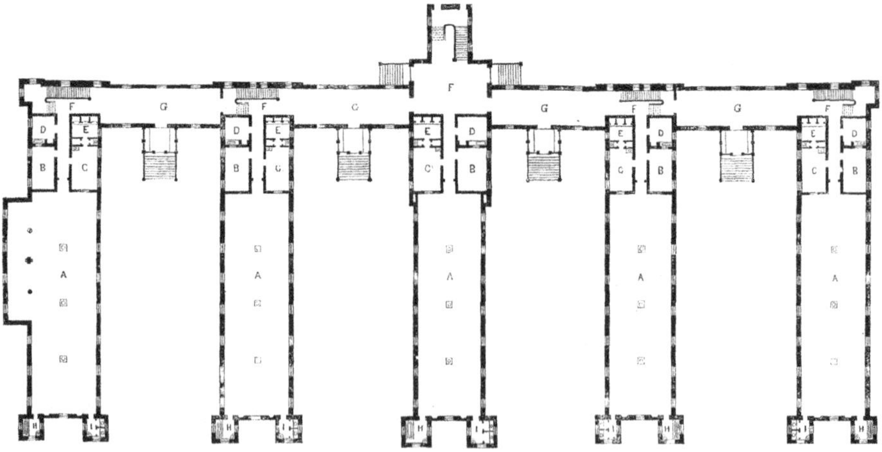

are used entirely as sleeping-rooms. It is, as its name indicates, a refuge for destitute immigrants, chiefly women and children, and will accommodate 450 persons.

New Barracks.—This is a plain brick building, three stories and basement, size 160×44 feet, with projection in the rear for boiler-rooms, bath-rooms, etc. It is devoted entirely to destitute male emigrants. The basement is used for exercise and protec ion in cold weather; the three upper floors for sleeping-rooms. Each floor is supplied with water-closets, bath-rooms, etc., and the uilding is heated with steam. It will accommodate 450 per- ons. New Barracks.

Dispensary Buildin.—This building is of the same size and appearance as the Nursery building, and, like it, was, in 1868, completely and thoroughly repaired. The basement is used for storage, kitchen, etc.; the first floor for the dispensary, apothecary, and clerks' apartments, dining-room for officers, and wash and bath rooms; the upper floors furnish sleeping-apartments for officers, also wards for males with chronic diseases. The capacity of the building is 250 patients. Dispensary.

New Dining Hall.—This was formerly two stories high, 25×125 feet. It was enlarged in 1868 by the addition of another building of the same size, connected with the old room by arches, thus giving four rooms of a total capacity of 10,000 square feet. This is used as a dining-room for the inmates of the Refuge, and will comfortably seat 1,200 people. Dining Hall.

Fever-Wards for Males.—These are in four brick buildings, one story and basement, each 25×150 feet, with bath-rooms, kitchens, etc., attached. They have each a capacity of forty-five patients. Male Fever-Wards.

Surgical Wards for Males.—This is a three-story brick building, 25×125 feet, and is used for male surgical cases. It has a capacity of 120 patients. Male Surgical Wards.

Protestant Chapel Building.—Is a two-story brick building, Protestant Chapel.

25×125 feet. The first floor is used as medical ward for women; the upper floor is a Protestant chapel and reading-room. The chapel, in general design and finish, is like the Catholic chapel. The reading-room is furnished with a large number of periodicals and papers. The first floor will accommodate forty-five patients.

Boys' Barrack.. *The Boys' Barrack.*—A two-story building, will accommodate eighty persons; size 25×125 feet.

Female Fever Wards. *Fever-Wards for Females.*—A three-story brick building, 35×125 feet; will accommodate 120 patients.

Lunatic Asylum. *Lunatic Asylum.*—Is a three-story and basement brick building, 25×125 feet in size. The basement is divided into close rooms for men or women, while the upper rooms are sleeping-apartments for both sexes; on each side are yards for the exercise of patients. This building will accommodate 125 persons. It is, however, not adapted to the proper treatment of lunatics, and will be replaced by one suited to the purpose.

Physicians' residences. *Physicians' Residences.*—Three in number, built together, and completed in 1868; are substantial brick houses; total size, 65×45 feet; three stories and basement.

Superintendent's house. *Superintendent's House.*—Three stories and basement, brick, 64×75 feet. The two large and spacious parlors on both sides of the hall serve as reception and dining rooms for the Commissioners and their guests, while the upper part of the building is occupied by the Superintendent. Just opposite is the

Deputy Superintendent's house. *Deputy Superintendent's House.*—Two stories and basement, frame, 27×44 feet; was thoroughly repaired in 1868.

Store-House. *Store-House on Dock.*—Frame building, one story, 28×85 feet; used for storage.

Boat-House. *Boat-House on the Dock.*—Frame building, 20×30 feet.

Stable. *Stable.*—A new stable was built in 1869, large enough to accommodate all the live stock required for the uses of the institution; also a new building for containing

Workshops, for the various branches of labor used on the island. Both of these buildings are constructed neatly and substantially of brick. Workshops.

The minor buildings consist of ice-house, dead-house, fowl-house, lumber-shed, tool-house, and gardener's house.

Ward's Island is reached from the foot of One Hundred and Tenth Street, by taking passage on a row-boat of the Commissioners, running to and from that point, or by a steamboat chartered by them, which leaves Castle Garden every day at one o'clock P.M. A sick or destitute emigrant who desires to go to the island has to apply at the Ward's Island Department at Castle Garden. After an examination has established his title to the privileges of the island, he receives a permit, which contains his name, age, nativity, date of arrival in this country, the name of the vessel, and the cause of application, which permit is delivered on landing and kept on record by the proper officer. Upon reaching the island, all the new-comers are brought to the reception office, where they have to pass a medical examination, which serves to determine whether they are to be sent to the Refuge or to the Hospital. After this examination and a thorough washing and cleaning, which in most cases is indispensable, they are admitted in the proper place. Access to Ward's Island.

The Ward's Island Institution is divided into the Refuge and Hospital Department, the general care of which is entrusted to a standing committee of six members of the Board, appointed annually by the President. The charge of the various departments devolves upon the Superintendent, under the general supervision of this committee. It is, however, hardly possible to separate one department from the other. The relations between them are so intimate, that the institution, although actually divided into two departments, appears and works as an integral whole. Administration of Ward's Island.

The Refuge Department, under the immediate direction of the Superintendent, has charge of all cases of destitution, in- Refuge Department.

cluding those newly arrived emigrants who, though in a healthy condition, are prevented from proceeding on their travels from want of funds or other causes. The inmates of this department perform a considerable amount of labor for the benefit of the institution, such as farming, grading, building stone walls, etc., etc. This department includes also those persons who from age or disease are infirm and incapacitated for labor; and, moreover, affords a refuge for all those persons discharged from the hospital who have no home or cannot obtain employment. A large number of persons of these different classes are constantly provided for during the winter season.

The buildings embracing the Refuge Department are plain but substantial, and well adapted to the purposes for which they are designed. Every possible provision is made for health and comfort. One of the buildings shelters the male sex, another the women and children. For nursing women and children without parents or protection, there is the nursery, in charge of a matron. It contains a school-room, where all newly arrived emigrant children at once have an opportunity to learn the English language. Boys from ten to fourteen years of age occupy their own quarters, and are employed on light, out-of-door labor.

Superintendent's duties.

In addition to the care of the Refuge Department, the Superintendent has charge of the entire property of the Commissioners of Emigration, and co-operates with the Medical Board in carrying out all measures affecting the well-being of the inmates; orders the supplies for the island, and is the chief executive officer to whom the heads of all the departments are obliged to report. As his duties are of a weighty responsibility and onerous, it requires not only talent and ability, but also a considerable experience to perform them.

Medical administration—its changes.

The medical administration of Ward's Island from the year 1847 up to the present time has experienced various changes until it assumed its present form, which experience has proved the most efficient. When the service was first organized on Ward's Island, the office of Superintendent and Physician was united in one person. Dr. John Snowden, who first occupied this position, a few months after his appointment fell a victim to his untiring devotion to the sick under his care. On April 19, 1848, Dr. E. Greene was appointed his successor. The largely increased hospital service, however, soon demanded the exclusive attention of a physician-in-chief, devoted solely to that duty. The former office of Superintendent and Physician was therefore divided. Dr. Theodore A. Tellkampf, in May, 1849, was appointed to the chief medical office, while Dr. Greene remained Superintendent of the Refuge Department, subordinate to the Physician-in-Chief in all matters respecting the sanitary and hygienic condition of the institution, as well as the economical affairs of the Hospital Department.

The institution was in a very bad condition, when, on June 6, 1849, Dr. Tellkampf took charge of the Hospital Department. He organized it with the efficient aid of the Ward's Island Committee, within a comparatively short time. Competent physicians, the majority of whom had been already assistant physicians or surgeons in other hospitals, were appointed. The places of incompetent orderlies and nurses were filled as speedily as possible by others, selected carefully from among the inmates of the hospital who had recovered. In order to secure an efficient corps of orderlies and nurses, they received monthly pay, after having been trained for their various duties. A head orderly and a matron were appointed.

Supplies. The so-called contract system was abolished with great difficulty, but since its abolition all articles requisite for the Hospital, for instance, medicines, meat, milk, vegetables, etc., have been of the best quality. The wards were newly furnished, and iron bedsteads introduced. A hospital kitchen was arranged; though deficient in some respects, an experienced cook with two or three assistants managed to supply all the patients—gradually increasing from 600 to about 1000—with the best diet, in full, half, and quarter rations, as ordered.

Croton water. The Croton water was introduced, and a wash-house built and furnished with all the modern improvements.

The various departments of the Hospital, namely, the Medical, Surgical, the Lying-in Department, and the Department for Diseases of Children, were meanwhile organized, each divided and subdivided; and all sick immigrants—curable as well as incurable cases—were admitted, except the insane and those suffering from small-pox.

Besides the more usual divisions, others were arranged, one for patients suffering from petechial typhus (ship-fever), another for cholera patients—the Asiatic cholera prevailing at that time—and still another for about 200 children infected with prevalent ophthalmia. In order to prevent the spreading of this contagious disease beyond the institution, the children were discharged from this division only when completely cured. A temporary building was erected for post-mortem examinations. All persons on their arrival at the institution were examined first by the Physician-in-Chief, and subsequently by the physician *du jour*, and those found to be sick were sent to their respective wards, after having complied (if possible) with the regulations made in regard to cleanliness, dress, etc.

In the spring of 1850, the Physician-in-Chief, who, in organizing the Hospital Department, had the direction of the economical affairs of that department as well as the direction and supervision of the treatment of all patients, and who performed, besides, all surgical and obstetrical operations, except such as he could entrust to his assistant-surgeons, proposed that his senior assistants should now be appointed physicians, to have charge of departments or divisions, subject to certain regulations and restrictions, and that each should have an assistant. This proposition was approved of by the Ward's Island Committee, but not formally acted upon by the Board, owing to the occurrence of some vacancies (two in the Ward's Island Committee, namely, one by the death of the Hon. David C. Colden, the other by the resignation of George E. Kunhardt, President of the German Society, both of whom had evinced a great interest in the organization and welfare of the institution).

Adoption of English plan of visiting physicians.

This change in the composition of the Board resulted in a new course of action. While the Physician-in-Chief was convalescent from petechial typhus, from which disease the majority of his assistants, one after the other, had also suffered, the Board resolved to introduce a so-called new plan—in fact, the old English plan—according to which visiting physicians and surgeons living from six to eight miles from the island, and young resident physicians, were appointed. The Physician-in-Chief, after having urged in vain that the hospital service required a permanent medical staff residing on the island, and that the contemplated change, for many weighty reasons, was objectionable, and sure to lead to most deplorable results, declined the position offered to him under the new system, and resigned.

The new plan, however, was carried into effect by the appointment of eight physicians and surgeons as visiting physicians to the institution, who formed together the Medical Board of Ward's Island.

This system soon proved its inefficiency, but was, nevertheless, kept up until 1855, when the Medical Department proper was again placed under the charge of a resident physician-in-chief, with two assistants, and the Surgical Department under the charge of a surgeon-in-chief, with the same number of assistants. This system has been in operation for the last fifteen years, with the simple change of one instead of two assistants in each department. The general supervision is exercised by the Medical Board, consisting of a Consulting Physician, Physician-in-Chief, and Surgeon-in-Chief. These offices are now filled by the following gentlemen: Dr. J. Murray Carnochan, Surgeon-in-Chief; Dr. Ernst Schilling, Consulting Physician; Dr. George Ford, Physician-in-Chief; Dr. Auguste Reimer, Assistant Physician; and Dr. John Dwyer, Assistant Surgeon; the three latter forming the resident medical staff. The former have been connected with the institution for a long series of years.

Inefficiency of same, and appointment of resident physicians and assistants, 1855.

Present Medical Board.

The regular routine business of the Hospital is about equally divided among the resident medical staff. A number of wards constitute the department of one physician or surgeon, to which his labor and attendance are mainly devoted. The Physician-in-Chief has the general supervision. The assistants have to report to and to consult with him, and to carry out his suggestions or orders. The Medical Board meets regularly every fortnight, to consult upon all matters relating to the Hospital and the welfare of its inmates; to deliberate upon general questions of health, and such suggestions as may be received from different quarters; to consider and decide upon changes and improvements, and to discuss new or difficult cases in practice. A record is kept of all its

Medical Board.

CHAPTER VIII.

CAPITAL VALUE OF IMMIGRATION TO THIS COUNTRY—ITS INFLUENCE ON THE POPULATION AND THE NATION'S WEALTH—IS IMMIGRATION A MATTER OF STATE OR NATIONAL CONCERN?

It is a common mistake of statisticians and writers on political economy to limit their enquiries to the amount of means which immigrants bring with them, to ascertain the aggregate thereof, and to conclude that the few millions thus obtained are the only addition to the nation's wealth.

Cash means of the emigrants.

In 1856, the Commissioners of Emigration in New York examined every immigrant as to the amount of his means, and the average cash of each of the 142,342 new-comers of that year amounted to $68 08. The Commissioners afterward discontinued this examination, for the reason that, in spite of all their endeavors, they could not obtain correct answers on the part of the immigrants, who were suspicious of their motives.

Kennedy's Report.

"The main object," says Superintendent Kennedy, in his report of January 14, 1858, "for enquiring of passengers the amount of cash means they possessed, was secured, when it was shown to the public that on the average they were in possession of a larger amount of such means than is held by the localized residents of any known community; and that, although a part of the immigration is among that class of persons who seek refuge on our shores, and subsistence by labor, with little or no cash means, yet a large portion bring with them of that kind of property a sufficient quantity to sustain themselves, and to aid in the enrichment of the country. It was justly apprehended that a continuance of the investigation might lead to mischievous results, from their manifest inaccuracy. For, while the table of 1856 presents the average amount of cash means at $68 08 per head, subsequent but reliable information showed that the concealment of large amounts had been constantly and successfully practised; and that, had full admission been made of the funds in possession, the average would have been at least double the amount reported."

Unreliable statements of emigrants.

I was myself at that time a witness of the unreliability of the statements of immigrants concerning their means. Being present when, in the summer of 1856, the passengers of a German ship were examined at Castle Garden, I observed an old farmer and his three adult sons, who, in answer to the enquiry of the Superintendent, opened their pocket-books, counted the contents of each, and hesitatingly declared it to be about $25. I interposed, and explained to these people, who evidently apprehended that they would be taxed on account of their money, the reason of the interrogatories, whereupon the old farmer showed me a bill of exchange of $2,700 on a New York banker, and remarked that each of his sons had about the same amount with him. These men had been entered as having about $100 together, while in fact they ought to have been credited with about $11,000.

German emigrants.

"German immigrants alone," says a report of the Commissioners of Emigration, December 15, 1854, on the subjects in dispute between the Commissioners of Emigration and the Almshouse Department of the city of New York, "have for the past three years, as estimated by the best German authorities, brought into the country annually an average of about eleven millions of dollars. A large amount of money in proportion to numbers is estimated to have been brought from Holland and other countries. The amount of money thus introduced into the country is incalculable."

Statistical facts.

These estimates are corroborated by statements which I happened to find among some German statistical tables. It appears from the statistical records of the grand duchy of Baden, that from 1840 to 1849 the ready cash which each emigrant carried with him amounted to 245 florins, or $98 gold. Again, of the Bavarian emigrants between 1845–1851, each was possessed of 233 florins, or $93 20 gold; between 1851–1857, each of 236 florins, or $94 40 gold; while the Brunswickers, who emigrated in 1853, had 136 thalers, or about $96 gold, each. The Würtembergers, in 1855, carried only $76 gold each with them; which sum in 1856 increased to $134 gold, in 1857 to $145 gold, and in 1858 even to $318 gold per head. Other official data concerning this I have not been able to obtain, but the instances just cited throw sufficient light on the subject.

Other property of emigrants.

The money, however, is not the only property which immigrants bring with them. In addition to it, they have a certain amount of wearing apparel, tools, watches, books, and jewelry. Assuming that their cash amounts to only $100 a head, I do not think I exaggerate in estimating their other property at $50, thus making $150 the total of the personal property of each immigrant. The total arrivals at New York for the year 1869 were 258,989 immigrants, and the amount added to the national wealth, through this port alone, in one year, did consequently not fall short of $38,848,350. Large as this sum appears, it is insignificant in comparison with the hundreds of millions which have been, and will be, produced yearly by the labor of immigrants. And here the question suggests itself: What is the economic value of each immigrant to the country of his adoption?

Economic value of emigrants.

We are perfectly familiar with the estimates which, during the existence of slavery, were made of the value of negroes. A good field hand was considered to be worth $1,200 and over; a good cook was valued higher; and a seamstress or housekeeper was, in some cases, held at even $1,500 or $2,000. In order to obtain a proper idea of the importance of immigration to the United States, we must endeavor to capitalize, so to speak, the addition to the natural and intellectual resources of the country represented by each immigrant.

Dr. Engel's theory.

A prominent German statistician, Dr. Engel, of Berlin, Director of the Prussian Statistical Bureau, in an able treatise on the price of labor, distinguishes three periods in the economic life of each man: two unproductive and one productive period. The first comprises the raising and education of the individual, and continues until he reaches his fifteenth year. It is, of course, not only unproductive, but causes considerable outlay. The second, extending from the fifteenth to the sixty-fifth year, is the productive time of life. The third comprises the unproductive years of old age after sixty. Dr. Engel calls the first the juvenile, the second the labor, and the third the aged period.

It is only during this productive period that man is able to subsist on the results of his own labor. In the juvenile period he is dependent on the assistance of others, and in the aged period he has to live upon the accumulated fruits of the productive years.

Whether or not the child in its first period lives at the expense of his parents, there must be means for its maintenance and education, and as nature does not spontaneously furnish these means, and as they cannot be provided by others without danger of impoverishment if not replaced, they must be obtained by labor. This labor is performed during the productive period, in which the following three objects should be attained, viz.: 1. The payment of the expenses incurred for the support and education of the child in the juvenile period. 2. The satisfaction of the daily wants, and the maintenance of the productive power of the individual. 3. The laying up of a surplus fund for his sustenance during the aged period. Thus, the cost of the bringing up and education of a man constitutes a specific value, which benefits that country which the adult individual makes the field of his physical and intellectual exertions. This value is represented by the outlay which is necessary to produce an ordinary laborer. An immigrant, therefore, is worth just as much to this country as it costs to produce a native-born laborer of the same average ability.

It is evident that the capital value which a grown-up, able-bodied immigrant represents is different according to his station in life and the civilization of the country whence he comes. The wants of a skilled and unskilled laborer from the same country differ widely. Those of the Englishman are different from those of the Irishman. The German must be measured by another standard than the Mexican or South American. Their mode of life, their economical habits and practical pursuits, have little in common; and hence the benefit to the country of their adoption varies according to their respective previous relations. It is certain, however, that each emigrant brings, independently of his personal property, a certain increase of wealth to this country, which increase is paid by the country from which he comes, and accordingly must be credited to it.

In order to arrive at the most accurate possible estimate of this addition of wealth, it is necessary to enquire into the cost of raising and educating, in this country, a man whose means of living are wholly derived from his physical labor. I shall not include in the following calculation the professional man, the scholar, the lawyer, the clergyman, the physician, the engineer, and others, who, in the course of years, have likewise come here by thousands, and added to the productive wealth of the country in proportion to the greater cost of their education; but I shall confine myself to the class named, which forms the great majority of immigrants.

Cost of raising a laborer.

Dr. Engel computes the cost of raising a manual laborer in Germany at 40 thalers a year for the first five years of his life; at 50 thalers for the next five years; and at 60 thalers from the eleventh to the fifteenth year, thus arriving at an average of 50 thalers per year, or 750 thalers in all. From my knowledge of German life, I consider this estimate as correct as it can be; and, assuming that in this country subsistence costs about twice as much as in Germany, I do not think I shall be far from the truth in doubling Engel's estimates, and in assuming the expense of bringing up an American farmer or unskilled laborer for the first fifteen years of his life to average 100 thalers per year, or a total of 1,500 thalers, equal to about $1,500 currency. Following Dr. Engel's estimate, an American girl will be found to cost only about half of that, or $750, for the reason that she becomes useful to the household from an earlier age. Allowance must be made, it is true, for the fact that about one-fifth of the emigrants are less than fifteen years old; but this is fully balanced by the great preponderance of men over women, and by thousands who represent the highest order of skilled labor. Hence I feel safe in assuming the capital value of each male and female emigrant to be $1,500 and $750 respectively for every person of either sex, making an average for both of $1,125. My friend, Mr. Charles Reemelin, one of the most prominent American political economists, confirmed these figures in a very able address, made before the German Pioneer Association of Cincinnati, on May 26, 1869, in which he estimated the value of each immigrant who had come to that city to live at $1,500, and the total value of the fifty thousand emigrants who have taken up their residence there in the last forty years at seventy-five millions of dollars.

Increase of national wealth by immigration.

The number of emigrants who have arrived at the port of New York from May 5, 1847, to January 1, 1870, is no less than 4,297,980. Adding to the capital value of $1,125 represented by every emigrant, $150 per head for the average value of personal property brought, as I have shown, by each, we find that immigration increased the national wealth, in the stated period, by more than five billions of dollars, or more than twice as much as the present amount of the national debt. The total immigration into the United States being now at the rate of 300,000 souls per year, the country gains nearly four hundred millions of dollars annually, or more than one million per day.

My friend, Mr. Charles L. Brace, in a very able communication which, on November 3, 1869, he addressed to the New York daily *Tribune*, has taken exceptions to these statements and estimates, which were contained in a paper read by me before the American Social Science Association. Mr. Brace's theory.

"Mr. Kapp," he says, "deserves high commendation for the ingenuity and industry he has shown in thus analyzing our emigration statistics, and proving the economical value of this current of population.

"But, in the light of science, we are compelled to point out what seem to us omissions in these economical reasonings, which will somewhat modify the results. The capital value of an object is not determined merely by the cost of its production, but also by another element—*the demand for it.* Thus, if a hundred new sewing-machines are produced, they are worth to the community not merely what they cost to make, but what the demand for them will bring. If there has been an overproduction of sewing-machines, or they are of poor quality, their worth sinks, and their money value to the community may fall below the cost of manufacture. The same is true of all articles which are parts of the capital of a country. Their money value or price is conditioned by cost of production and the relation of demand to supply. It is true also of animals. A cow or a horse is worth not alone what it costs to produce it, but what the demand will bring. Some, from adventitious circumstances, will fall below the cost of production; some will rise above it. Many fine horses, which cost no more to raise than poor ones, are worth far more to the country, because the demand for them is greater, while many poor ones sink below their cost, because the demand is unreasonably small. So with human beings, if we look at them purely as instruments of production. An idiot costs as much, perhaps more, to raise as a lad of ordinary intelligence; but he is of no capital value. A farmer's boy, whose brain has worked intensely as he broke the sod, though costing no more in education than a dull clodhopper in the next house, finds himself at fifteen worth double the other in his market value, solely because the demand for his labor is greater. The wages or salary of men in the professions is not measured solely by the cost of their education, but by the price which their services will bring in the market; and this is determined mainly, though not entirely, by demand and supply.

"When an emigrant lands in this country, his capital value is conditioned by these two elements, cost of production and demand. There are, probably, every year among the emigrants, a few thousand of poor, ignorant, and rather weakly women who become sewing-women in the great cities. These, on Mr. Kapp's estimate, should be worth $750 each. But, owing to the crowded state of the market for such instruments of production, and to their own ignorance, and the consequent small demand for each seamstress, those women are probably of scarcely any pecuniary value to the community, and are often a burden. On the very property of the Commissioners of Emigration there will be, this winter, some thousands of able-bodied men, who not only produce nothing, but are supported by the contributions to the Emigration Fund of their more industrious fellows. These certainly are not worth $1,175 capital to the nation. Then take the very considerable number of the four million emigrants who have been entirely non-producers, being either paupers, or criminals, or diseased, or who have, as neglected children, fallen into the hands of the public authorities, or whose labor, as destitute women, has not supported themselves. When these are all subtracted from the four millions, there will be a very considerable deduction from Mr. Kapp's enthusiastic estimates of the value of this golden tide.

"We do not question, however, the general conclusion of the Commissioner's paper—the immense value of this current of labor to the production and development of the country. We would only diminish somewhat his numerical estimate of the pecuniary worth of each emigrant.

"Articles which are in universal demand, such as gold and silver, depend for their value mainly on the cost of production. So universal is the demand here for ordinary male labor, that its value will not vary much from the expense of its production in this country. This cost Mr. Kapp has probably exaggerated in making it double that of Germany. It would be safe, however, reckoning from the expense of supporting a laborer's male child in Germany, to call the capital value of the most ordinary farm-hand at least $1,000 or $1,100 in the United States.

"This estimate alone would justify all the Commissioner's enthusiasm as to the pecuniary value of emigration.

"It is a little less than was the old market value of the male slave, for the reason, probably, as Mr. Olmsted has shown, that the pecuniary value of slaves was somewhat speculative, based *on the expectation of profit* from the best cotton lands.

"There is another method of obtaining 'the capital value' of the male emigrant, which we throw out for the consideration of your readers interested in questions of political economy.

"Each laborer is worth (pecuniarily) to the country the profits from his production over and above the expense of his support. His average cost to his employer is, say, $20 per month and 'keep,' or about $400 per annum. It is believed that an ordinary profit on common labor upon a farm is from 15 to $18\frac{3}{4}$ per cent. This would leave the gain to the country from $60 to $75 annually. This, at seven per cent. interest, would represent just about the capital value estimated above, or about $1,000 or $1,100 for an average male laborer."

Reply to Mr. Brace's argument.

So far Mr. Brace. I freely admit that the economical principles set forth by him are incontrovertible; but, on the other hand, I claim that actual experience has established the correctness of the position I have assumed. The basis for my statements and estimates is chiefly this:

In a comparatively new country like the United States, with its immense area and the rapid development of its resources, the demand for labor is always greater than the supply. There are, it is true, some pursuits in which this is not the case. During the winter, too, in large cities, hundreds and thousands of emigrants are often unable to find suitable employment or an adequate reward for their labor; but this state does not continue for any length of time. Seamstresses who cannot find work in their line turn to other occupations, such as housemaids, nurses, etc. The character of the European workingwoman in this respect is just the reverse of that of the American. While the latter considers labor in a factory to be of a more elevated character, and would never descend to common housework, the former is content to exert herself in any decent sphere of labor.

But for argument's sake, let me admit that every year there are a few thousand poor, ignorant, and incapable men or women who become a burden to the community. What proportion does their number bear to the total immigration of a whole year? The New York Commissioners of Emigration have annually to support an average of about 2,000 sick and destitute in their institutions, and, besides, a few hundred criminals, who are confined at their cost in the city prisons; but all this does not amount to one per cent. of the entire immigration. It must be borne in mind that the poorer emigrants remain in New York City, and that, consequently, it cannot be presumed that any large number of the others become a burden to the several States.

However, I will even go so far as to admit that the number of those who not only produce nothing, but are supported by the contributions of States or counties, reaches 5 per cent. Taking the number of immigrants in 1869 as a basis, this percentage would give between 12,000 and 13,000 non-producers. But even such a percentage would be more than counterbalanced by the large number of emigrants better educated than the ordinary laborers who form the basis of my computation.

An emigrant population contains a very small percentage of helpless and incapable individuals. Apart from the law which prohibits the landing of cripples, blind, deaf, and aged persons, it is self-evident that only the strong, the most courageous and enterprising natives of a country emigrate to a foreign land. The unequal representation of the several ages and sexes among emigrants is due to this fact. Out of the whole immigration to the United States from 1819 to 1860, more than 22 per cent. were from one to fifteen years old; a little over 50 per cent. were from fifteen to thirty years of age; more than 73 per cent. were less than thirty years old; more than 46½ per cent. were from twenty to thirty-five; more than 60 per cent. were from fifteen to thirty-five, and nearly 90 per cent. less than forty years old. Moreover, the sexes approach equality only among children and youths. Of individuals under twenty years of age, about 18 per cent. were males, and 17 per cent. females, while the male immigrants from twenty-five to forty years of age were double the number of females of the same age.

Of the total immigration to the United States within the above-mentioned period (1819 to 1860), amounting to 5,459,421, the occupation of 2,978,599, including 2,074,633 females, is not stated, while 1,637,154 are put down as farmers and laborers, leaving 843,688 persons who were either mechanics or professional men. In the census tables for that period, we find 407,524 mechanics, 4,326 clergymen, 2,676 lawyers, 7,109 physicians, 2,016 engineers, 2,490 artists, 1,528 teachers, 3,120 manufacturers, 3,882 clerks, and 5,246 seamstresses and milliners, enumerated among the immigrants. This enumeration, incomplete as it is, shows that about 15 per cent. of the immigration belong to that class of population which produces more than the common laborer, and that therefore the 5 per cent., if so many, of helpless and unproductive emigrants are more than balanced by the percentage of higher mechanical and professional ability.

Influence of immigration on the population and wealth of this country.

We will next consider not only the increase of population by the immigrants proper, but also that produced by their descendants. It is the great merit of Mr. L. Schade, of Washington City, to have first applied the proper principle in computing the gain of population in this country from immigration. As he has shown, if it had been the policy of the Government to exclude all aliens from our shores, the growth of the population of the United States would represent simply the excess of births over deaths. In 1790, the population of the United States, exclusive of slaves, was 3,231,930. In the census returns for 1850, we find that among the white and free colored population, the number of births was 548,835, and the number of deaths 271,890. The excess of the former over the latter—276,945—represented the increase of population for 1850. The whole population of whites and free colored persons in 1850 was 19,987,573. This increase, therefore, was at the rate of 1·38 per cent. I cannot find in the small edition of the Census for 1860 the number of births; but in 1860 the percentage of increase is nearly, if not precisely, the same as in 1850—the total increase of population from 1840 to 1850 being 35·87, and from 1850 to 1860 35·59 per cent.

That this estimate of 1·38 as the yearly rate of increase of the population without immigration cannot possibly be an understatement appears evident when we compare it with the percentage of the yearly increase of the population of other countries. In England, the rate was only 1·25; in France, 0·44; in Russia, 0·74; in Prussia, 1·17; in Holland, 1·23; in Belgium, 0·61; in Portugal, 0·72; and in Saxony, 1·08. This increase of 1·38 added each year to the aggregate of the preceding year, down to 1865, would give us the population of the United States as it would have been if the policy of excluding immigration had been followed. The whole white and free colored population in the year 1790 having been 3,231,930, it would have amounted, if increased only by the excess of births over deaths:

In	1800	to	3,706,674,	while in fact it was,	exclusive of	slaves,	4,412,896
"	1810	"	4,251,143	"	"	"	6,048,450
"	1820	"	4,875,600	"	"	"	8,100,056
"	1830	"	5,591,775	"	"	"	10,796,077
"	1840	"	6,413,161	"	"	"	14,582,008
"	1850	"	7,355,423	"	"	"	19,987,563
"	1860	"	8,435,882	"	"	"	27,489,662
"	1865	"	9,034,245	"	"	"	about 30,000,000

Deducting 9,034,245 from 30,000,000, the remainder, or 20,965,755, represents the population of foreign extraction gained by the United States since 1790. If the influx of aliens had been stopped in that year, the population in 1865 would have been very nearly what it was in 1825. Immigration, therefore, has enabled this country to anticipate its natural growth some forty years. The increase of wealth in every branch of national activity has been, too, in the exact ratio of the increase of population. Official statistics show, indeed, that the augmentation of imports, exports, tonnage, and revenues has been most rapid during the periods of the largest immigration. The following tables give ample proof of this fact:

Year.	Imports.	Exports.	Tonnage.	Revenues.
	VALUE OF			
1800	$91,252,768	$70,971,780	972,492	$12,451,184
1810	85,400,000	66,757,974	1,424,783	12,144,206
1820	74,450,000	69,691,699	1,280,166	20,881,493
1830	70,876,920	73,819,508	1,191,776	24,844,116
1840	131,571,950	104,805,891	2,180,764	25,032,193
1850	178,136,318	151,898,720	3,535,454	47,649,388
1860	362,168,941	400,122,293	5,353,868	76,752,034

The number of immigrants between	1819–1829 was	128,502
" " "	1830–1839	538,381
" " "	1839–1849	1,427,337
" " "	1849–Dec. 31, 1860	2,968,194
Total in 41¼ years,		5,062,414

Immigration a matter of State not of national concern.

We hear it often said that immigration is to the country, not to a State; that it has a national bearing; and that in more than one respect we stand in absolute need of a national board of emigration. I do not agree with this. Immigration is undoubtedly a matter of national importance, but it is a matter of State concern also. I will endeavor to state the grounds on which this opinion rests.

Ever since immigration has attained greater proportions, legal questions have grown out of the financial interests connected with it, which have turned on the point whether a single State has or has not the right to tax the immigrant on his arrival for sanitary purposes and for his protection. As this tax, or commutation money, of $2 50, which is levied on each immigrant landing at New York, amounts to between one-half and three-quarters of a million per year, it will easily be understood that the magnitude of the amount involved induced a reference of the questions to the highest tribunals of the land. Lately, this same question has again been taken up by Western newspapers, and by some Western members of Congress. They demand that the commutation money which immigrants pay at the several ports of entry be distributed, *pro rata*, among the States where they settle; and to effect this purpose they insist that the United States Government should take the whole business of immigration in its own hands; that the Secretary of the Treasury make all needful rules and regulations, and appoint the proper officers in the same manner in which the Custom House officers are appointed; thus doing away entirely with all State institutions which have been established in the course of years for the protection of immigrants. I believe not only that existing laws authorize the single State to exercise an exclusive control over immigrants, but that the real interest of the country requires this exclusive State control to be continued.

It is a well-known fact that New York is the principal port of entry for immigrants, and that more than five-sevenths of them are landed there. Whether directly pointed out or not, it is the port and State of New York against which the attacks of those who wish to give to the General Government the exclusive power of dealing with immigration are directed. Now, the State of New York is, as far as my knowledge extends, the only one which heretofore has organized a proper system for the protection of immigrants. As has been stated, it took years to effect a wholesome reform in the former management of immigration, and to create the Board of the Commissioners of Emigration of the State of New York.

All that can be admitted in regard to the question of State or national control is, that the Congress of the United States has not only the right, but is absolutely bound, in the interests of humanity, to protect the immigrant on the high seas, in his transit from foreign countries, and to make for that purpose international treaties, which Congress alone can do. But the authority of the federal legislative power extends no further in the premises, and completely ceases after the immigrant has landed and put himself under the operation and protection of the State laws. For Congress to attempt, then, to collect from him any tax, or to assume his support, would be not less absurd than if it were to undertake to license the boarding-house where he puts up, to appoint the policeman who protects him, or to provide him with transportation to his railway depot. The care of the immigrant, after he lands, is purely a police regulation, in which the people of the State where he lands are so exclusively interested as to have, beyond a doubt, the best right to provide for him. The harbor of the city of New York, while of national importance, is still of State concern, and so it is with foreign immigration.

But granting, for the sake of argument, that immigration is a matter of national concern, it is doubtful if anything but evil would result from abandoning a system which has fully realized its purpose—which has been tried and perfected by the experience of nearly a quarter of a century; whose operations are greatly facilitated by being concentrated upon a comparatively small area, and the agents under which are few, practised, and under the immediate supervision of a Board of unsalaried and non-partisan Commissioners, located and laboring on the spot. To replace such a system by the clumsy machinery of a central board, or by a single Commissioner, stationed at an inland city, remote from the chief objective points of foreign immigration, with an unwieldy multitude of subordinates scattered over the land, whose irresponsibility would inevitably increase in the direct ratio of their distance from the seat of authority, would be worse than unreasonable. The transfer to the National Government of the control of the immigrant would lead to quarrels, heart-burnings, and jealousies among the States, as the controlling officers would certainly be required to use their power to influence the current of immigration. The effect would undoubtedly be to so increase the cost of supporting the immigrant, as either to quadruple the present tax, and then make it virtually a prohibitory one, or to impose the burden on the national treasury, and thus make the immigrant the nation's pauper.

It is obvious that the General Government would encounter a great many more insurmountable obstacles and be called upon to remedy more evils than are met with under the present system. In the first instance, the institutions for the protection of the immigrant would have to be largely extended, and instead of one place like Castle Garden, a dozen would be required. Besides the Eastern and Southern and Western ports, the large inland cities, like Cincinnati, Chicago, St. Louis, Milwaukee, and St. Paul, would have to be provided with the same proportionate facilities as New York. Thus the General Government would be obliged to sustain ten establishments, while the income derived from the commutation would remain the same. At a very low estimate, the Government would have to pay at least one million of dollars per year out of its coffers for this purpose. In itself, this sum is insignificant when expended for such an object; but every cent spent from the national treasury for the immigrant can only injure his condition and the proper appreciation of his value. Again, we all know the tendency of originally small public expenditures to grow into large ones. While one million might suffice at first, many millions would be required in the end. One of the worst consequences would be that immigration would speedily become a political question, and as such the subject of strife among demagogues, and that cry against the "importation of foreign paupers" would doubtless soon be raised by which the condition of the immigrants would be deeply affected. Again, it is not clear to me how the United States can establish hospitals and houses of refuge for the small percentage of sick and destitute among immigrants, unless the fundamental law of the country is changed. This difficulty would, in all probability, lead to a division of the duties for the protection of the immigrant between the General and State governments, so that the several States would be charged with the duty of nursing the sick and supporting the destitute. Whether they would or could do this, is a matter about which I have considerable doubt.

There is another weighty objection to a transfer of the control of immigration to the General Government. The proper care of the immigrant requires a staff of efficient officers, having well-trained employees acting under them. Experience has shown that even the best organized minds require months and years to master this task.

The best and most efficient agents of the Commissioners of Emigration have served under them from May 5, 1847, that is, from the birth of the Commission. They have educated themselves and others to a proper comprehension and discharge of their duties. They are familiar with all the minutiæ of the service, and are consequently able to perform their work more speedily and efficiently than inexperienced new-comers. The uniformity and stability of the system, the undisturbed march of progress and reform, the absence of sudden changes, form an indisposition to try new experiments, constitute, indeed, the main reasons of the success of the New York Commission of Emigration, which would never have been attained if, with the advent of every na tiona.. administration, a change of officers and clerks had taken place.

It is a well-known fact that the mode in which the General Government appoints its officers is very far from giving security for the proper discharge of their duties. We have seen about ten or twelve different collectors of the New York Custom House since 1847, and in all probability each new administration would have paid off part of its political liabilities by appointments to offices in connection with immigration. The place of general agent or treasurer of the Commission would have been eagerly sought after, as the salary connected therewith is larger than that of any one subaltern of the Collector of Customs in New York. The interest of the ruling party would have been paramount, of course, to the interest of the immigrant. And how many clerks and assistants rotated into office would withstand the temptations held out in the immigration business, which would be greater than in any other branch of the civil service? When, according to the statement of a Commissioner of Internal Revenue, it costs one hundred millions in bribes, theft, and embezzlement to collect three hundred millions of revenue, I do not think I exaggerate when I state that the immigrant, if handed over to the mercy of the regular office-holder, would not leave New-York without having been fleeced out of at least one-half of his property. Certainly, so long as Mr. Jenckes's Civil Service Bill, or some such measure, has not become the law of the land, it will be a cruelty and an aggravation of the existing evils to make the change referred to.

While New York has to endure nearly all of its evils, the other States reap most of the benefits of immigration. New York protects and shields the immigrant in his health and property, and the rising communities of the West flourish upon the fruits of her vigilant care. Our State acts, so to speak, as a filter in which the stream of immigration is purified: what is good passes beyond; what is evil, for the most part, remains behind. Experience shows that it is the hardy, self-reliant, industrious, wealthy immigrant who takes his capital, his intelligence, and his labor to enrich the Western or Southern States. As near as a calculation can be made, it has been ascertained that out of one hundred

account. For, whenever the poor immigrant is fleeced by rogues, his judgment is impaired, his energy is diminished, and in general that moral elasticity lost which he needs more than ever to start well in a strange land; and thus a heavy injury is inflicted on his adopted country, which, instead of self-relying, independent men, receives individuals who are broken in spirit, and, at least for a time, useless, who are burdensome to themselves and to others. From this point of view, every one who has the interest of his fellow-being and of his country at heart, has the strongest interest in having the immigrant efficiently protected, and in co-operating with those who are officially called upon to provide for this protection.

If the same people who engage our attention on their landing here crossed our path in their native country while in their old accustomed track of life, the task would be comparatively easy, for in that case they would much more readily understand their interest and advantage; they would not be confused by a hundred new impressions; and the majority of them would distinguish the honest man from the scoundrel. Upon emigrating, however, the masses enter into entirely new relations, into a new world; two-thirds of them do not know the language of the country, and all receive in one single hour more new notions and ideas than formerly in years. Thus, they find themselves without proper guidance, and fall the easier into the hands of impudent impostors, perhaps for the very reason that they have been warned against them. This sudden transition from one country into another, this change of old homelike surroundings, with new conditions of life, all of which, strange and some offensive to the immigrants, often stuns them temporarily, and creates a general bewilderment, which even makes an intelligent man appear awkward and stupid.

Whatever we may do, we cannot absolutely protect the immigrant against the practices of sharpers as long as we cannot obstruct the sources from which credulity and ignorance flow. We can take some precautionary measures, we can point out the right way, but it is just as impossible entirely to cure the evil as it is to put an end to human depravity in general. The Commissioners cannot be expected to accomplish an impossibility. In New York, a special detective would have to be assigned to each immigrant, in order to render him absolutely secure against all attempts to swindle him. What a board like that of the Commissioners can do is to give the immigrant the best possible protection, and this duty they are certainly discharging.

CHAPTER IX.

IMMIGRATION AS AFFECTED BY THE CONSTITUTION OF THE UNITED STATES.

Constitutional power of States to legislate on emigration.

In concluding this essay, it is proposed to examine, in the light of the decisions of the court of last resort, the constitutional power of the several States to legislate on the subject of emigration, and especially to derive a revenue from immigrants.

Decisions of Supreme Court.

There are but three cases in which the Supreme Court of the United States has had the question before them. The first was that of the City of New York against George Milne, reported in 11 Peters, 102, in which the decision was rendered at January term, 1837; the second was that of James Norris *vs.* The City of Boston; and the third and last, that of George Smith *vs.* William Turner, Health Commissioner of the Port of New York. The two latter were decided at the December term of 1848. The three cases can be summed up in a few words.

City of New York *vs.* Geo. Milne.

In the first case, the Corporation of the city of New York had instituted an action of debt, under the Statute of February 11, 1824, against George Milne, as consignee of the ship *Emily*, for the recovery of certain penalties imposed by this act. The declaration alleged that the *Emily* arrived in New York in August, 1829, from a country out of the United States, and that one hundred passengers were brought in the ship, on the voyage, and that the master had not made the report required; it therefore claimed that the amount of $15,000 as penalties had become due in consequence of the breaches of the statute referred to. The defendant demurred to the declaration, and the question finally presented to the Supreme Court was, whether or not the act of the Legislature of the State of New York assumed to regulate trade and commerce between the port of New York and foreign ports, and, if so, was it unconstitutional and therefore void?

The two other cases are the same in principle, and have consequently been considered together.

The plaintiff in the case of Norris *vs.* The City of Boston was an inhabitant of St. John's, in New Brunswick, an English colony. He arrived at the port of Boston, in June, 1837, in command of a schooner belonging to St. John's, having on board nineteen alien passengers. He was compelled to pay to the City of Boston the sum of two dollars for each passenger before he could obtain permission to land them. This amount of thirty-eight dollars was paid under protest that the exaction was illegal. An action was thereupon brought against the City of Boston, in the Court of Common Pleas, to recover back this money; under the instructions of the court, the jury found a verdict for the defendant, on which judgment was entered, and which was affirmed on a writ of error to the Supreme Court of Massachusetts. The case was then taken to the Supreme Court of the United States. Norris *vs.* City of Boston.

The demand was made, and the money received from the plaintiff in pursuance of the following act of the Legislature of Massachusetts, passed on April 20, 1837, the third section of which reads as follows: "No alien passenger shall be permitted to land until the master, owner, consignee, or agent of such vessel shall pay the regularly appointed boarding officer the sum of two dollars for each passenger on landing, and the money so collected shall be paid into the treasury of the city or town, to be appropriated as the city or town may direct, for the support of foreign paupers."

In the case of George Smith *vs.* Turner, the plaintiff in error was master of the British ship *Henry Bliss*, which vessel touched at the port of New York in the month of June, 1841, and landed two hundred and ninety steerage passengers. The defendant in error brought an action of debt against the plaintiff to recover one dollar for each of the above passengers. A demurrer was filed on the ground that the statute of New York was a regulation of commerce, and in conflict with the Constitution of the United States. The Supreme Court of the State overruled the demurrer, and the Court of Errors affirmed the judgment. This brought before the United States Supreme Court the constitutionality of the New York statute, which, under the general denomination of health laws in New York, provides that the Health Commissioner George Smith *vs.* Turner.

shall demand and be entitled to receive, and in case of neglect or refusal to pay shall sue for and recover, in his official name, from the master of every vessel that shall arrive at the port of New York from foreign ports, one dollar for each steerage passenger, mate, sailor, or mariner.

Clauses of Constitution involved in enquiry.

The subject of this enquiry is complicated with, and depends on, the construction of the first, second, fourth, and fifth clauses of the eighth section, the first and fifth clauses of the ninth section, and the second clause of the tenth section of the first article; of the first clause of the second section of the fourth article of the Federal Constitution, and with the ninth and tenth articles of the amendments to that instrument.

The first and second clauses of the eighth section of the first article, so far as in point here, read as follows:

"1. The Congress shall have power,

"2. To lay and collect taxes, duties, imposts, and excises; to pay the debts and provide for the common defence and general welfare of the United States; but all duties, imposts, and excises shall be uniform throughout the United States."

Construction of eighth section, first article, as not applicable to taxation.

Upon the construction of this section, the point is made that the collection of taxes is a power substantively vested in Congress, and not incident to the power to regulate foreign and inter-State commerce. The regulation of commerce vested in Congress was not, therefore, understood by the framers of the Constitution to apply to any species of taxation, and is not to be resorted to for any argument respecting the continuance in or ademption from the several States of the power to impose any kind of taxes. The *Federalist*, No. 32, asseverated that the several States would retain their taxing power absolutely undiminished except by the express prohibitions on State taxation, which is incompatible with an implied curtailment of those powers by virtue of the clause vesting Congress with the regulations of commerce.

Opinion of J. Daniels.

This point is strongly put by Daniels, J., in his dissenting opinion in Smith *vs.* Turner, 7 Howard, U. S. R., p. 429, who cites Gibbons *vs.* Ogden, 9 Wheaton, 201, in support

J. McLean.

of it. The correctness of the citation is admitted by McLean, J., of the majority in Smith *vs.* Turner, but the soundness of the doctrine is disputed on the ground that the uniformity of duties, imposts, and excises throughout the Union is incompatible with their imposition by other than the general power. This objection must be regarded as exploded by the subsequent practice of the Government in the matter of *excises.* That practice proceeds on the assumption that the mandate that excises must be uniform is addressed to Congress only. C. J. Taney, also of the minority in Smith *vs.* Turner, is likewise clear (7 Howard, 479) that Congress takes all its power of indirect taxation from this clause, and none (except the right to tax slaves imported) from any other, and says that this view, under which the Constitution was adopted, has been frequently confirmed by the Supreme Court (Marshall, C. J., in Billings *vs.* Providence, 4 Peters, 561). The same view is taken by Woodbury, J., also of the minority in Smith *vs.* Turner (7 Howard, 549) C. J. Taney.

It would appear to be still an open question, unless impliedly closed by the majority vote in Smith *vs.* Turner, whether Congress derives its power of indirect taxation from other sources than the present clause. If this is the sole source, it is clear that it is not exclusive, because the power of the States to tax indirectly has never been disputed, and has been constantly exercised. And if this is the sole source of the taxing power of Congress, that power, as applied to immigrants, is not only not exclusive in Congress, but it is probably not vested in Congress at all. The power to levy taxes, duties, imposts, and excises is not general, but is restricted to such as are laid for the payment of the debts or common defence or general welfare of the United States. Power of indirect taxation vested in Congress; whence derived.

The general welfare of the United States does not include the protection of the tax-payers of New York from exorbitant poor taxes. See 9 Wheaton, 199, 206, cited by Woodbury, J., in Smith *vs.* Turner, 7 Howard, 550. Now, if Congress is without power to effect an end necessary for the public safety and comfort, it cannot be pretended that that power is taken from the States.

The provision that duties, imposts, and excises shall be uniform throughout the United States is invoked by McLean, J., to prove that the power to impose them must necessarily be exclusively in Congress. This point has been already referred to. Judge

Woodbury (7 Howard, 546) holds that legislation respecting foreign paupers is not required to be uniform.

Fourth clause of eighth section of first article of Constitution interpreted.

The fourth clause of the eighth section of the first article provides that Congress shall have power "to regulate commerce with foreign nations, and among the several States, and with the Indian tribes."

J. McLean.

Is or is not this power vested in Congress to the exclusion of the States? The affirmative is held by McLean, J., of the majority in Smith *vs.* Turner, on the ground that the idea of its being vested concurrently in Congress and in the States involves a total repugnancy (Holmes *vs.* Jennison, 14 Peters, 517), and because two wills cannot be compatibly exercised respecting the same subject at the same time (Houston *vs.* Moore, 5 Wheaton, 23). He says that in Gibbons *vs.* Ogden, 9 Wheaton, 196, Johnson, J., expressly, and the majority of the court impliedly, held that the power was exclusive, and that Judge Story drew the same result from Gibbons *vs.* Ogden in New York *vs.* Milne, 11 Peters, 156 (Judge Story there also says that he knew C. J. Marshall [then deceased] agreed with him). To the same effect, he says, Marshall, C.J., reviewed the whole ground in Gibbons *vs.* Ogden. The Constitution restricts the power of the States to lay duties on imports, and this was admitted and acknowledged in Gibbons *vs.* Ogden to admit the existence of a power to tax in the States. "But," says Judge McLean, "I do not think it admits the power of the States to regulate commerce." He refers to Wilson *vs.* The Blackbird Creek Marsh Co., 2 Peters, 250, and says "that it does not decide, as contended, that a State may regulate commerce, but only that where a creek otherwise navigable falls into the sea, but is of so limited an extent that it may well be doubted whether the general regulation of commerce will apply to it, and a State causes it to be dammed for the sake of the public health, the Supreme Court of the United States will not overrule such a State law until Congress expressly exercises federal jurisdiction over the subject. Judge Wayne, of the majority in Smith *vs.* Turner, says (7 Howard, 410) that the exclusiveness is unquestionable since Gibbons *vs.* Ogden, and (p. 415) that the States have given away all control of commerce, except the regulation of their internal trade. Admitting that the opinion delivered by Judge

J Wayne.

Barbour as that of the Court, in 1837, in New York *vs.* Milne (11 Peters, 130), militates against this view, he says that opinion never had the majority, but was assented to by three judges (Barbour, Taney, C.J., Thompson) only out of seven (Baldwin, McLean, Wayne, Story). The opinion in that case of Judge Baldwin, which was accidentally excluded from the report, but published the same year in Baldwin's "Views of the Constitution," also declares the power exclusive. At the first consultation of the Judges, Thompson, J., was directed to write the opinion of the Court. When he read his production, it was objected to on another ground, that is, on the ground that Thompson declared a State might regulate commerce wherever there was at the time no conflicting Congressional legislation, whereas the majority of the Court preferred to leave that point open. He then said he would read it as his own opinion. Barbour then undertook to deliver the opinion of the *Court.* Without a further consultation, he read it, just before the Court separated. J. Baldwin.

Baldwin immediately objected, on the ground that Barbour said persons were not the subjects of commerce, and not imported goods; privately, but in vain. Wayne says there was no intention in New York *vs.* Milne to deviate from Gibbons *vs.* Ogden or Brown *vs.* Maryland (12 Wheaton, 438). He admits that, in Grove *vs.* Slaughter (15 Peters, 549), Baldwin spoke approvingly of New York *vs.* Milne, but that, so far from denying the exclusiveness, he, in that very opinion, asserted it to have been conclusively settled by Gibbons *vs.* Ogden and Brown *vs.* Maryland. Judge Grier, likewise of the majority in Smith *vs.* Turner, evidently regards the question of the exclusiveness of this power as still open.

Daniels, J., of the minority in Smith *vs.* Turner, admits that in Gibbons *vs.* Ogden Judge Johnson pronounced for exclusiveness, but remarks that the majority in that case expressly disclaim an intention to pass upon the point. He contends that Story, J. (one of the majority in Gibbons *vs.* Ogden), held, in Houston *vs.* Moore, 5 Wheaton, 48, the direct contrary of what in New York *vs.* Milne, 11 Peters, 158, he pronounces to be the law as settled in Gibbons *vs.* Ogden (see 13 Barb., 206; People *vs.* Huntington, 4 New York Leg. Obs., 187). Judge Barbour, Judge Thompson, and J. Daniels

Baldwin, of the supposed majority, and Story, J., of the minority, in New York *vs.* Milne (1837), died before Smith *vs.* Turner, McLean and Wayne of the majority, and Taney, of the minority, survived. Judge Catron, of the majority in Smith *vs.* Turner, incidentally declares the power exclusive (7 Howard, 448), but does not dwell on the point. Taney, C.J., of the minority in Smith *vs.* Turner, evades the direct question of exclusiveness, but says that the passage objected to in Thompson, J.'s opinion in New York *vs.* Milne, was that in which he said that a State might regulate commerce, while the power so to do in Congress, respecting a particular matter, was dormant, and that the reason of the objection was that the majority desired to leave that question open.

J. Catron.

C. J. Taney.

Nelson, J., in Smith *vs.* Turner, concurs in all points with Taney. Woodbury, J., of the minority in Smith *vs.* Turner, holds that the power is not exclusive (7 How., 554), because there is no express prohibition on the States, and because the power is not in its nature necessarily exclusive (Federalist, 82; 14 Peters, 575), and cites many other authorities (p. 555). Where the doctrine is apparently contravened, he says it is in the application, not in principle. The regulation of commerce has been expressly held *not* exclusively vested in Congress, so as to prevent the States from regulating bridges and ferries (cites authorities, p. 556), fisheries (*ib.*), pilots (p. 557). He says it has been nowhere decided that the power to regulate commerce is exclusive (p. 559), that the contrary has been held in the License Case (5 Howard, 504). He contends that much of the regulation of trade is necessarily local, and the nature of the power does not require it to be exclusive.

J. Nelson

J. Woodbury.

Cases cited to show regulation of commerce not exclusively vested in Congress.

That the regulation of commerce is not exclusively vested in Congress is also laid down in Cooley on Constitutional Limitations, p. 486, citing Cooley *vs.* Board of Wardens (12 Howard, 299; Sin Ling *vs.* Washburn, 20 Cal., 534; Crandall *vs.* Nevada, 6 Wall; State *vs.* Delaware, etc., 1 Vroom, 413).

The latter case decides that a State may tax the business of a railroad, incorporated by a sister State, transporting across the taxing State, graduating the tax by the number of passengers and weight of goods carried. The contrary appears, however, to have been decided between the same parties (on appeal?), 30 New Jersey Reports, 531.

In *ex parte* Crandall it was decided (1 Nev., 294) that a State may tax passengers leaving the State.

A State may tax a State steamship company plying to and from Brazil, on its capital (People *vs.* Commissioner of Taxes, 48 Barb., 157).

Authorities conflicting.

It is almost impossible to say on which side the scale of authority turns. The question, however, may be evaded, without avoiding to decide the question here involved.

Because it is not disputed that where Congress has regulated commerce the States cannot interfere by conflicting regulations (Gibbons *vs.* Ogden, 9 Wheaton, 195; Grier, J., of the majority in Smith *vs.* Turner).

But, has Congress regulated commerce in this particular? "Aye," say Judge McLean and Judge Grier, of the majority in Smith *vs.* Turner, "it has regulated it, by willing that this trade should be free." "Aye," says Judge Catron, "because they have exempted the property of emigrants" (Act March, 1799, § 46), and because they expressly allow the emigrant to appear at the Custom House with his goods (17 Howard, 443), and to come into the federal courts and sue (444).

"No," says Taney, C.J., of the minority, "because the Act of 1799 only *presupposes* the landing." It does not repose the decision of who shall be allowed to inhabit the country in a shipmaster (p. 471). Nelson agrees with Taney.

Woodbury, J., says, very forcibly, that it is arguing in a circle to contend that a power is exclusive if Congress speaks, and, therefore, if Congress is silent, that silence is a speech, because the power is exclusive. The power must first be shown to be exclusive before it can be said that the silence of Congress speaks (p. 559). On the hypothesis of exclusiveness in all mere grants, what becomes of concurrent power under any circumstances?

Are passengers subject of regulations of commerce?

Are passengers the subject of regulations of commerce? The majority of the Court (McLean, Grier, Wayne, Catron, McKinley) in Smith *vs.* Turner, says Yes. McLean says commerce does not relate exclusively to "commodities," unless they include passengers. Says that has been settled in Gibbons *vs.* Ogden.

But Taney, C.J., says that this clause has nothing to do with the admission of foreigners (p. 483); it was adopted to prevent one State from making citizens for another.

First clause, ninth section—its interpretation.

The first clause of the ninth section of the first article reads: "The migration or importation of such persons as any of the States now existing shall think proper to admit, shall not be prohibited by the Congress prior to the year 1808, but a tax or duty may be imposed on such importations not exceeding ten dollars for each person."

"This clause," says McLean, J., of the majority in Smith *vs.* Turner, "proves that the regulation of commerce covers voluntary as well as involuntary immigration." McKinley, J., says it distinguishes between migration and importation, by subjecting the latter only to taxation, but that it declares them both subjects of commercial regulations. It impliedly allows Congress to prohibit immigration into all new States even before 1808, and therefore forbids the States to tax it. Wayne, J., agrees with him.

Daniels, J., contends this clause applies purely to the slave-trade (*Federalist*, No. 42). Taney, C.J., the same (7 Howard, 474; Madison Papers). The power to prohibit voluntary immigration could not have been intended to be conferred, because all the States were in favor of it. All the States then admitted voluntary immigrants. This shows the clause relates to slaves only. "Migration" was used lest "importation" might not aptly apply to human beings. At all events, there is no power to compel the States to admit emigrants. Woodbury, J., says that the power to tax is conferred only respecting slaves. A special clause was introduced for that purpose, because it was doubtful whether such a tax was an impost (1 Blackstone, by Tucker, p. 231). Besides, this class does not *confer* a power, but limits it (p. 541).

Fifth clause, ninth section.

The fifth clause of the ninth section of the first article reads (as far as in point here):

"No preference shall be given, by any regulation of commerce or revenue, to the ports of one State over those of another; nor shall vessels bound to or from one State be obliged to enter, clear, or pay duties in another."

McLean, J., of the majority in Smith *vs.* Turner, says that, if foreigners are thus to be taxed, as well might passengers who come from another State. This is unconstitutional because of the clause cited; but this does not protect passengers, except by the same implication as does the clause respecting the regulation of foreign commerce.

The second clause of the tenth section of the first article reads: **Second clause, tenth section—its application to passengers.**

"No State shall, without the consent of Congress, lay any imposts or duties on imports or exports, except what may be absolutely necessary for executing its inspection laws; and the net produce of all duties and imposts laid by any State on imports or exports shall be for the use of the treasury of the United States. No State shall, without the consent of Congress, lay any duty of tonnage."

In Smith *vs.* Turner, Grier, J., of the majority, says an act imposing a tax on passengers from foreign ports before landing might be called an act to raise revenue off vessels transporting passengers. It is a duty on the vessel, producing a like result as a tax on tonnage. That the tax is really paid by the passenger is no answer. Such is any indirect tax. A State, says Catron, Jr., "cannot raise duties on imports as a revenue measure for her own treasury." The passengers had not yet come under State jurisdiction, because they could not be taxed without either taxing tonnage or imports. In New York *vs.* Milne, Barbour, giving what appears as the opinion of the Court, says that passengers are not imported goods. But this, says Wayne, is what made Baldwin say he liked this opinion less than Thompson's, and which was contrary to the opinion of five of the judges. But in Smith *vs.* Turner this opinion is held by Daniels, Taney, Nelson, and Woodbury. That passengers are not imports, says Taney, C.J., was decided in New York *vs.* Milne. But at all events this tax was necessary for the inspection of these imports (477, 481). Woodbury, that passengers are not imports, cites Brown *vs.* Maryland (McCulloch, Dictionary, article Passengers; 5 How., 594, 614). If they were, they would be dutiable as non-enumerated. Whether a tax is imposed on shipboard or in a hotel, cannot make a void tax valid or a valid tax void.

First clause, second section, fourth article—its interpretation.

The first clause of the second section of the fourth article reads as follows:

"The citizens of each State shall be entitled to all privileges and immunities of citizens in the several States."

Woodbury, J. (7 Howard, 525), says that but for this clause each State would have the right to exclude the citizens of every other State, and that, as respects foreigners, the original right of each State to exclude all except its own citizens is unimpaired.

Taney, C.J. (p. 491), says: "I believe only so much of this act as taxes passengers coming from foreign ports is constitutional. The citizens of one State have free access to Washington, etc., and to pursue slaves," etc.

Second section, sixth article.

The second section of the sixth article of the Constitution says:

"This Constitution, and the laws of the United States which shall be made in pursuance thereof, and all treaties made, or which shall be made, under the authority of the United States, shall be the supreme law of the land."

"Whenever a right grows out of or is protected by a treaty, it is sanctioned against all the laws and judicial decisions of the States; and whoever may have this right, it is to be protected." 5 Cr., 348; 4 Am. Law Reports, 604; 6 Opin., 291, Walker; Cr., 129; 1 Doug., 546.

Opinions of judges.

"By Art. 14 of Treaty of 1794 with England," says McLean, J., in Smith *v.* Turner (7 Howard, 468), "the people of each country may freely come into the other." "But," says Daniels, J., of the minority, "in the first place, treaties are not supreme unless made within the authority legitimately exercised by the Federal Government. A treaty can't cede away a right of a single State reserved in the Constitution. In the second place, that article cannot be so construed as to prohibit such taxation." Taney, C.J., also of the minority (p. 471), says the treaty admits foreigners, *subject to our laws.*

The ninth and tenth articles of the Amendment to the Constitution read as follows: Ninth and tenth articles of Amendment; its construction in Smith *vs.* Turner.

"9. The enumeration in the Constitution of certain rights shall not be construed to deny and disparage others retained by the people.

"10. The powers not delegated to the United States by the Constitution, nor prohibited by it to the States, are reserved to the States respectively, or to the people."

See 1 Story, Constitution, § 447; 1 McLean, 234; 5 Harris (Remd.), 119.

In Smith *vs.* Turner, Grier, J., of the majority, says: "This is not the case of a police regulation to repel paupers, lunatics, or criminals. That right was vindicated in New York *vs.* Milne, 1837, 11 Peters, 102, but no more. Here the claim is not a fee or toll for some service rendered, nor a license to become citizens. It is by no means a fact that most of the foreigners who afterwards become paupers remain in the seaports. This tax is founded on the claim of power in a State to exclude all persons from passing through her territory. The same power, if existing, might be exercised by every State through which an emigrant was compelled to travel. This would thwart the cherished policy of the General Government. It is not a necessary appurtenant of the police power. The exclusion of criminals and paupers may be necessary, like that of putrid or pestilential goods, while that of emigrants and sound merchandise is perfectly harmless. The right to tax and exclude does not follow from the right to punish crimes. Else a State might exclude all persons and all vessels."

"This," says McLean, J., same side, "is not a health law. New York *vs.* Milne does not sustain this act. The acts there under consideration simply *exacted* reports of all passengers, and imposed a penalty for not reporting. It was an internal police regulation. It did not impose a tax as a prerequisite to the introduction of passengers. Except to guard against diseases and paupers, a State cannot prohibit the introduction of foreigners. It may deny them a residence unless they shall give security to indemnify the public should they become paupers." (Grove *vs.* Slaughter, 15 Pet., 549.) "The police power of the States cannot draw within its jurisdiction objects which lie beyond it."

"The police power," says Catron, J., same side, "proves too much, and does not apply to persons in good health and of good character. The object cannot sanctify the means. The act is not in execution of any supposed State right to exclude all aliens, because nothing of the sort is attempted. No such right exists; it would be incompatible with the exclusive right of Congress to make war, peace, and treaties, regulate commerce, and naturalize aliens. The persons and property taxed had not yet come under State jurisdiction, because they could not be taxed without taxing either tonnage or imports."

"The States," says Wayne, J., same side, "have given away all control of commerce, except that of regulating internal trade. The motive cannot save a law if it practically operates in a regulation of commerce. Milne's case established no more than the right of each State to be informed of the name and quality of every foreigner that arrives. The States have retained no more police power than is necessary to their internal government. No point was ruled in Milne's case which gives any support to the law now in question. The fear that the decision (of the majority) will be held to prevent the slave States from forbidding the introduction of freedmen from the West Indies is unfounded. That case would be an exception to the present rule, because the Constitution must be interpreted according to its subject-matter. The fundamental idea was, that slavery should remain undisturbed by the Federal Government. What had the majority of the judges in Milne's case was the point that the duty to report was a police regulation, and, therefore, not unconstitutional. The court never intended, in Milne's case, to derogate from Gibbons *vs.* Ogden or Brown *vs.* Maryland." The dissenting opinions, however, assume exactly contrary grounds. "The fundamental question," says Taney, C.J. (p. 464), "is: Has the Federal Government power to compel States to receive, and suffer to mingle with its citizens, any person or class of persons? I had thought the negative established by Holmes *vs.* Jennison, 14 Peters, 540; Grove *vs.* Slaughter, 15 Peters, 449; Prigg *vs.* The Common-

Dissenting opinions.

wealth, 16 Peters, 539. These cases decide that the States have the power to expel and exclude. There can be no concurrent power respecting such a subject-matter. Such a power is necessarily discretionary. Massachusetts fears foreign paupers; Mississippi, free negroes. The rightfulness of taking bonds is incontrovertible—self-defence against European almshouses. The Constitution does not distinguish between different grades of aliens. We cannot enquire whether their persons were paupers or not. The Act of Congress of 1819 keeps carefully within Federal jurisdiction. It says nothing about the landing of passengers, nor about their health or condition, which it would have done had it meant to vindicate a right to landing anybody. This act of Massachusetts only exacts security against pauperism. We cannot admit emancipated slaves. This act of New York is a quarantine law, and no more. The provisions for making it self-supporting are legitimate incidents."

Nelson, J., fully concurred with Taney, C.J. "States," says Woodbury, J., also of the minority, "may keep off foreign paupers, even paupers from other States." (Revised Statutes of New Hampshire, chapter 67; 5 Howard, 629; Colonial Charter of Massachusetts, 1639, p. 113, and 1692, p. 252). Indemnity from shipmasters has been required in Massachusetts since 1701, and has assumed its present form in 1837, after the Milne decision. The present measure is one of police regulation, and fair. The money is wholly applied to the support of foreign paupers. That money is called for as security, and not a bond, is no objection. Police measures have not been ceded to the Federal Government, but are open to the States, if honestly administered as such (License cases, 5 Howard, 624; Baldwin's Views, 184-188; United States *vs.* Bedford Bridge, 1 Wood *vs.* Minn, 423). The principle was settled in Milne. All governments may exclude foreigners (Vattel, chapter 19, § 201; 5 Howard, 328). The alien act (June 17, 1798, 1 St. at L., 571) was considered unconstitutional, because it was believed this right had not been surrendered (4 Elliott, Debates, 581, Virginia Resolutions of 1798). The old Congress in 1787, after the adoption of the present Constitution, requested the States to exclude foreign malefactors. As against foreigners, the States have never surrendered this power.

Power cannot be taken from the States by mere implication. Congress has no power to maintain paupers. Poor-laws belong to the States (Vanderbilt *vs.* Adams, 7 Wendel, 349 ; 1 Blackstone's Com., by Tucker, 249), although not strictly referable to sanitary or other police. The States have exclusive power to lay taxes for the support of paupers (9 Wheaton, 206). The Constitution of Kentucky, sanctioned by Congress, says States have power to exclude slaves as merchandise; the States have not ceded their ports for taxing or other purposes. The regulation of the number of passengers by Congress is not inconsistent with the imposition of terms on their landing by a State to support paupers, replenish her treasury, or exclude criminals. Though the means may be very similar, the powers are not identical (Marshall, C. J., 9 Wheaton, 204). Hides may be imported, and yet destroyed by the State if noisome. To recapitulate:

Unsettled points.

It must be regarded as still unsettled—

Whether the power to regulate foreign and inter-State commerce is vested in Congress to the exclusion of the States.

Whether a State law passed for a legitimate purpose, or whether a State tax, not otherwise objectionable, is unconstitutional, if it tends incidentally to regulate foreign or inter-State commerce.

Whether taxes or imports are intended, by the Constitution, to be included among regulations of commerce.

Whether passengers from foreign ports are in such a sense the subjects of commerce that taxes imposed on them, and exacted as a prerequisite to their landing, are regulations of commerce.

Whether passengers from foreign ports, after their arrival in a home port, but before landing, are imports.

Whether Congress has so legislated as impliedly to regulate commerce in foreign passengers by willing that it shall be free.

Whether single States have the right to exclude aliens from their boundaries.

Whether States may impose a tax per head on passengers from foreign ports, payable by the master before his being permitted to land them.

Whether States may exact bonds from ship-masters or others,

conditioned that passengers from abroad, now in good health, shall not become chargeable as paupers.

Whether States may circuitously impose a tax, by first exacting such bonds, and then permitting them to be commuted for a specified sum of money.

On the other hand, the following points may be regarded as well settled:

A State has the right to deny foreign paupers, or foreigners likely to become paupers, a residence on its borders. **Settled points.**

A State has jurisdiction of its own ports for purposes of port regulations and harbor police, sanitary police, quarantine administration, pilotage, and the support, maintenance, and regulation of paupers, foreign and domestic.

A State has the right to be informed of the name and quality of every foreigner coming within its limits, and to impose a penalty on any ship-master failing to comply with a State law requiring him to make such report.

A State has the right to maintain paupers, foreign and domestic, and to lay a tax for that purpose on foreigners or others, when undoubtedly within its jurisdiction, and not imports or subjects of commerce.

The Federal Government has no power to maintain paupers, foreign or domestic, or to levy taxes for that purpose.

A law of Congress, regulating commerce, is paramount to any State law purporting or pretending to do the same.

A State law pretending to subserve a legitimate object of State legislation, but in fact aiming at and effecting a disturbance of commercial regulations made by Congress, is unconstitutional and void.

A State cannot impose a tax on passengers coming into its ports from the ports of other States.

And it seems to be the better opinion, that a State cannot legislate for the regulation of foreign or inter-State commerce on the ground that it does not interfere with any existing act of Congress.

APPENDIX.

I. SUFFERINGS OF EMIGRANTS WHILE AT SEA.

REPORT OF ANDREAS GEYER, JR.,

ON THE CONDITION OF GERMAN REDEMPTIONERS ON BOARD OF THE AMERICAN SHIP *GENERAL WAYNE*, CAPTAIN JOHN CONKLIN, ADDRESSED, ON APRIL 27, 1805, TO HON. H. MUHLENBERG, PRESIDENT OF THE GERMAN SOCIETY OF PHILADELPHIA.*

SIR: Having just returned from the errand sent upon by you and the other officers of the German Society, relative to the German Redemptioners lately arrived at Perth Amboy, I have thought proper without loss of time to communicate to you in writing, for your and their information, how far I proceeded with the business entrusted me, respecting the said German redemptioners.

I left the city on Friday last, and in the evening arrived at New Brunswick, when I waited on Mr. Robert Eastburn, and presented him the letter you addressed him. Mr. Eastburn appears to be a gentleman of humanity and of feeling. After he read the letter, he observed a willingness to accompany me to Amboy; he did so the next morning, as also did Mr. Kladey. Both of them behaved with the greatest politeness towards me, and with great liberality towards the German Redemptioners at Amboy. Immediately on our arrival at Amboy we went to the river with an intention of going on board the ship *General Wayne*, or with an expectation of seeing some of the redemptioners on shore. However, we saw none of them at the time, and the ship was weighing anchor, and soon after set sail for New York. By enquiry we found the passengers were deposited in the Jail of Amboy, however not closely confined, having permission granted them by the agent to walk about the place or town. From what I could learn, the captain began to be uneasy, as some of the inhabitants had spoken to him with respect to the malconduct exercised by him towards those unhappy beings, and resolved to leave Amboy and go to New York.

I went to visit those unfortunate people, and in truth they may be called unfortunate. And I must confess I have seen a number of vessels at Philadelphia with redemptioners, but never did I see such a set of miserable beings in my life. Death, to make use of the expression, appeared to be staring them in

* Copied by the author from the Records of the German Society in Philadelphia. The English of the original has not been changed.

the face. The complaints were numerous which they made against the captain respecting the bad treatment they received from him on and during the passage. The complaints which I conceive are of the greatest importance I shall briefly state. My intention was to have had them confirmed with their oaths, but as they are made by every one of the passengers I thought it unnecessary. They are that they left Hamburg some time in November last, and arrived at Tönningen, where lay the ship *General Wayne*, John Conklin, Master, bound for New York, with whom they entered into a certain agreement, on condition that he, the said Conklin, would take them to New York, that during the passage they should be allowed a certain quantity of bread, meat, peas, fish, vinegar, butter, potatoes, tobacco, etc., as also a dram in the morning, as will appear by a reference to the agreement itself, each passenger having one. About fourteen days after they left Tönningen they put into an English port near Portsmouth, where they remained about four weeks; that during that time a British recruiting officer came on board the ship, when the captain informed them that they now had an opportunity of enlisting, that those who so chose to do might, as the recruiting officer was on board the ship. Ten men consented, and entered their names, giving to the other passengers their reasons for so doing, namely, that, having been already put on allowance by the captain, they were apprehensive that, should they stay on board the ship, they should be starved before they arrived in America. Amongst those that enlisted was a man who had a wife and child on board the ship; that eight days after they had thus entered their names they were taken from the ship by the recruiting officer, although some of them wished to withdraw their names, but to no effect; go they must. The woman and her child are now at Amboy, lamenting the loss of the husband and father.

On the last day of their remaining in this British port, the same recruiting officer came the third time on board the ship, when the mate called four or five of the passengers by name, and told them, in the presence of the captain, they must be soldiers and go with the officer. They replied they had no intention of being soldiers, they wished to go to America; whereupon the captain and mate seized one of them by name Samuel Vogel, and threw him into the boat belonging to the recruiting officer, which was alongside of the ship. However, Vogel got back again into the ship, went below, and hid himself, but was again compelled to come forward with his clothes, when the recruiting officer, observing him weep, declared he would not have him, and left the ship, mentioning that he should not have again come on board had not the captain, the day before, pressed him so to do. The captain was highly dissatisfied with these men for refusing to go, and declared that they should not have anything to eat on board the ship, that they might starve, and ordered one of them to be flogged for refusing, which was performed, too, in a cruel manner. That the whole of the passengers, when at this British port, complained to the captain that the treatment they received was not such as was agreed to between them at Tönningen. He replied they were not then in Tönningen, neither were they in America, but in England. They then set sail, and after fourteen days had elapsed the captain informed them that they would get nothing to eat except bread and meat. After this each person received two biscuits, one pint of water, and the eighth part of a pound of meat per day. This regulation continued for two or three weeks, when they one and all declared they could not any longer exist on the small allowance they received; that they must, without doubt, perish. The hunger and thirst being at this time so great, and the children continually crying out for bread and drink, some of the men, resolved, at all events, to procure bread, broke open the apartment wherein it was kept, and took some. This was discovered by the captain, as were also those who did the same, when each of them was ordered to, and actually did, receive, after being first tied, a number of lashes on their bare backs well laid on. The whole of the passengers were also punished for this offence. The men received no bread, the women but one biscuit. This continued for nine days, when the men were again allowed one biscuit per day; however, the captain would at least make or proclaim a fast day. In this situation their condition became dreadful, so much so that five and twenty men, women, and children actually perished for the want of the common necessaries of life, in short, for the want of bread. The latter were ten in number, all at the time at the breasts of their mothers. The hunger was so great on board that all the bones about the ship were hunted up by them, pounded with a hammer and eaten; and what is more lamentable, some of the deceased persons, not many hours before their death, crawled on their hands and feet to the captain, and begged him, for God's sake, to give them a mouthful of bread or a drop of water to keep them from perishing, but their supplications were in vain; he most obstinately refused, and thus did they perish. The cry of the children for bread was, as I am informed, so great that it would be impossible for man to describe it, nor can the passengers believe that any other person excepting Captain Conklin would be found whose heart would not have melted with compassion to hear those little inoffensive ones cry for bread. The number of passengers, when the ship arrived at Amboy, amounted to one hundred and thirty-two. Fifty-one remain there still; the others have been disposed of.

The passengers further state that they did not receive the tobacco, the fish, nor the potatoes, as they ought to have received, and which they were entitled to as by their contract with the captain, neither did they receive their dram but four or five times during their passage, and no butter after they left the British port until within three or four days ago.

The foregoing are the principal causes of complaint, and indeed they appear very serious ones too to me. However, I having heard those complaints, and understanding from a number of citizens of Amboy that the captain's intention was to take the ship to New York, leave her, as also the State of New York, and go to his native State, Rhode Island, I was at a loss to know how to act or what to do, as my instructions were not for New York. However, after reflection I determined to push on for New York, and there inform the German Society of his conduct. I did so, and on Sunday arrived there, when, after some little enquiry, I found the President of the society, Mr. Philip I. Arcularius. To him I communicated the whole of this disagreeable affair. His feelings can be more easily conceived than described. He, however, gave directions to have the officers of the society summoned to meet the next day, which was done, and they all attended, excepting one of the assistants, and, after hearing the circumstances relative to those unfortunate people, they appointed three of their members, officers, to act in such way as they should, after taking legal advice, think best to bring the captain to that punishment which his conduct should merit.

THE IRISH EXODUS.

From Maguire's "Irish in America."

I HAVE more than once referred to the unfavorable circumstances under which the vast majority of the Irish arrived in America, and the difficulties with which, in a special degree, they had to contend ; but the picture would be most imperfect were not some reference made to the disastrous emigration of the years 1847 and 1848—to that blind and desperate rush across the Atlantic known and described, and to be recognized for time to come, as the Irish Exodus. We shall confine our present reference to the emigration to Canada, and track its course up the waters of the St. Lawrence. A glance even at a single quarantine—that of Grosse Isle, in the St. Lawrence, about thirty miles below Quebec—while affording a faint idea of the horrors crowded into a few months, may enable the reader to understand with what alarm the advent of the Irish was regarded by the well-to-do colonists of British America ; and how the natural terror they inspired, through the terrible disease brought with them across the ocean, deepened the prejudice against them, notwithstanding that their sufferings and misery appealed to the best sympathies of the human heart.

On the 8th of May, 1847, the *Urania*, from Cork, with several hundred immigrants on board, a large proportion of them sick and dying of the ship-fever, was put into quarantine at Grosse Isle. This was the first of the plague-smitten ships from Ireland which that year sailed up the St. Lawrence. But before the first week of June as many as eighty-four ships of various tonnage were driven in by an easterly wind ; and of that enormous number of vessels there was not one free from the taint of malignant typhus, the offspring of famine and of the foul ship-hold. This fleet of vessels literally reeked with pestilence. All sailing-vessels—the merciful speed of the well-appointed steamer being unknown to the emigrant of those days—a tolerably quick passage occupied from six to eight weeks ; while passages of ten or twelve weeks, and even a longer time, were not considered at all extraordinary at a period when craft of every kind, the most unsuited as well as the least seaworthy, were pressed into the service of human deportation.

Who can imagine the horrors of even the shortest passage in an emigrant ship crowded beyond its utmost capability of stowage with unhappy beings of all ages, with fever raging in their midst ? Under the most favorable circumstances it is impossible to maintain perfect purity of atmosphere between decks, even when ports are open, and every device is adopted to secure the greatest amount of ventilation. But a crowded emigrant sailing-ship of twenty years since, with fever on board!—the crew sullen or brutal from very desperation, or paralyzed with terror of the plague—the miserable passengers unable to help themselves, or afford the least relief to each other; one-fourth, or one-third, or one-half of the entire number in different stages of the disease; many dying, some dead; the fatal poison intensified by the indescribable foulness of the air breathed and rebreathed by the gasping sufferers—the wails of children, the ravings of the delirious, the cries and groans of those in mortal agony! Of the eighty-four emigrant ships that anchored at Grosse Isle in the summer of 1847, there was not a single one to which this description might not rightly apply.

The authorities were taken by surprise, owing to the sudden arrival of this plague-smitten fleet, and, save the sheds that remained since 1832, there was no accommodation of any kind on the island. These sheds were rapidly filled with the miserable people, the sick and the dying, and round their walls lay groups of half-naked men, women, and children, in the same condition—sick or dying. Hundreds were literally flung on the beach, left amid the mud and stones, to crawl on the dry land as they could. "I have seen," says the priest who was then chaplain of the quarantine, and who had been but one year on the mission, "I have one day seen thirty-seven people lying on the beach, crawling on the mud, and dying like fish out of water." Many of these, and many more besides, gasped out their last breath on that fatal shore, not able to drag themselves from the slime in which they lay. Death was doing its work everywhere—in the sheds, around the sheds, where the victims lay in hundreds under the canopy of heaven, and in the poisonous holds of the plague-ships, all of which were declared to be and treated as hospitals.

From ship to ship the young Irish priest carried the consolations of religion to the dying. Amidst shrieks, and groans, and wild ravings, and heart-rending lamentations—over prostrate sufferers in every stage of the sickness—from loathsome berth to loathsome berth, he pursued his holy task. So noxious was the pent-up atmosphere of these floating pest-houses, that he had frequently to rush on deck, to breathe the pure air or to relieve his overtaxed stomach; then he would again plunge into the foul den, and resume his interrupted labors.

There being, at first, no organization, no staff, no available resources, it may be imagined why the mortality rose to a prodigious rate, and how at one time as many as 150 bodies, most of them in a half-naked state, would be piled up in the dead-house, awaiting such sepulture as a huge pit could afford. Poor creatures would crawl out of the sheds, and, being too exhausted to return, would be found lying in the open air, not a few of them rigid in death. When the authorities were enabled to erect sheds sufficient for the reception of the sick, and provide a staff of physicians and nurses, and the Archbishop of Quebec had appointed a number of priests, who took the hospital duty in turn, there was of course more order and regularity; but the mortality was for a time scarcely diminished. The deaths were as many as 100 and 150 and even 200 a day, and this for a considerable period during the summer. The masters of the quarantine-bound ships were naturally desirous of getting rid as speedily as possible of their dangerous and unprofitable freight; and the manner in which the helpless people were landed or thrown on the island aggravated their sufferings, and in a vast number of instances precipitated their fate. Then the hunger and thirst from which they suffered in the badly found ships, between whose crowded and stifling decks they had been so long pent up, had so far destroyed their vital energy that they had but little chance of life when once struck down.

About the middle of June the young chaplain was attacked by the pestilence. For ten days he had not taken off his clothes, and his boots, which he constantly wore for all that time, had to be cut from his feet. A couple of months elapsed before he resumed his duties; but when he returned to his post of danger the mortality was still of fearful magnitude. Several priests, a few Irish, the majority French Canadians, caught the infection; and of the twenty-five who were attacked, seven paid with their lives the penalty of their devotion. Not a few of these men were professors in colleges; but at the appeal of the Archbishop they left their classes and their studies for the horrors and perils of the fever sheds.

It was not until the 1st of November that the quarantine of Grosse Isle was closed. Upon that barren isle as many as 10,000 of the Irish race were consigned to the grave-pit. By some the estimate is made much higher, and 12,000 is considered nearer the actual number. A register was kept, and is still in existence, but it does not commence earlier than June 16, when the mortality was nearly at its height. According to this death-roll, there were buried, between the 16th and 30th of June, 487 Irish immigrants "whose names could not be ascertained." In July, 941 were thrown into nameless graves; and in August, 918 were entered in the register under the comprehensive description—"unknown." There were interred, from the 16th of June to the closing of the quarantine for *that* year, 2,905 of a Christian people, whose names could not be discovered amidst the confusion and carnage of that fatal summer. In the following year 2,000 additional victims were entered in the same register, without name or trace of any kind to tell who they were or whence they had come. Thus 5,000 out of the total number of victims were simply described as "unknown."

REPORT ON THE CONDITION OF THE SHIP LEIBNITZ,

OF SLOMAN'S HAMBURG LINE.

EMIGRANT LANDING DEPOT, AND OFFICES OF THE
COMMISSIONERS OF EMIGRATION, OF THE STATE OF NEW YORK.
CASTLE GARDEN, NEW YORK, Jan. 22, 1868.

At a regular meeting of the Board of Commissioners of Emigration, held Wednesday, the 22d day of January, 1868, the Vice-President, Frederick S.

Winston, Esq., in the chair, and a quorum being present, the following resolutions were, on motion, adopted:

Resolved, That the Report of Commissioners Kapp and Bissinger, in relation to the mortality on the sailing-ship *Leibnitz*, be accepted and adopted, and be referred to the Special Committee, Messrs. Kapp, O'Gorman, and Bissinger, and said Committee be requested to draft a bill, subject to the approval of this Board, to be presented to Congress for adoption.

Resolved, That official copies of the Report be transmitted to the Honorables the Secretaries of State and of the Treasury of the United States, Baron Von Gerolt, as the Diplomatic Representative of the North German Confederation, to the Consul-Generals of Prussia and Mecklenburg, and to the daily press of this city.

Resolved, That one thousand copies of the above Report be printed for circulation.

The following is the Report of Messrs. Kapp and Bissinger, referred to in the foregoing resolutions:

To the Board of Commissioners of Emigration:

GENTLEMEN: Although not expressly authorized, yet, because the emergency arose since your last meeting, the undersigned deemed it their duty to go on board the ill-fated ship *Leibnitz*, and to enquire into the condition of her passengers transferred to the hospital-ship *Illinois*, in the Lower Bay.

Dr. Swinburne, the Health Officer, kindly placed the steamer *Fletcher* at our disposal. On Wednesday, Jan. 15, we went down the bay, accompanied, among others, by the physicians of the German Society, Drs. Pieper, Schwarzenberg, and Krause, who volunteered their services for the examination of the cause of the sickness.

The *Leibnitz*, originally the *Van Couver*, is a large and fine vessel, built at Boston for the China trade, and formerly plying between that port and China. She was sold some years ago to the house of Robert M. Sloman, and has since sailed under her present name.

We were informed that her last trip was her second with emigrants on board. Last summer, she went to Quebec with about seven hundred passengers, of whom she lost only a few on her passage; this time, she left Hamburg, Nov. 2, 1867, Capt. H. F. Bornhold, lay at Cuxhaven, on account of head-winds, until the 11th, whereupon she took the southern course to New York. She went by the way of Madeira, down to the Tropics, 20th degree, and arrived in the Lower Bay on Jan. 11, 1868, after a passage of 61 days, or rather 70 days—at least, as far as the passengers are concerned, who were confined to the densely crowded steerage for that length of time.

The heat, for the period that they were in the lower latitudes, very often reached 24 degrees of Réaumur, or 94 degrees of Fahrenheit. Her passengers 544 in all—of whom 395 were adults, 103 children, and 46 infants—came principally from Mecklenburg, and proposed to settle as farmers and laborers in Illinois and Wisconsin; besides them, there were about 40 Prussians from Pomerania and Posen, and a few Saxons and Thuringians.

It is not proven by any fact, that the cholera (as has been alleged) raged or had raged in or near their homes when or before they left them. This statement appears to have been made by or in behalf of those who have an interest in throwing the origin of the sickness on its poor victims. Of these 544 German passengers, 105 died on the voyage, and three in port, making in all 108 deaths—leaving 436 surviving.

The first death occurred on Nov. 25th. On some days, as for instance on Dec. 1, nine passengers died, and on Dec. 17, eight. The sickness did not abate until toward the end of December, and no new cases happened when the ship had again reached the northern latitudes; five children were born; during the voyage some families had died out entirely; of others, the fathers or mothers are gone; here, a husband had left a poor widow, with small children; and there, a husband had lost his wife. We spoke to some little boys and girls, who, when asked where were their parents, pointed to the ocean with sobs and tears, and cried, "*Down there!*"

Prior to our arrival on board, the ship had been cleansed and fumigated several times, but not sufficiently so to remove the dirt, which, in some places, covered the walls. Mr. Frederick Kassner, our able and experienced Boarding Officer, reports that he found the ship and the passengers in a most filthy condition, and that when boarding the *Leibnitz* he hardly discovered a clean spot on the ladder, or on the ropes, where he could put his hands and feet. He does not remember to have seen anything like it within the last five years. Captain True, who likewise boarded the ship immediately after her arrival, corroborates the statement of Mr. Kassner.

As to the interior of the vessel, the upper steerage is high and wide. All the spars, beams, and planks which were used for the construction of temporary berths had been removed. Except through two hatchways and two very small ventilators, it had no ventilation, and not a single window or bull's-eye was open during the voyage. In general, however, it was not worse than the average of the steerages of other emigrant ships; but the lower steerage, the so-called orlop-deck, is a perfect pest-hole, calculated to kill the healthiest man. It had been made a temporary room for the voyage by laying a tier of planks over the lower beams of the vessel, and they were so little supported that they shook when walking on them. The little light this orlop-deck received came through one of the hatchways of the upper-deck. Although the latter was open when we were on board, and although the ship was lying in the open sea, free from all sides, it was impossible to see anything at a distance of two or three feet. On our enquiring how this hole had been lighted during the voyage, we were told that some lanterns had been up there, but that on account of the foulness of the air, they could scarcely burn. It had, of course, much less than the upper-deck draft or ventilation, and was immediately over the keel, where the bilge-water collects, and adjoining part of the cargo, which consisted of wool and hides. And in this place about 120 passengers were crowded for 70 days, and for a greater part of the voyage in a tropical heat, with scanty rations and a very inadequate supply of water, and worse than all, suffering from the miasma below, above, and beside them, which of itself must create fever and pestilence!

The captain himself stated to us that the passengers refused to carry the excrements on deck, and that "the urine and ordure of the upper-steerage flowed down to the lower." As the main-deck was very difficult of access from the orlop-deck, the inmates of the latter often failed to go on deck even to attend to the calls of nature. There were only six water-closets for the accommodation of all the passengers. They have been cleansed, of course; but the smell that emanated from them was still very intense, and corroborates the statement of the above-named officers—that they must have been in an extraordinary frightful condition.

When the ship *Lord Brougham*, belonging to the same line, arrived on the 6th of December last, from Hamburg, and had lost 75 out of 383 passengers, we personally examined the majority of the survivors, and found them not only healthy and in good spirits, but, at the same time, in every respect satisfied with the treatment they had received on board.

The present case, however, is different. There was not a single emigrant who did not complain of the captain, as well as of the short allowance of provisions and water on board. As we know, from a long experience, that the passengers of emigrant ships, with a very few exceptions, are in the habit of claiming more than they are entitled to, we are far from putting implicit faith in all their statements. There is as much falsehood and exaggeration among this class of people as among any other body of uneducated men. We have, therefore, taken their complaints with due allowance, and report only so much thereof as we believe to be well founded.

All the passengers concur in the complaint that their provisions were short, partly rotten, and that, especially, the supply of water was insufficient, until they were approaching port. We examined the provisions on board, and found that the water was clear and pure. If the whole supply during the voyage was such as the samples handed to us, there was no reason for complaint as to quality. But, in quantity, the complaints of the passengers are too well founded; for they unanimously state, and are not effectually contradicted by the captain, that they never received more than half a pint of drinkable water per day, while by the laws of the United States they were entitled to receive three quarts. Some of the biscuit handed to us were rotten and old, and hardly eatable; other pieces were better. We ordered the steward to open a cask of corn-beef, and found it of ordinary good quality. The butter, however, was rancid. Once a week herrings were cooked instead of meat. The beans and sauerkraut were often badly cooked, and, in spite of hunger, thrown overboard.

The treatment of the passengers was heartless in the extreme. The sick passengers received the same food with the healthy, and high prices were exacted for all extras and comforts. A regular traffic in wine, beer, and liquors was carried on between the passengers on the one side and the steward and crew on the other. A man by the name of Frederick Hildebrand, from Wirsitz, in Posen, who lost two children, paid 35 Prussian thalers extra for beer and wine to sustain himself and his sick wife. A bottle of rum cost him one dollar; a bottle of bad wine even more. "This extortion, at such a time, cannot be too strongly condemned," says Captain True, in his report, which confirms the information received by us from the passengers.

When the first deaths occurred, the corpses were often suffered to remain in the steerage for full twenty-four hours. In some cases the bodies were covered with vermin before they were removed.

There was no physician on board. Although we found a large medicine-chest, it was not large enough for the many cases of sickness, and was, in fact, emptied after the first two weeks of the voyage.

The captain seems to have been sadly deficient in energy and authority in matters of moment, while he punished severely small offences; as, for instance, he handcuffed a passenger for the use of insulting words; but he did not enforce the plainest rules for the health and welfare of his passengers. Instead of compelling them, from the first, to come on deck and remove the dirt, he allowed them to remain below, and to perish among their own excrements. Of the whole crew, the cook alone fell sick and died, as he slept in the steerage. Three passenger girls who were employed in the kitchen, and lived on deck, enjoyed excellent health, during the whole voyage.

The physicians above mentioned, to whose report we refer for particulars, most positively declare that it was not the Asiatic cholera, but intestinal and stomach catarrh (*catarrh ventriculi et intestinorum*), more or less severe, and contagious typhus, which killed the passengers. From what we saw and learned from the passengers, we likewise arrive at the conclusion that the shocking mortality on board the *Leibnitz* arose from want of good ventilation, cleanliness, suitable medical care, sufficient water, and wholesome food.

The present case is another instance of the mortality on board the Hamburg sailing-vessels, and increases their bad reputation. Of 917 passengers on board of two ships of the Sloman line, not less than 183 died within one month! As often as complaint has been made here, it has not induced them to make any improvement. It appears that the Hamburg authorities either did not care to examine the merits of the charges brought against their ships or that they were imposed upon by their officials. On the other hand, local interests, friendly feelings, family connections, and other personal considerations, usually prevailing in small political communities, seem to stand in the way of energetic administration of the police of emigrant ships, and of the removal of the several grievances. While the average deaths that take place in the Bremen sailing-vessels amount to one-eighth or one-fourth of the total number of emigrants forwarded, the proportion on board the Hamburg sailing-vessels is *more* than two per cent.!!

Thus, of 11,264 steerage-passengers who arrived, in 1865, in our port, from Hamburg, 128 died on the passage; of 14,335 who arrived in 1866, 387; and of 8,788, in 1867, not less than 199.

In our opinion, it is of great importance for the interest of humanity, in which both Europe and this country are concerned, and as a matter of political economy, that the transportation of emigrants across the Atlantic to this port should be confined to steam-vessels, as they not only convey the passengers more comfortably and land them in better health, but, in consequence of the regularity and rapidity of the passage, save an immense amount of labor for their own benefit and that of this country.

We are sorry to say that our laws afford very inadequate relief for the punishment of these crimes against humanity, and that, in the majority of cases, the institution of legal proceedings for redress, and the prosecution of the guilty parties, is almost an impossibility.

Much of the suffering, disease, and death on board of emigrant ships could have been prevented, and a recurrence of such abhorrent scenes might hereafter be avoided, by proper enactments of Congress, enforced by suitable penalties.

We would therefore propose to petition Congress for an amendment of the Emigrant Passengers' Act, of March 3, 1855, enacted by Congress on the representation of the Commissioners of Emigration of this State, incorporating into the same the following provisions:

I. THE APPOINTMENT OF A PHYSICIAN OR SURGEON ON BOARD OF ALL EMIGRANT VESSELS WITH MORE THAN FIFTY PASSENGERS.—Thus far there is no law requiring it in the statute-book of the United States. The failure to have on board a physician, whose skill and good character should be fully vouched for by unquestionable evidence, should be punished by the infliction of a penalty of at least $5,000, one-half of such penalty to be paid over to the passengers *pro rata*, and the other half to the Collector of the Customs at the port of New York for the benefit of the Emigrant Fund.

II. THE DOING AWAY WITH THE ORLOP-DECK ON BOARD OF EMIGRANT SHIPS.—In case of contravention, the penalty should be at least $5,000; and, in addition, passengers roomed in the orlop-deck should have double the amount of their passage money refunded.

III. A MORE STRINGENT RULE FOR ENFORCING THE PAYMENT OF THE PENALTY FOR THE DEAD PASSENGERS.—With a view to protecting emigrants against the rapacity of ship-owners, the 14th section of the present law requires the payment of $10, as a penalty, for every passenger, other than cabin passengers, and over the age of eight years, who shall have died on the voyage from natural disease; for the non-payment of which penalty within twenty-four hours after arrival, a further penalty of $50 is imposed, to be recovered by the United States in any Circuit or District Court. Under this wording of the law, no particular officer of the United States appears to be authorized to prosecute or enforce the collection, and consequently many of the penalties are not paid, and the law, to some extent, becomes a dead letter. We would, therefore, suggest that the section be amended for this port by authorizing and directing a prosecution by the District Attorney of the Southern District, on complaint being made by the Commissioners of Emigration of the State, and making such penalties a lien on the ship or vessel, and the owner or consignee liable therefor.

IV. THE POWER OF OBTAINING REDRESS TO BE LODGED IN THE HANDS OF THE PARTIES INJURED—THE EMIGRANTS THEMSELVES.

V. SUMMARY PROCEEDINGS FOR THE RECOVERY OF DAMAGES.

As to the two latter provisions, we would state that the efforts which have been made by legislation at Washington and at Albany to protect the lives and health of emigrant passengers from the rapacity of ship-owners have been attended with but a very limited share of success. The regulation to which the owners of ships are required to conform are, with some exceptions, precisely those called for by the exigency of the case, as is best proved by the fact that the accidents and disasters which continue to happen are almost always traceable to the disregard of some of these provisions; but the fact that they are disregarded proves, in its turn, that the law must remain a dead letter until more effective remedies are provided against its violation.

The Act of 1855 provides that, if some of its provisions are violated, the master shall be guilty of a misdemeanor; and that, if others of its directions are not complied with, the master or the owners, or both, shall forfeit money penalties against the ship by the *authorities of the United States.*

It is found that indictments are not feared, and that suits for the recovery of penalties are never instituted.

To make the law effective, the power of obtaining redress must be lodged in the hands of the emigrants themselves.

The law gives them an action against the ship for marine *torts* and for breaches of marine contracts; but this action must be prosecuted through the dilatory form of admiralty practice. The ship is bonded, and goes on her way. The emigrant, poor, friendless, and often emaciated by disease, is kept loitering in a crowded city, dancing attendance on the delays of litigation, while the Western fields, which he came to till, lie fallow. The loss falls immediately on himself, but indirectly likewise on the entire country, which receives and detains a languishing pauper, when it needs industrious and able-bodied laborers.

It is absolutely necessary to authorize a summary proceeding, simple and expeditious, such as the case of the emigrant requires. A commissioner should be appointed for the especial purpose of hearing and passing upon these complaints. He might be appointed by the Chief Justice of the United States, under the precedent established in the case of the Register in Bankruptcy. His authority, however, must be to hear and determine. An appeal from his decision should not operate to supersede execution upon his judgment; but the losing party should be cast upon his chances of obtaining restitution.

It will also be necessary to establish certain principles of remedial law, not now considered established.

The owner of a ship should be made responsible in damages to the natural representatives of persons dying in the course of a voyage from causes produced by misconduct of such owner, or his agent. Such claims must be declared liens on the ship, recoverable by action *in rem* in the admiralty form.

The contracts to convey passengers must be declared contracts of absolute insurance, not to be qualified by written or printed stipulations dictated by the ship-owner.

The ship-owner must be prevented from pleading that the emigrants, having seen the ship when they came on board, had assumed their own risks, and precluded themselves against bringing suit for damages occasioned by its imperfections.

Damages merely compensatory will not suffice to recompense sufferers for the annoyance arising from insufficient food or air, or other ill treatment, not causing definite pecuniary loss.

A stated minimum of the damages should be fixed by law in such cases, such as the amount of the passage money, or of double or treble that amount.

We do not think that any of the legislators of the nation will object to the passage of such a bill. One of the greatest sources of the nation's income in wealth and population has been the vast emigration from Europe, and it should therefore be protected by appropriate national legislation. Every principle of public policy, looking to the welfare of the country, as well as every sentiment of humanity, demands this at the hands of Congress.

Under the present system, the emigrants are treated more like beasts of burden than like human beings, starved and crowded together in ill-ventilated, ill-fitted, ill-supplied, and ill-manned vessels.

The arrival of an emigrant ship in our ports, if it does not bring disease and pestilence among us, often occasions great apprehension and alarm, disturbing the regular business of our city, and creating an indefinable prejudice against the worthy emigrant, instead of extending to him, as he truly deserves, a kind and hearty welcome.

The Commissioners of Emigration are the trustees as well of the emigrant as of the State of New York and of the United States in general. Although appointed by the State authority for State purposes, their line of duty is not confined to the boundaries of the State, but extends over the whole country, inasmuch as they have to encourage and protect the emigrant until he reaches his new home. It would betray a narrow-mindedness, of which no member of this Board is guilty, if they did not look at emigration from this national point of view. Whenever they succeed in doing away with a grievance, or achieving a result favorable to the emigrants, it is a national gain, and an advantage won for the whole country.

Hence, every consideration in relation to the comfort and protection of the emigrant is of a national character, and demands the serious attention of a good and enlightened statesmanship.

FRIEDRICH KAPP,
PHILIP BISSINGER,
Commissioners.

NEW YORK, January 21, 1868.

II. PROTECTION OF EMIGRANTS AND CARE TAKEN OF THEM.

REPORT OF THE GRAND JURY ON THE MODE OF DOING BUSINESS AT CASTLE GARDEN.

GRAND JURY ROOM, September 9, 1856.

THE Grand Inquest of the county of New York, in the discharge of their duty, have been called upon to investigate certain complaints which have been preferred against certain employees of the railroad companies doing business with the emigrants landing at Castle Garden. In the discharge of this duty they have felt called upon to visit the Landing Depot itself, with a view to give a personal inspection to the mode of doing business within its enclosures. The landing and despatching of a cargo of upwards of 400 passengers, taking place at the time of their visit, afforded a favorable opportunity to watch the whole proceeding. The passengers were brought from the ship on a barge, towed by a steamboat, persons and property sheltered from the rain by the upper deck of the barge. They landed in an orderly manner, having evidently been instructed by the officers from Castle Garden as to the nature of the Landing Depot and its arrangements. They passed over the deck, answered the enquiries of the examining physician, whose duty is to note cases whose age or condition requires special bonds from the ship for their support in case of need, and to detect cases of sickness which may have escaped the notice of the Health Officer at Quarantine. On entering the large rotunda of Castle Garden, they were registered by a clerk of the Commissioners of Emigration, who took down the names of the heads of families and single persons, whence they came, the State of their destination, their cash means, and the relatives (if any) they were going to join. The annual statistics of the current of emigration are made up from these notes. The passengers then passed on to the next desk, where clerks of the Transportation Companies ascertained the places of destination they wished to go, laid maps of the various routes of travel before them, explained the difference in time and price of travel by the various routes; and, after a selection was made by the passengers, provided them with an order on the cashier, setting forth the number of tickets required, the route selected, and the price of passage and of over-freight per one hundred pounds by such route. The cashier, on receiving this order, issued the class of tickets it called for, and received the price therefor. The passengers were then shown by a different way from that by which they had entered the rotunda back to the dock, and there produced to the weigh-master the checks they held for baggage, which they had received on board of the vessel which brought them into port previous to passing their trunks into the hands of the officers from Castle Garden. The property having the corresponding checks was then taken from the barge and weighed, each piece being labelled with a conspicuous label, having a certain number and the place of destination printed thereon, the passenger receiving a baggage ticket with the corresponding number, and on which were inserted the number of pieces of baggage delivered, the route it had to be transported, the gross weight, and the amount of freight to be collected thereon after deducting the amount to which each passenger is entitled. This freight was then paid to the collector, having his office at the scales, who copied the whole ticket into a book kept for reference, and then receipted for the money at the foot of the baggage ticket. The baggage was then taken on board of a steamboat employed to transport the passengers and their property, free of charge, from Castle Garden to the starting-places of the various railroads and steamboat lines; and the passengers, having now fully prepared themselves at the usual hour of the day, had ample time to enjoy themselves in the depot by taking their meals, cleansing themselves in the spacious bath-rooms, or promenading on the galleries or on the dock. The utmost order prevailed throughout; every requisite information was given passengers by officials conversing in different languages; letters from friends were transmitted to landing passengers, bringing them money or directions how to proceed, etc.

The Grand Inquest, having thus personally witnessed the whole mode of doing business at the Landing Depot of Castle Garden, and having become satisfied that every care was taken of the emigrant that philanthropy could suggest, and devotion to a good cause, realized by perseverance and daily care, made further enquiries about the arrangements made for special cases which might not then have arisen or been witnessed by them. They learned that it is a frequent occurrence that passengers land expecting to find the means to pursue their route into the interior of the country without delay, but are disappointed. In such cases advances are made on the luggage of passengers, who, being thus enabled to escape the necessity of waiting in expensive boarding-houses for communications from their friends, leave immediately for their destination, and after a short while send the amount advanced to them, without interest or charge for storage, and have their trunks sent after them. The amount of money saved to emigrant families by this beneficial arrangement, in keeping them out of boarding-houses, is immense; for it embraces not only the reasonable board for a few days. Before the establishment of Castle Garden, emigrants in such difficulties would go to a boarding-house, and write to their friends for "money," not specifying amounts; the friends would send what they thought would pay for the passage, which was then swallowed up by the boarding-house bill, leaving the emigrant still without means to travel. The boarding-house keeper would probably extend a new credit on the security of the luggage (but not a cash advance thereon), and when thus all the means of the emigrant had been exhausted, he would be turned into the street a pauper, and a fit subject for the charities of the public institutions. This is proved by the statistics of Ward's Island Emigrant Refuge, which, at the time of the establishment of Castle Garden, had 3,000 inmates, whose number has, in one year, been reduced to about 1,000—the protection afforded by Castle Garden having cut off the supply of paupers.

Another admirable feature, to which the attention of the Grand Inquest was called, is the special arrangement of a large, airy, and well-ventilated room for the accommodation of lying-in women, or such as have been confined so recently before the arrival of the ship as to require rest before travelling. They have all the necessary care of medical attendance and nursing, at the expense of the Commissioners of Emigration, and are not under any necessity of going to boarding-houses and expending money which will take them to their destination as soon as their strength is sufficiently established to bear the fatigues of a journey.

On enquiring into the causes of certain published attacks on the Emigrant Landing Depot, the Grand Inquest have become satisfied that they emanate, in the first instance, from the very interested parties against whose depredations Castle Garden affords protection to the emigrant, and who are chiefly runners, in the employ of booking-agents, boarding-house keepers, and others, who have lost custom by the establishment of a central depot, where the railroad companies have their own business done by their own clerks, and without the extensive intervention of passage brokers, etc.

This class has thrown great difficulties in the way of the proper development of affairs in Castle Garden, by constituting a noisy crowd around the gates, whose behavior is utterly lawless, and endangers the personal safety not only of the passengers who have to leave Castle Garden to transact business in the city, but also the employees of the Landing Depot, and of individual Commissioners of Emigration, who are continually insulted in the public grounds surrounding the depot, and have been obliged to carry loaded fire-arms in self-defence against the violence which has frequently been offered to them.

This same class will swarm in boats around the ships in the bay, and bias the minds of passengers against the Landing Depot, and, when driven off by the police officers stationed by the Commissioners of Emigration on such ships, will abuse these officers in the most violent manner, and will lodge complaints against such officers in the Mayor's office, and such complaints will be listened to as though they emanated from respectable citizens.

The Grand Inquest witnessed a crowd of this class hovering around the gates of Castle Garden, and they learned with regret that, in spite of repeated representations to the municipal authorities, the police utterly ignore the disturbances caused by this mob, who will pounce upon every person leaving the enclosures of Castle Garden, and, if they do not rob them of their money, valuables, tickets, baggage-checks, or the like, or commit gross assault and battery upon such as will not enter into conversation with them, will induce them, by force or argument, to go with them to places where they will be required to spend part or all of their money before they can find a chance to escape.

With a proper attention to their obvious duty on the part of the police, there can be no doubt that this motley, noisy, and dangerous crowd could be entirely broken up, and prevented from reassembling.

The Grand Inquest have learned with regret that this obvious duty of the police is absolutely neglected, to the great detriment of the emigrants, and to the great annoyance of the Commissioners of Emigration, who superintend the business of the Emigrant Landing Depot.

The Grand Inquest, having become satisfied that the latter in all its operations is a blessing, not only to the emigrants, but to the community at large, would feel remiss in the performance of a sacred duty if they failed to recommend this important philanthropic establishment to the fostering care of the municipal authorities; and they have dismissed the complaints preferred against certain employees of the Castle Garden, satisfied that they are not sustained by law, and have their origin in a design to disturb, rather than to further, the good work for which the establishment has been called into life by an act of Legislature of April, 1855.

HOWELL HOPPOCK, *Foreman of Grand Jury.*

III. The Inland Voyage,

AND BOOKING OF PASSENGERS IN EUROPE.

Office of the Commissioners of Emigration
of the State of New York,
New York, November, 1848.

The Legislature of the State of New York, admonished by the rapid increase of immigration at the port of New York, and considering the important interests connected therewith, has established a Board of Commissioners, acting under the authority of the State, and entrusted with the general care and supervision of the subject. The protection of the emigrant against the tricks and dishonesty of persons with whom he must necessarily come in contact immediately on his arrival, is one of the principal objects of the Commission; and, in furtherance of this object, the undersigned have been appointed a committee to notice a great and frequent abuse, which is practised upon the emigrant even before he leaves the Old World.

The number of passengers arrived at this port since the beginning of this year is nearly 160,000; and it may be assumed that at least 130,000 thereof have proceeded to the distant parts of the country at the West, and that the money paid here for their passage amounts to more than half a million of dollars. As may be supposed, there are many people engaged in the business of forwarding these emigrants, and the individuals or companies thus engaged employ a host of clerks or servants, called "runners," who try to meet the new-comer on board the ship that brings him, or immediately after he puts his foot on shore, for the purpose of carrying him to the forwarding offices for which they respectively act. The tricks resorted to, in order to forestall a competitor and secure the emigrant, would be amusing, if they were not at the cost of the inexperienced and unsuspecting stranger; and it is but too true that an enormous sum of money is annually lost to the emigrants by the wiles and false statements of the emigrant runners, many of them originally from their own country, and speaking their native language.

Of late the field of operation of these "emigrant runners" is no longer confined to this city; it extends to Europe. Some have appeared there sent from here by forwarding offices, others have been engaged on the spot, and again others have commenced and are carrying on the business on their own account and responsibility; but all have the same object in view, namely, to make money out of the emigrant. They generally call themselves agents of some transportation or forwarding bureau, and endeavor to impress the emigrant who intends going farther than New York with the belief that it is for his benefit, and in the highest degree desirable, to secure his passage hence to the place of his destination before he leaves Europe.

It is well known that emigrants frequently arrive at the seaports in Europe, without having engaged their passage across the ocean, and not finding a vessel ready to take them on board, they are compelled to stop, at a considerable expense, until an opportunity offers to proceed on their voyage; and it also happens that, even when they have secured a passage before going to the port of embarkation, they are delayed, and subject to perplexities and charges which they did not anticipate. This circumstance is taken advantage of by the so-called agents of New York transportation and forwarding houses, to induce the emigrant to take his passage from this port to his ulterior destination, before leaving Europe. He is told that, unless he does so, he runs great risk of being detained, or having to pay exorbitant prices.

These statements, and all similar ones which may be used for the purpose, *are not true*, and whoever believes them, and acts upon such belief, is sure to be deceived.

There are but two routes hence to the West; the one is by way of Albany and Buffalo, the other by way of Philadelphia and Pittsburg, and to these places there is no more than one conveyance daily, all the year through. There is never any difficulty in getting away from New York, and so numerous are the establishments engaged in the business of forwarding passengers, that exorbitant or high prices of passage are entirely prevented by the competition among said establishments, and the traveller will never be exposed to them, if he will only be careful *not* to make an arrangement with the first comer, but will take some pains to find out which is the safest and cheapest office to apply to.

It is invariably the case, that those who in Europe take passage tickets for inland places in America pay more, generally considerably more, than others, who wait until they are here. The agents in Europe who sell such tickets must have a compensation therefor, and this compensation, be it much or little, is added to the regular price of passage, and the emigrant has to pay it. Instances have come to the knowledge of the Commissioners, where the difference amounted to three dollars a person! But this is not all. The cases are by no means rare in which the tickets prove entirely worthless. They bear the name of offices which never existed, and then, of course are nowhere respected; or the offices whose name they bear will be found shut up, and are not likely ever to reopen; or the emigrants are directed to parties refusing to acknowledge the agent who issued the tickets, and in all these cases the emigrant loses the money paid for them.

It is to be hoped that this publication will receive the attention it deserves. It would be gratifying to the Commissioners, and entirely for the interest of the emigrants, if the respective Governments in Europe would prohibit the business alluded to; in any event, the Commissioners trust that emigrants will heed this warning, and henceforward will not pay or arrange for passage to the interior of America until they are here.

On their arrival here, they should not give ear to any representations, nor enter into any engagements, without obtaining first the advice and counsel of either the Commissioners of Emigration, or the Emigrant Society of the nation to which they belong, or its consul; and in enquiring for the office of the society, or consul, or the commissioners, they should be careful not to be carried to the wrong place. There are many individuals sufficiently unscrupulous intentionally to mislead the stranger. If the latter, for instance, enquire after the agency of the German Society, the person applied to will say that he is the agent, or that he will take the stranger to the office of the German Society, but, instead of doing so, will take him to a place where he is almost sure to be defrauded. As a general rule, if the emigrant is urged to take passage, or has to pay for the advice he asks, he may take it for granted that he is not at the place where he wishes to be; and he should bear in mind to look for the names of the persons or office he is in search of, at the door of the houses into which he is shown. All the foreign consuls, and the emigrant societies, as well as the Commissioners of Emigration, have signs over the doors of their offices. The office of the German Society is No. 95 Greenwich Street, of the Irish Emigrant Society at 22 Spruce Street, and of the Commissioners of Emigration in one of the public edifices of the city, in the Park.

Finally, we would remark that, if the emigrant be so situated as to render his immediate departure hence necessary, without having an opportunity to apply for advice to any of the places indicated, he should be careful not to take his passage for the whole distance he has to go, but should do so only to the first station of the route, say to Albany or Philadelphia. He should bear in mind that the passage hence to Albany is fifty cents, and to Philadelphia two dollars and twenty-five cents a person, and *no more.*

The Commissioners trust that this advice will be received and acted upon with that confidence to which it is entitled, from being given by persons who have no interest but that of the welfare of the emigrant, whose duties make them perfectly familiar with the subject, and who act not as private citizens, but under the authority and supervision of the Government of the State.

In behalf of the Commissioners of Emigration,

GULIAN C. VERPLANCK,
President of the Board.
LEOPOLD BIERWIRTH,
President of the German Society.
JOHN H. GRISCOM,
General Agent.
} *Committee.*

New York, November 2, 1848.

Hon. JAMES BUCHANAN, Secretary of State:

SIR: I have the honor to address you on behalf of the Board of Commissioners of Emigration of the State of New York.

This Board (as you may perhaps be already informed) is a commission appointed by the authorities of this State, for the assistance and protection of foreign emigrants arriving in this State, by providing for the sick and destitute, and protecting all from imposition while here, and aiding them to their ultimate destination. We have lately learned from unquestionable authority (among others from the United States Consul at Havre) that an organized system of imposition exists at the principal points of emigration from Europe, in the ports of Great Britain and Ireland, as well as those of the Continent, by which great and frequent frauds are committed in relation to the passages of emigrants to the interior of the United States. A circular has been accordingly prepared, under the authority of this Board, with the design of exposing these frauds, thus setting the emigrants on their guard against them. (A printed copy is herewith enclosed.) It has occurred to the Commissioners that this communication would be far more likely to promote its objects if it received the aid and sanction of the Government of the United States.

This being a subject strictly relating to our intercourse with foreign nations, and in which other States must feel as much interest as that which first receives the emigrant; it appears to be legitimately within the constitutional sphere of the General Government. It is, therefore, respectfully suggested that copies of the enclosed circular should be transmitted to the several consuls of the United States, at all the points of great emigration to this country, with a note from the Department of State, recommending the subject to their especial attention, and requesting them to give publicity to the information and advice of the Commissioners.

Should this suggestion meet your approval, printed copies of the circular will be furnished and forwarded as the Department may direct.

I am, with great respect, your obedient servant,

G. C. VERPLANCK, *Pres't of Comm'rs of Emigration.*

DEPARTMENT OF STATE,
Washington, November 6, 1848.

Hon. G. C. VERPLANCK, New York :

SIR : I have received your letter of the 2d inst., addressed to me on behalf of the Board of Commissioners of Emigration of the State of New York, referring to the existence of "an organized system of imposition at the principal points of emigration from Europe, in the ports of Great Britain and Ireland, as well as those of the Continent, by which great and frequent frauds are committed in relation to the passages of emigrants to the interior of the United States, together with a printed copy of a circular, prepared under the authority of the Board, with the design of exposing these frauds, thus setting the emigrants on their guard against them."

In the promotion of an object so honorable and benevolent, your Board may fully rely upon all the aid and support which this Department can properly afford.

In reply to your suggestion that copies of this circular be transmitted to the several consuls of the United States, at all the points of great emigration to this country, and your offer to furnish them for that purpose, I have to state that I will, with great pleasure, cause them to be so addressed, with such instructions as may be best calculated to ensure the results you have in view.

I am, sir, respectfully, your obt. servant,

JAMES BUCHANAN.

MEMORIAL.

THE present respectful address to the august Governments of those European states from which a regular annual emigration takes place purposes to invoke their powerful assistance in the philanthropic work of protecting emigrants landing upon these shores, for which the memorializing Commission was constituted by a law passed by the Legislature of the State of New York, in the year 1847.

This law creates a fund by the payment of $1 50 a head (since raised to $2 50), in lieu of special bonds for the support of persons likely to become a public charge, on all passengers landing at the port of New York, such fund to be applied for the relief of immigrants who should become unable to support themselves within the first five years after landing, by sickness, want of employment, or other causes, and to be administered by a board of Commissioners of Emigration, consisting of six Commissioners appointed by the Governor of the State, of the Mayors of the cities of New York and Brooklyn, and of the Presidents of the Irish and German Societies of the city of New York.

Under this law the memorialists have erected extensive hospitals and houses of refuge, and disbursed vast sums of money for temporary relief, during a period of eight years, securing the immigrant against distress, and the State at large against the charge of a great number of paupers, by healing the sick, sheltering the houseless, and finding employment for thousands of people able to earn their living, but unable to find employment for themselves, by means of extensive and well organized intelligence offices, where labor is provided without charge to the seeker.

But the efforts of the Commissioners of Emigration have not been limited to the work of *relief* alone. Their attention has also, from the beginning of their activity, been directed towards the *prevention* of suffering among immigrants, and they have from time to time suggested the passage of laws by the Legislature for the protection of immigrants against systematic fraud, to which they were exposed, from persons profiting by their ignorance of the condition of things in this country, or of its laws or language, and subjecting them to heavy losses of money or property, thereby reducing them to a condition calling for relief.

The most fruitful source of misery among immigrants has ever been the lawless action of a numerous class of people engaged directly or indirectly in the business of forwarding immigrants landing at this port to their destination in the interior. The schemes resorted to by this class for practising fraud and extortion upon the newly arrived immigrant beggar the liveliest imagination, and a variety of remedies for this evil, tried by this Commission and various benevolent societies, invariably called forth renewed efforts of invention on the part of the offenders, which again baffled the intentions and exertions of the friend of the immigrant for his protection.

The growing evil has finally led to the adoption of means for a radical cure, by placing the landing of the entire immigration under the direct supervision of the Commissioners of Emigration. A law was passed by the Legislature of the State, in April, 1855, compelling all vessels bringing emigrant passengers to this port to land them at one wharf, to be designated by the Commissioners of Emigration, and imposing a heavy fine for any deviation from the rule thus established.

The object of this law is to break up the system of barter and sale of passengers which prevailed to a large extent, by rendering it impossible for captains of vessels to sell their cargo of passengers to one or other gang of passenger brokers, known as runners, who were employed at an enormous expense by hotel-keepers, forwarding agents, and railroad and steamboat companies, for the purpose of securing to them respectively the largest possible share of the profits to be made out of the unsuspecting immigrant.

Under this law, the memorialists selected and designated as the only landing place for emigrants the wharf adjoining the extensive old fort situated at the Battery, on the southern part of the city, and known as *Castle Garden*, and fitted up the fort itself as an "Emigrant Landing Depot," affording ample accommodations for landing and forwarding several thousand emigrants in a day, and for the safe-keeping of their baggage until forwarded. They surrounded the whole ground with a high and strong fence, shutting out effectually the class of persons whose depredations against the property of emigrants had, for years, been a source of a great deal of misery among emigrants landing in New York.

They also induced the directors of the principal railroad and steamboat lines to the West to organize at Castle Garden a central and joint ticket office for the sale—at the regular published prices—of passage tickets for emigrants to their several places of destination in the interior, and to place such office, and the entire business of forwarding persons or property, under their own immediate supervision.

Under this arrangement the passenger is landed with his baggage, as security for which checks are issued acknowledging responsibility for its safety. He finds in Castle Garden a vast hall, well ventilated and comfortably warmed, when the season requires it, in which he can rest and refresh himself; large bath-rooms, whose use is free of charge; frugal meals at cost price; responsible and disinterested officials, speaking his own language, to give him advice as to the best mode of travelling, or the easiest and quickest way of finding employment; he can there buy his ticket for the line of travel by railroad or steamboat which he may choose, and have his baggage labelled and numbered, receiving therefore a receipted check which calls for the baggage therein described at the place of destination, and he is finally transported with his baggage by water, free of charge, to the starting place of the line he has chosen. He is thus entirely guarded against the necessity of going into the streets of the city, and of exposing himself to the dangerous snares which the runner has in readiness for him, as soon as he comes in contact with him. Even the collection of his bills of exchange on merchants in the city may, if he choses, be done for him through the cashier's office, and the money is then paid over to him under the supervision of one of the Commissioners of Emigration. He can thus proceed to his Western destination without being exposed to the least danger of loss from imposition.

Desperate efforts are being made by the runners and their backers to break down this beneficent institution. No calumny is left untried in order to excite public opinion against it. But all this has proved of no avail, for the immense benefit which the immigrant derives from the protection afforded him by this institution is too clearly demonstrable to admit of a doubt in any observing and unbiassed mind.

The clamorers finding themselves unable to prove the Emigrant Landing Depot at Castle Garden a nuisance, endangering the health and prosperity of the city, and equally unable to make their usual iniquitous profits out of the emigrants protected by its walls, have resorted to a means which threatens in a measure to paralyze the beneficial action of this institution, by circumventing its protective operation.

The means alluded to is the *system of contracting with emigrants in Europe for their inland passage from New York to their places of destination in the interior of the United States or in Canada.* This system has been lately revived to a considerable extent. Runners and forwarding agents of this city, finding their occupation gone by the establishment of the Emigrant Landing Depot of Castle Garden, have removed to European ports, and even inland towns, or have there revived or established agencies for booking passengers to places in the interior previous to their leaving the European ports, or even their inland homes, and for receiving part or the whole of the price of such inland tickets in advance.

It is self-evident that these agencies, carried on at considerable expense, are not content to charge a legitimate commission on the net prices of tickets merely. Overcharges on the personal tickets are the rule, pretty generally varying from 25 to 50 per cent. above the established rates of transportation companies, and very often being fully double the proper charge; whilst full and unlimited facilities are left open for the consignees in this country, their runners and baggagemen, to defraud the passenger on the charges for his baggage after he arrives here. False representations, amounting almost to coercion, are not unfrequently resorted to, in order to induce emigrants to contract for inland passage before leaving Europe. Assertions of the most absurd description are made to the emigrant, such for instance as that it would be impossible to travel inland unless on tickets issued by the agent making the assertion, and such assertions are conveyed in such language, and with such a show of apparently corroborative evidence, as to inspire confidence, and to mislead the inexperienced emigrant. Some of these agencies, more especially in England, have gone so far as to represent themselves as agents for the Commissioners of Emigration, and have grossly defrauded passengers under the shelter of the name of the memorialists, thus endeavoring indirectly to shake public faith in the Commissioners of Emigration.

The effect of this system is calculated to destroy the protection which Castle Garden throws around the immigrant, for the passenger landing with a contract in his pocket, on which he has made payment, in part or in full, at once leaves Castle Garden for the city, to find the consignee who is to fulfil the contract made in Europe. He thus passes by the institution planned and arranged by the Legislature of the State for his protection, and falls into the very hands against whom he would have been effectually protected. He has to pay heavy cartage for the transportation of his baggage, for whose safety, moreover, his own vigilance will be the only guarantee. He will again be detained, on various pretences, in the taverns until his last dollar is expended, and a small debt incurred, which furnishes a pretext for seizing part or the whole of his luggage, and, thus plucked, he will again be turned heartlessly into the street, to become a charge to benevolence, instead of going directly into an independent and useful activity, as he would if he had proceeded at once from the Landing Depot to his final place of destination, without being robbed of his means and of his property by useless and fraudulent delays, caused by interested parties taking advantage of his ignorance.

It is to prevent this dangerous system of "*booking in Europe*," that the memorialists most respectfully ask for the assistance and co-operation of the Governments of Europe. The care which the European Governments have evinced for the protection of their individual subjects, by stringent laws regulating, superintending, or forbidding every species of business, calculated to offer scope to the swindler, inspires the memorialists with the hope that their representations will be favorably considered, and that the Governments addressed will be pleased to assist them in their efforts to protect the landing emigrants, by adopting such measures as will render it impossible for the reckless speculator upon the property of the emigrant to frustrate, in the manner indicated, the desire of the Legislature of the State of New York to extend to him, through the memorialists, a complete protection against fraud and imposition when he lands in this port.

The memorialists, being aware of the accomplished business-tact, and of the easy, insinuating, and gentlemanly address of the more prominent among the passenger agents who have gone to Europe, and are now travelling or residing there, engaged in forwarding the interests of the concerns of this city with which they are connected, would respectfully caution the Governments of Europe against the plausible statements which such men are in the habit of making to further their own ends, and would respectfully solicit a thorough investigation of the protective establishment under the charge of the memorialists, by the representatives in this country of the European Governments, envoys, ministers, consuls, or commercial agents.

Recommending their memorial to the favorable consideration of the august Governments, the undersigned have the honor to subscribe themselves most respectfully,

NEW YORK, November, 1855.

THE BOARD OF COMMISSIONERS OF EMIGRATION,

GULIAN C. VERPLANCK, President.

JOHN A. KENNEDY, JAMES KELLY,
ELIJAH F. PURDY, E. D. MORGAN,
JOHN P. CUMMING, } Commissioners.

FERNANDO WOOD, Mayor of New York.

GEO. HALL, Mayor of Brooklyn.

ANDREW CARRIGAN, President Irish Society.

RUD. GARRIGUE, President German Society.

OFFICE OF THE COMMISSIONERS OF EMIGRATION,
New York, January 23, 1857.

Hon. WM. L. MARCY, Secretary of State, Washington City :

SIR : At the last meeting of the Commissioners of Emigration of the State of New York, I was instructed to communicate to you their request that another effort should be made to induce the Governments of those countries of Europe whence emigration to this port chiefly flows, to prohibit altogether the booking of passengers for inland passages or transportation in the United States, or selling abroad passage tickets or contracts for passage tickets to be used on this side of the Atlantic.

On this subject, permit me to refer you to a letter from a Committee of this Board to yourself, of October 12, 1855, to your reply thereto, and to the printed circulars issued in consequence thereof, and circulated abroad through the facilities afforded by the Department of State.

The apprehensions expressed in the letter of the Committee, that the seat of depredation on the emigrant would be changed from this port to the port of embarkation, have been more than realized.

The chief operators in this system of fraud have not only opened offices in the several seaports where emigrants to this country usually embark, but have also established agencies in towns in the interior of those countries, and in the very villages whence families are likely to emigrate.

The effect of these agencies has been to renew, and even increase, the evils which have been checked by the establishment of an exclusive landing-place for emigrants at Castle Garden.

The more remote the place where the emigrant is induced to purchase a ticket for inland transportation in this country, the greater is the opportunity for imposition and fraud, and this is seldom suffered to pass unused.

The efforts made by our Government heretofore for protecting emigrants from such frauds abroad, have hitherto had little effect on the European Governments, with the exception only of Hamburg and Bremen. Not only is the privilege of booking passengers for distant inland points in the United States continued, but in some places it has been aided (it is hoped not intentionally) by means of government licenses, giving an official character to the business, well calculated to mislead the ignorant. These are grossly overcharged for real tickets, or as often imposed on by fraudulent ones. After which, they are consigned to continued depredations by other confederates in this city and elsewhere in the United States.

These are facts of daily occurrence, which our official position brings constantly to our notice, but seldom enables us to arrest or remedy.

There is a marked contrast in passengers coming by way of Hamburg and Bremen and those by other European ports. It rarely occurs that passengers from either Hamburg or Bremen are unable, on their arrival here, to pay their way to their destination in the interior, or to secure all proper comforts and conveniences on the way. Very many of those from other ports are first defrauded of their means, by being induced to purchase tickets for railroad and water travel in this country, at high prices, which, when presented here, are found to be either quite worthless, or to carry the holders only to some point in the interior far short of their destination, where they are left destitute.

Other tickets are genuine, but are found to have been paid for at prices very far above the actual cost at the offices here.

It appears to us that the claims of humanity and justice and the comity of nations require and authorize our Government to invoke the aid of other Governments in protecting their own subjects during their pilgrimage from an overcrowded home to a region where vacant acres invite and reward the hand of industry.

To show the manner in which the business of the emigrant landing-place at Castle Garden, New York, under the exclusive control of this Commission, and established in pursuance of a special enactment of our Legislature, has been conducted, I enclose copies of a presentment* by a recent grand jury of this county. It will probably speak for us better than we can for ourselves on one of the most important points of our administration of the trust confided to us by the State of New York.

am, with much respect, your obedient servant,

G. C. VERPLANCK, *President.*

DEPARTMENT OF STATE,
Washington, January 31, 1857.

HON. G. C. VERPLANCK, President Board of Commissioners of Emigration:

SIR: I have received your communication of the 23d inst., with its enclosures, calling the attention of this department to the impositions practised upon emigrants to the United States in the countries from which they depart, and suggesting that the aid of those Governments should be invoked to protect their subjects from the arts of designing and unprincipled individuals.

The motives which led to the establishment of the Board of Commissioners by the State of New York are in the highest degree philanthropic and praiseworthy, and, accordingly, to further the objects which you have in view, I have addressed a circular letter, of which a copy is herewith enclosed, to the diplomatic and consular agents of the United States in those countries of Europe from which emigrants chiefly proceed, and instructed them to bring the subject of your communication to the notice of the Governments to which they are respectively accredited, or of the authorities of the places where they reside, and to ask for the adoption of such measures on their part as may be required by the claims of humanity and the comity of nations.

I have likewise had the pleasure of conferring with Mr. Murray, the agent of the Board, and have furnished him with facilities for the accomplishment of the purposes of the Commissioners in his proposed visit to Europe.

I am, sir, respectfully, your obedient servant,

W. L. MARCY.

* For presentment, see page 196.

CIRCULAR.

No. 17.

DEPARTMENT OF STATE,
Washington, January 31, 1857.

SIR: The attention of this department having been recently called to the abuses to which emigrants are subjected in the countries from which they proceed, and on their arrival at certain seaports in the United States, it has been deemed advisable to bring the subject to your notice. I accordingly herewith transmit, in a printed form, a copy of a communication addressed to this department, on the 23d instant, by the President of the Board of Commissioners of Emigration at New York, in which a mode of correcting the existing evils is suggested.

You are instructed to bring this subject, which is fully set forth in the annexed letter of Mr. Verplanck and its accompaniment, to the notice of the Government to which you are accredited, or of the authorities of the place where you reside, and to ask for the adoption of such measures on their part as may be considered necessary for the protection of those intending to emigrate to this country. A step in this direction would no doubt be of service in correcting the evils complained of, and a regard for the interests of humanity demands that it should be taken.

I am, sir, your obedient servant,

W. L. MARCY.

IV. Rules and Regulations.

EMIGRANT LANDING DEPOT, CASTLE GARDEN.

I.—EMIGRANTS.

1. ALL emigrant passengers arriving at the Port of New York, and their luggage, after being checked, must be landed at the Emigrant Landing Depot, Castle Garden, free of expense. Passengers are earnestly requested to take personal charge of all their property not checked.

2. After landing, the passengers will be examined for the purpose of ascertaining if any are liable to be bonded, or in such condition of health as to require hospital care, and will then be assembled in the enclosure, and the name, occupation, age, birthplace, and destination of each, with other necessary particulars, recorded.

3. Emigrants desiring to take any Railroad or Steamboat route for which tickets are sold in this Depot, will communicate with the officers of the Railroad Agency, and select such route as they prefer. The agent of said route shall be required to transport such emigrants and their luggage to the Railroad Depot or Steamboat Landing, by water conveyance when feasible, by land when not, but in either case free of charge.

4. Before the removal of luggage of emigrants having bought tickets of the Railroad Agency, the same shall be weighed, and each piece labelled and checked to its place of destination, with a common number for all the pieces of luggage of any one passenger, and a proper check given to the owner, setting forth, *in ink*, the number of his luggage ticket, the number of pieces of luggage, the gross weight, the overweight, and the charge he is liable to for its transportation to the point of destination; which check shall be signed in ink as a receipt for the luggage by an authorized representative of the Railroad Agency.

5. The names of all emigrants expected by friends and relatives will be announced, and all answering to their name will be transferred to such friends and relatives as may be waiting for them.

6. The galleries and floor of the Depot will be open for the free use of recently arrived emigrants, until ready to take their departure; and they are requested to make use of the wash-rooms before leaving the premises.

7. Emigrants desiring board and lodging are advised to communicate with the keepers of boarding-houses having permission in this Depot, and who will be allowed on the floor for this purpose. Every boarding-house keeper, when soliciting an emigrant for his house, must hand such emigrant a card, setting

forth his name and residence, the prices, in gold and paper money, of board and lodging, by the day and week, and for single meals and night's lodging.

8. Emigrants wishing to buy food can purchase at the bread stands and restaurant in the Depot at prescribed rates, as stated on cards at such stands.

9. Emigrants remaining in the city of New York or vicinity must defray the expense of removing their luggage from the Depot, and are informed that for this purpose a Baggage Express is admitted to the Depot.

10. Emigrants seeking employment are requested to apply to the Superintendent of Labor, and to make use of the Labor Exchange attached to the Depot.

11. Emigrants desiring to deposit money or valuables over night are advised to do so in the office of the General Agent and Superintendent, who will give a receipt therefor. Employees are forbidden to take charge of such money or valuables of emigrants, unless the same be handed them after business hours; in which case report shall be made as soon as possible to the General Agent.

II.—BOARDING-HOUSE KEEPERS.

Boarding-house Keepers, having permission to enter the Landing Depot to solicit Boarders, must observe the following Rules:

12. Every Boarding-house Keeper must wear his badge in a conspicuous place on his breast when entering the Depot, and keep it so exposed while in the premises.

13. Every Boarding-house Keeper must present to passengers, when soliciting such passengers for his house, a card setting forth his name and residence, and the prices in gold and paper money charged for board and lodging by the day and week, and for each meal and night's lodging; and he must also furnish emigrants with a bill setting forth all charges incurred for board, etc., before receiving pay therefor; and must make to this department a daily return of all passengers taken out of the Depot.

14. Boarding-house Keepers are required to direct to this Depot emigrants wishing to communicate with their friends, or seeking employment, or desiring advances on luggage.

15. Every Boarding-house Keeper having permission in this Depot must post in Castle Garden and in his house, in a conspicuous place, where the same may be seen at all times by emigrants, a card containing a list of prices for board and lodging by the day and week, and for single meals and night's lodging, and setting forth whether such prices are in gold or paper money. Prices charged to emigrants must conform with the prices set forth on said lists, and on the card handed to the emigrant, as required in Rule 13.

16. Boarding-house Keepers must behave in an orderly manner while in the Depot, and remain seated in the place assigned them until admitted on the floor.

III.—MISSIONARIES

And Representatives of Religious Bodies and Societies, admitted to the Landing Depot, are to observe the following Rules:

17. They may distribute religious books and papers among the emigrants, and give them all necessary advice of a spiritual nature; and shall report to the officers of the Commissioners of Emigration any wants of emigrants other than of a religious nature, coming under their notice; and shall not interfere in the secular requirements of the emigrants, or the secular matters of the Department, but shall direct all such emigrants to the proper officers of the Commissioners of Emigration.

18. They may visit any sick emigrants in the Hospital as often as their presence is required by such emigrant, and when called by the nurse or other officer of this Department.

IV.—GENERAL RULES

For the Government of the Landing Depot:

19. The business of the Depot will commence at 7 o'clock A.M. from May 1 to Nov. 1, and at 8 o'clock A.M. from Nov. 1 to May 1; and the clerks of the Letter Department shall also be present at all times, after the landing and registering of passengers, to write to friends of emigrants desiring to acquaint them of their arrival, and request funds for their inland journey, or for any purpose.

20. No person shall be admitted within the enclosure except the officers and employees of this Department and the officers and employees of the Railroad Agency, except on permission of the Superintendent.

21. No person shall be employed by any party occupying an office within the enclosure as clerk, ticket-seller, interpreter, or in any other capacity, unless first approved by the Castle Garden Committee; and no employee or other person having privilege in this Depot shall, under any pretence whatever, receive from emigrants or others any recompense for any service rendered.

22. Every employee of this Department will be furnished with a badge setting forth his position, which he shall wear and exhibit while on duty.

V.—RULES AND REGULATIONS

For the Government of the Information Office, for Friends of arriving Emigrants.

23. This office will be open for business from May 1 to November 1 at 7 o'clock A.M., and from November 1 to May 1 at 8 o'clock A.M., and remain open as long as the Superintendent may direct. All persons having relations or friends whom they wish to receive, are requested to report to the clerk the names of the passengers expected by them, and the vessel on which they arrived, with their own names and residences. They will then remain seated until such passengers are brought, and on receiving them they are requested to leave the premises, so as to avoid obstructing the business.

24. Emigrants wishing to have their baggage transported by the Express Company at the Depot (referred to Rule 9) are requested to leave the proper directions at the Express Office before leaving the premises. Those desiring to take away their baggage can receive it on the day after landing, and are requested to apply for it themselves, for the purpose of identifying their property.

25. All services rendered by the officers and employees are without charge or expense to emigrants or their friends, or to any person having business with the office.

VI.—RULES AND REGULATIONS

For the Government of the Labor Exchange and Intelligence Office.

26. This office will be open for business from May 1 to November 1 at 7 o'clock A.M., and from November 1 to May 1 at 8 o'clock A.M., and remain open as long as the Superintendent may direct; and shall be free for the use of employers and of emigrants seeking employment.

27. Emigrants and their employers are requested, after making their contracts and before leaving the office, to leave on record in the Office Register the particulars of such contract, the emigrant's name, age, and date of arrival, and the employer's name and residence.

VII.—RAILROAD DEPARTMENT.

28. It shall be the duty of the clerks and employees of the Railroad Agency to be at their respective stations on the landing of passengers, and so long thereafter as their services may be required, to attend to the wants of emigrants desiring to leave the city by any of the routes for which tickets are sold in the Depot; and in every way to conform to all rules regarding them heretofore or hereafter adopted.

29. It shall further be the duty of the clerks and employees of the Railroad Agency to refer all emigrants desiring information other than regarding the purchase of tickets to the proper officers of the Commissioners of Emigration.

30. The Railroad Agency and its officers are permitted to accept in payment for Railroad tickets and for overweight of luggage gold and silver, allowing for such gold and silver in current funds within one per cent. of the market rate, and furnishing to the emigrant a printed slip, setting forth the number and denomination of the coins purchased, the respective rates paid therefor, and whole amount paid.

31. The Railroad Agency will be required to report monthly to the Castle Garden Committee the number of emigrants transported each month over the several Railroads represented by said Agency and their connecting lines to the chief points to which emigrants go, together with the routes by which such emigrants are sent.

32. No person shall be employed by the Railroad Agency in any capacity whatever, except by and with the consent and approval of the Castle Garden Committee.

VIII.—EXCHANGE BROKERS.

33. Every Exchange Broker admitted to this Depot shall be required to be at his desk while emigrants are landing, in order to attend to the wants of such emigrants as wish to have money exchanged.

34. They shall post in a conspicuous place every day the current market rates of gold and silver, and the prices paid by them for gold and silver of every denomination, domestic and foreign, and shall pay in current funds for all gold and silver bought by them from the emigrants within one per cent. of the current market rates of such gold and silver.

35. They shall furnish to every emigrant, from whom they purchase gold or silver, a printed slip setting forth the name of the broker and the number and denominations of the coins purchased, the respective rates paid therefor, and the whole amount paid.

IX.—RESTAURANT AND BREAD-STANDS.

36. The Keepers of the Restaurant for the use of emigrants within the Depot shall be required to open the same at 6 A.M. in the summer and 7 A.M. in the winter, and to keep open as long as the emigrants require their services; and shall expose in a conspicuous place a list of prices charged by them for all articles supplied, which list of prices must be submitted to the Castle Garden Committee for examination and approval monthly.

X.—WASH-ROOMS.

37. The Wash-rooms shall be open from 6 A.M. to such an hour in the night as emigrants need their use.

XI.—HOSPITALS.

38. The Hospital Rooms are for the use of the sick alone.

39. When any emigrant becomes sick in or is brought sick to the Depot during the night, it shall be the duty of the Night Watchman to have such patient transferred to the Hospital and put in charge of the nurse, and to procure the attendance of the Medical Officer of the establishment without delay.

N. B.—It is earnestly requested that immediate complaint be made to the General Agent and Superintendent of any violation of these Rules.

Adopted by the Board of Commissioners of Emigration of the State of New York.

EMIGRANT LANDING DEPOT, CASTLE GARDEN,
New York, May 18, 1867.

STATE EMIGRANT REFUGE AND HOSPITAL, WARD'S ISLAND.*

[The Establishment at Ward's Island, under the control of the Commissioners, shall be known as and styled THE STATE EMIGRANT REFUGE AND HOSPITAL.]

I.—THE SUPERINTENDENT.

THE SUPERINTENDENT shall have charge of the Emigrant Refuge and Hospital at Ward's Island, all the buildings and grounds connected therewith, the control of the inmates, and of all subordinate officers; he shall be held responsible for the cleanliness, good order, and proper management of the Establishment; and he shall have a general supervision of all the property of every description belonging to the Commissioners at Ward's Island.

2. He shall receive all persons to whom permits have been given for admission into the Refuge or Hospital, by the Vice-President, or his Deputy for that purpose, or by any Commissioner. No other person will be admitted as an inmate. It shall be his duty to see that all persons having permits for the Hospital are at once transferred to that department. He shall cause the transportation of sick persons in the Refuge to the Hospital; but no person shall be continued or allowed to remain in the Hospital after they cease to need Medical treatment.

3. He shall take charge of all money or other valuable articles, except religious books and emblems, belonging to inmates, and shall cause a receipt for the same to be given to the person from whom they may be taken, and enter the name of the owner, a description of the articles, the date when, and the circumstances under which they were taken, shall be entered in a book kept for that purpose.

4. He shall cause to be kept a Register of all admissions into and discharges from the Establishment, distinguishing the Hospital and Refuge, under their several dates, and shall make a weekly return to the Commissioners of each day's admissions and discharges, and also of the births and deaths, accompanied by such remarks as may be called for by any case of admission, discharge, birth, or death. Every Monday he shall make a return to the Commissioners of the whole number of persons in all the departments of the Establishment, designating by actual count the number in each; the number of children under twelve years of age, and a summary of the births and deaths for the preceding week; also, of the number of orphan children of each sex, their ages, etc.

5. He shall give to every adult inmate applying for it a discharge in writing, except insane persons, or those he may consider unable to earn a living

* These rules were adopted by the Commissioners of Emigration, June 16, 1858. It is sufficient for our purpose to give only those portions of them which have reference to the Superintendent and the Hospital. The duties of the subordinate employees, such as clerks, watchmen, stewards, policemen, matrons, teachers, cockswain, apothecary, nurses, and orderlies do not differ from the ordinary duties performed by such persons.

or take care of themselves, or such as may be retained for disorderly conduct. He shall take care that no person employed in the Establishment, and no inmate, leaves the Island without his permission.

6. He shall make to the Commissioners monthly reports of all inmates who ought to be or wish to be discharged, and who desire to be sent to any place out of the city of New York, but who have not sufficient means for their transportation, and of such children (orphans or others) who should be indentured as apprentices, or placed at general service. These reports must be accompanied by a statement of the age and condition of each party named in them, and his opinion of the best disposition to be made of each; and any decision by the Board as to the disposition of the parties named in the reports, the Superintendent must see carried into effect without delay.

7. The Superintendent shall make weekly written requisitions for the supplies of every description required for the use of the Hospital and Refuge; and these requisitions, countersigned by the Steward, together with the Apothecary's requisition, countersigned by the Physician, must be delivered at the office of the Commissioners every Monday.

8. He must see that an exact account is taken of all goods and supplies furnished for the use of the Establishment, and proper receipts given for the same; that the goods and supplies are properly taken care of; and should any deficiency in quality or quantity occur, forthwith to report the same to the Board.

9. He shall see that proper facilities are afforded the inmates for writing to their friends; or, when necessary, that letters are written for them, and that all letters for inmates are promptly delivered to them. When notified that any inmate of the Hospital, or is aware that any inmate of the Refuge, is desirous of conversing with a religious person other than the Chaplains, he shall invite such person of such denomination as the said inmate shall require, to visit the inmate; and while such person is present he shall see that due decorum is observed by the other inmates of the Ward.

10. With the exception of the Chaplains and Physicians, he shall select and appoint all officers, nurses, and employees necessary for the various departments of the Refuge and Hospital, to hold their respective places during the pleasure of the Superintendent, who shall report to the Board all appointments and discharges when made.

11. He shall have the control and direction of all the officers and persons employed in and about the Refuge and Hospital, except the Chief Physician and Chief Surgeon; and all officers and other persons so employed must conform to his directions, and must be governed by his decisions in any difficulties which may arise in the discharge of their respective duties.

12. He shall endeavor at all times to find employment for such of the inmates as are able to work; and all inmates who are capable of working shall be employed, as well to inure them to labor as to contribute to their support. At stated hours, they shall repair to their proper apartments, or places on the ground allotted for them, where they shall work in an orderly manner, and at such labor and as many hours as the Superintendent may direct. And in case any inmate able to labor shall refuse to comply with the directions of the

Superintendent, he may confine such inmate in the "Lock-up," or discharge such inmate from the Island.

13. When notified by any person of any theft within the Hospital or Refuge, or the grounds connected therewith, he shall immediately take the necessary steps for the recovery of the stolen property, and to secure the offender and bring him to justice; and he must at all times maintain a strict police throughout the Establishment. He shall make out a monthly pay-roll of every person employed, including Physicians and Surgeons, with the name, occupations, salary or wages, amount due, etc., and deliver the same to the Commissioners at the close of every month for approval.

DEPUTY SUPERINTENDENT.

It shall be the duty of the Superintendent to select and employ one person, who shall be styled "Deputy Superintendent," who shall be his Principal Assistant, and, in the absence of the Superintendent, clothed with and exercise all his power. He shall reside on the Island, and examine daily into the state of the Institutions; visit every apartment, and see every person therein, as often as good order and necessity require. He shall exercise a general supervision and direction in regard to the discipline and police of the Island, and to the business concerns thereof; and shall superintend all the business carried on, and labor done, in and upon the buildings, or land belonging to or connected with the Island. He must spend the whole day in a general supervision of the Assistants and inmates, direct them in their duties and labors, and report to the Superintendent all neglect of duty on the part of any of the Assistants; receive reports from the Assistants of all disobedience or violation of the *Rules*, and report the same to the Superintendent, and see that his orders and directions are strictly and promptly observed; and to this end he must be always present on the Island, by day and by night, that he may be able, during the evening and night, to see that all is safe.

It shall be his duty, generally, to see that the whole Establishment exhibits throughout neatness, good order, and cleanliness.

It shall be his duty to see that all the dead deposited in the Dead-house are carefully removed for burial as speedily as may be proper, and that the proper certificates of death are signed by a Physician of the Establishment.

II.—THE HOSPITAL.

1. There shall be appointed by the Commissioners of Emigration, a Chief Physician and a Chief Surgeon, who shall have charge of the Medical and Surgical treatment of inmates in their respective departments, and shall be held responsible by the Superintendent and the Commissioners of Emigration for the proper performance of their duties.

2. The Chief Physician and Assistant Physicians and Surgeons shall reside on the Island, in a residence or rooms to be designated by the Superintendent or the Commissioners of Emigration.

3. The Chief Surgeon shall visit the Island at least every other day, prescribe for the patients under his care, and perform such operations as may be

deemed necessary at the request of the patient; but no surgical operation shall be undertaken without the consent of the patient; and all capital operations, endangering the life or the limb of the patient, shall be decided on by consultations with the Chief Physician and the Superintendent. In surgical cases requiring immediate treatment, the Superintendent is required to send for the Chief Surgeon, and, when unable to obtain his services, the Superintendent is authorized to call in Doctors Valentine Mott, Willard Parker, Gurdon Buck, Alfred C. Post, John Watson, or W. H. Van Buren, any of whom may perform such surgical operations as he may deem necessary.

4. All persons afflicted with diseases requiring Medical or Surgical treatment, shall be sent to their respective departments by the Examining Physician, and no patients shall be transferred from the Surgical or Medical Wards until cured of the malady for which they were admitted into it, unless subsequently attacked with a strictly pestilential disease; but no person shall be kept or retained in the Hospital Wards who does not require Medical or Surgical treatment, without the consent of the Superintendent.

5. The Chief Physician and Chief Surgeon shall appoint, with the approval of the Commissioners of Emigration, such number of Assistant Physicians and Surgeons as may be deemed necessary for the proper care, and Medical and Surgical treatment of the inmates of the Institution.

6. The Chief Physician and Chief Surgeon shall make such regulations for the sanitary treatment of the patients and inmates as may be found necessary, and prescribe and regulate the duties of the Assistant Physicians and Surgeons.

7. The Assistant Physicians and Surgeons shall be subject to the Rules and Regulations of the Institution, and shall perform all duties in the line of their profession that shall be required of them by their superiors.

8. They may be suspended by the Superintendent, Chief Physician or Chief Surgeon, and be removed from office by the Board of Commissioners of Emigration, and no assistant removed for cause shall be reappointed.

9. The Physicians and Assistant Surgeons shall make one regular daily morning visit to each patient in the wards under their charge, and shall also visit those afflicted with acute diseases as often as may be necessary. They shall report to the Superintendent, in writing, or to his Deputy, every Monday, Wednesday, and Friday, the names of all convalescent, or partially insane, who are able to work, and, in case they neglect this duty, the Superintendent may use his own judgment in setting those to work whom he may consider able. They shall make an afternoon visit to all patients received during the day. In no case shall an Assistant Physician or Surgeon absent himself from the Island, without the consent of the Chief Physician and the knowledge of the Superintendent. Non-observance of this rule will be considered equivalent to a resignation.

10. The Chief Physician and Chief Surgeon shall regulate the diet of the patients in the Hospital, as well as the hours of eating, and the mode of cooking the food; for this purpose, a regular diet table shall be prepared, which shall be revised as occasion may require, to be signed by the Superintendent.

11. No post-mortem examination shall be held without the assent of the Chief Medical or Surgical Officer of the department to which the patient belonged, and the Superintendent.

12. The Physicians and Surgeons shall make weekly report to the Superintendent of all admissions and discharges, elopements, births, and deaths during the preceding week ; and in all cases of smallpox, or other contagious diseases, they shall report such cases at the Superintendent's office immediately, that they may be removed without delay to the Marine Hospital.

REVISED RULES FOR THE STATE AGENCIES AND COUNTIES.

(*Adopted in January*, 1870.)

TO ALL ALMSHOUSE COMMISSIONERS, SUPERINTENDENTS, AND OVERSEERS OF THE POOR OF THE SEVERAL COUNTIES, CITIES, AND TOWNS OF THE STATE OF NEW YORK:

Notice is hereby given, that the Commissioners of Emigration, by virtue of the several Acts passed by the Legislature of this State on and since May 5, 1847, concerning passengers on vessels coming to the City of New York, and all other Acts passed by said Legislature of the State of New York in relation to the Commissioners of Emigration, have established the following *Revised* " Rules and Regulations," for the purpose of ascertaining the right, and the amount of the claim, of any city, town, or county, to indemnity from the fund created by the provisions of the aforesaid Acts, for the support of any persons, not citizens of the United States, who may have landed at the City of New York within the last five years.

RULE I.

Applications from the Superintendents or Overseers of the Poor of any city, town, or county, to the Commissioners of Emigration for indemnity for expenses incurred, can be received only in cases of persons who have arrived at the Port of New York within five years previous to the date of their application for relief, and who have not been absent from this State for twelve consecutive months, and for whom commutation money was paid or bonds given.

RULE II.

Applications to the Commissioners of Emigration must be accompanied by a statement of the name of the person in reference to whom it is made, his or her age, occupation, last place of residence before he or she came to this country, the name of the ship or vessel by which he or she arrived, the name of the Master or Commander of such ship or vessel, the foreign port at which he or she embarked, and the date of his or her arrival at New York; all of which must be verified by the oath of the party in whose behalf it is made, or, in case of his or her disability, by the oath of any other person cognizant of the facts; and no claim for indemnity will be allowed, unless the name of the person in respect to whom indemnity is sought shall be found in the "Report" of the Master of the vessel in which such person is said to have arrived, such "Re. port" having been sworn to by said Master before the Mayor of the City of New York, and on file in the Office of the Commissioners of Emigration.

RULE III.

Every application for indemnity must be accompanied by a statement, signed by the Relieving Officer: that the person in reference to whom it is made is unable to support himself or herself; from what cause his or her inability proceeds; whether such inability is likely to be temporary or permanent, and that he or she has no relations in this country able, at their own charge, to support him or her.

RULE IV.

Persons, in respect to whom applications for indemnity may be properly made, must be sent to and maintained in the poor-house of the city, town, or county; they must be required to work under the same circumstances and to the same extent as other inmates of such poor-houses; the account for their support must be rendered at the cost of their subsistence, after deducting the value of the work which they may be able to do and have performed—stating these particulars—and the account must be verified by the oath of the Superintendent or Overseer of the Poor that it is accarate and just.

RULE V.

No temporary or out-door relief, beyond one night's board and lodging, will be allowed, except on the affidavit of the Attending Physician that the person for whose relief indemnity is sought could not with safety be removed to the County House. A similar affidavit to accompany every bill containing similar charges.

RULE VI.

Superintendents of Poor, having claims against this Commission for medical attendance, must state, under oath, the whole amount paid for such attendance outside the County House during the year, the entire number who received that attendance, and how many of them were emigrants chargeable to the Commissioners of Emigration, and they will be allowed for, *pro rata*.

RULE VII.

The Commissioners of Emigration will reimburse the counties, etc., etc., the actual cost of support of emigrants under the foregoing "Rules," but will not pay for the services of Superintendents or Overseers of the Poor, or of any other officer not appointed by said Commissioners of Emigration.

RULE VIII.

Within ten days after the first day of every month a report must be made by the Superintendent or Overseer of the Poor of each city, town, or county, and be submitted to the Commissioners of Emigration, containing a statement of the emigrants who have been admitted and discharged during the previous month; the date of these admissions and discharges, with an account of their present condition and the expense incurred in their behalf; and unless this rule is strictly complied with, no expense incurred for emigrants previous to the time herein mentioned will be allowed.

V. An Act

FOR THE MORE EFFECTUAL PROTECTION OF EMIGRANTS ARRIVING AT THE PORT OF NEW YORK.

Chapter 857.

[Passed June 5, 1868, three-fifths being present.]

The People of the State of New York, represented in Senate and Assembly, do enact as follows:

Sec. 1. Each Commissioner of Emigration shall have power to administer an oath to, and examine under oath, any witness respecting any complaint made by any person relative to the ship in which any passenger was brought to the United States, or the treatment of any passenger during the voyage, or the food or drink furnished to any passenger on the voyage, or the death on the voyage of any passenger; but to entitle the same to be read upon the trial of any person accused of any crime or offence, such examination shall be made in the presence of the person complained of, who shall have a right to cross-examine every such witness.

Sec. 2. Such Commissioner shall cause such testimony to be reduced to writing before him, and shall sign and certify the same, and shall deliver such depositions, so signed and certified, to the Clerk of the County of New York, who shall file the same of record in his office, and shall enter a docket or minute of such filing, on payment of a fee of one dollar.

Sec. 3. The said clerk shall deliver a certified copy of such deposition to any person applying for the same, upon payment of a fee of twenty-five cents for such certificate, and of five cents for every folio of one hundred words therein contained.

Sec. 4. Such deposition and certified copies thereof shall be evidence in any action then or thereafter pending, between any of the passengers on such voyages, and the said ship, or her owners, master or charterers, victualling, manning, and navigating her for such voyage, upon any claim involving the facts therein testified to.

Sec. 5. Before taking such testimony, such Commissioners shall cause at least six hours' written notice thereof to the said vessel, her owners, master, or charterers, to be served on the owners personally, or on the master personally, or by handing a true copy thereof to the person found in charge of such vessel. The said notice, with an affidavit of service, which may be made before such Commissioner, shall be attached to the deposition; but such notice need not name the owner, master, or charterer, and such owner, master, or charterer, or their agent, may cross-examine said witness; but no examination shall be adjourned for more than twenty-four hours, unless by reason of sickness of such witness.

VI. MEMBERS OF THE COMMISSION

FROM ITS ORGANIZATION, 1847, TO 1870.

1847.

WM. F. HAVEMEYER, President, elected June 15, 1847.
GULIAN C. VERPLANCK.
JAMES BOORMAN.
JACOB HARVEY, died May 10, 1848.
ROBERT B. MINTURN.
DAVID C. COLDEN.
LEOPOLD BIERWIRTH, ex officio, Pres't German Society.
GREGORY DILLON, ex officio, Pres't Irish Em. Society.
WILLIAM V. BRADY, ex officio, Mayor City of New York.
FRANCIS B. STRYKER, ex officio, Mayor City of Brooklyn.

1848.

GULIAN C. VERPLANCK, President, elected March 1, 1848, vice Wm. F. Havemeyer, resigned.
JAMES BOORMAN, term expired May 5, 1849.
DAVID C. COLDEN.
ROBERT B. MINTURN.
ANDREW CARRIGAN, vice Wm. F. Havemeyer, resigned February 9, 1848.
WILLIAM McARDLE, vice Jacob Harvey, died May 10, 1848.
LEOPOLD BIERWIRTH, ex officio, Pres't German Society.
GREGORY DILLON, ex officio, Pres't Irish Em. Society.
WM. F. HAVEMEYER, ex officio, Mayor City of New York.
FRANCIS B. STRYKER, ex officio, Mayor City of Brooklyn.

1849.

GULIAN C. VERPLANCK, President.
CYRUS CURTISS, appointed June, 1849, vice James Boorman, term expired.
DAVID C. COLDEN.
ROBERT B. MINTURN.
ANDREW CARRIGAN, resigned Dec., 1849.
WILLIAM McARDLE.
GEO. E. KUNHARDT, Pres't German Soc'y.
GREGORY DILLON, Pres't Irish Em. Soc'y.
CALEB S. WOODHULL, Mayor City of New York.
EDWD. COPELAND, Mayor City of Br'klyn.

1850.

GULIAN C. VERPLANCK, President.
ROBERT B. MINTURN.
CYRUS CURTISS.
WM. McARDLE, term expired May, 1851.
ABRAM R. LAWRENCE, appointed vice David C. Colden, died April, 1850.
JOHN E. DEVELIN, appointed vice Andrew Carrigan, resigned Dec., 1849.
ADOLPH RODEWALD, Pres't German Soc'y.
GREGORY DILLON, Pres't Irish Em. Soc'y.
CALEB S. WOODHULL, Mayor City of New York.
SAMUEL SMITH, Mayor City of Brooklyn.

1851.

GULIAN C. VERPLANCK, President.
JOHN E. DEVELIN, resigned Dec., 1851.
CYRUS CURTISS.
ABRAM R. LAWRENCE, resigned Dec., 1851.
CHARLES H. MARSHALL, vice William McArdle, term expired.
ELIAS HICKS, vice Robert B. Minturn, resigned May, 1851.
FERDINAND KARCK, Pres't German Soc'y.
GREGORY DILLON, Pres't Irish Em. Soc'y.
A. C. KINGSLAND, Mayor City of New York.
CONKLIN BRUSH, Mayor City of Brooklyn.

1852.

GULIAN C. VERPLANCK, President.
CYRUS CURTISS.
CHARLES H. MARSHALL.
JAMES KELLY, appointed vice Abram R. Lawrence, resigned Dec., 1851.
GEORGE W. BLUNT, appointed vice John E. Develin, resigned Dec., 1851.
CALEB BARSTOW, appointed vice Elias Hicks, resigned Nov., 1852.
JOHN C. ZIMMERMANN, Sen., Pres't German Society.
GREGORY DILLON, Pres't Irish Em. Soc'y.
A. C. KINGSLAND, Mayor City of New York.
CONKLIN BRUSH, Mayor City of Brooklyn.

1853.

GULIAN C. VERPLANCK, President.
CHARLES H. MARSHALL.
THOMAS DUNLAP, appointed vice Caleb Barstow, term expired May, 1853.
TERENCE DONNELLY, vice George W. Blunt, nomination withdrawn.
JAMES KELLY.
JOHN A. KENNEDY, vice Cyrus Curtiss, resigned Oct., 1853.
JOHN C. ZIMMERMANN, Sen., Pres't German Society.
GREGORY DILLON, Pres't Irish Em. Soc'y.
JACOB A. WESTERVELT, Mayor City of New York.
EDWD. A. LAMBERT, Mayor City of Br'klyn.

1854.

GULIAN C. VERPLANCK, President.
CHARLES H. MARSHALL.
JAMES KELLY.
JOHN A. KENNEDY.
THOMAS DUNLAP.
ELIJAH F. PURDY, vice Terence Donnelly, resigned May, 1853.
R. A. WITTHAUS, Pres't German Society.
ANDREW CARRIGAN, President Irish Em. Society.
JACOB A. WESTERVELT, Mayor City of New York.
EDWD. A. LAMBERT, Mayor City of Br'klyn.

1855.

GULIAN C. VERPLANCK, President.
JAMES KELLY.
ELIJAH F. PURDY.
E. D. MORGAN, appointed May 7, 1855, vice Chas. H. Marshall, resigned.
JOHN A. KENNEDY.
JOHN P. CUMMING, appointed April 25, 1855, vice Thos. Dunlap, nomination withdrawn.
GUSTAV SCHWAB.
RUDOLPH GARRIGUE, President German Society, vice Gustav Schwab, resigned in March.
ANDREW CARRIGAN, President Irish Em. Society.
FERNANDO WOOD, Mayor City of N. York.
GEORGE HALL, Mayor City of Brooklyn.

1856.

GULIAN C. VERPLANCK, President.
ELIJAH F. PURDY.
JOHN P. CUMMING.
E. D. MORGAN.
CYRUS CURTISS, appointed March, 1856, vice James Kelly, resigned.
WILSON G. HUNT, appointed May, 1856, vice John A. Kennedy, resigned.
RUDOLPH GARRIGUE, President German Society.
ANDREW CARRIGAN, President Irish Em. Society.
FERNANDO WOOD, Mayor City of N. York.
GEORGE HALL, Mayor City of Brooklyn.

1857.

GULIAN C. VERPLANCK, President.
ELIJAH F. PURDY.
CYRUS CURTISS.
JOHN P. CUMMING.
E. D. MORGAN.
WILSON G. HUNT.
RUDOLPH GARRIGUE, President German Society.
ANDREW CARRIGAN, President Irish Em. Society.
DANIEL F. TIEMANN, Mayor City of New York.
S. S. POWELL, Mayor City of Brooklyn.

1858.

GULIAN C. VERPLANCK, President.
ELIJAH F. PURDY.
CYRUS CURTISS.
JOHN P. CUMMING.
WILSON G. HUNT.
EDWIN D. MORGAN.
WM. JELLINGHAUS, Pres't German Soc'y.
ANDREW CARRIGAN, President Irish Em. Society.
DANIEL F. TIEMANN, Mayor City of New York.
SAM. S. POWELL, Mayor City of Brooklyn.

1859.

GULIAN C. VERPLANCK, President.
ELIJAH F. PURDY.
CYRUS CURTISS.
JOHN P. CUMMING.
WILSON G. HUNT.
A. A. LOW, appointed vice E. D. Morgan, resigned Dec., 1858.
WM. JELLINGHAUS, Pres't German Soc'y.
ANDREW CARRIGAN, President Irish Em. Society.
GEORGE OPDYKE, Mayor City of N. York.
SAM. S. POWELL, Mayor City of Brooklyn.

1860.

GULIAN C. VERPLANCK, President.
ELIJAH F. PURDY.
CYRUS CURTISS.
JOHN P. CUMMING.
WILSON G. HUNT.
A. A. LOW.
WM. JELLINGHAUS, Pres't German Soc'y.
ANDREW CARRIGAN, President Irish Em. Society.
GEORGE OPDYKE, Mayor City of N. York.
SAM. S. POWELL, Mayor City of Brooklyn.

1861.

GULIAN C. VERPLANCK, President.
CYRUS CURTISS.
A. A. LOW.
WILSON G. HUNT.
JOHN P. CUMMING.
ELIJAH F. PURDY.
WM. JELLINGHAUS, Pres't German Soc'y.
ANDREW CARRIGAN, President Irish Em. Society.
GEORGE OPDYKE, Mayor City of N. York.
SAM. S. POWELL, Mayor City of Brooklyn.

1862.

GULIAN C. VERPLANCK, President.
CYRUS CURTISS.
ELIJAH F. PURDY.
JOHN P. CUMMING.
WILSON G. HUNT.
A. A. LOW.
E. VON DER HEYDT, President German Society.
ANDREW CARRIGAN, President Irish Em. Society.
GEORGE OPDYKE, Mayor City of N. York.
MARTIN KALBFLEISCH, Mayor City of Brooklyn.

1863.

GULIAN C. VERPLANCK, President.
CYRUS CURTISS.
ELIJAH F. PURDY.
JOHN P. CUMMING.
WILSON G. HUNT.
A. A. LOW.
E. VON DER HEYDT, President German Society.

ANDREW CARRIGAN, President Irish Em. Society.
C. GODFREY GUNTHER, Mayor City of New York.
—— —— Mayor City of Brooklyn.

1864.

GULIAN C. VERPLANCK, President.
CYRUS CURTISS.
JOHN P. CUMMING.
WILSON G. HUNT.
A. A. LOW.
ELIJAH F. PURDY.
A. SCHNIEWIND, Pres't German Society.
ANDREW CARRIGAN, President Irish Em. Society.
C. GODFREY GUNTHER, Mayor City of New York.
ALFRED M. WOOD, Mayor City of Brooklyn.

1865.

GULIAN C. VERPLANCK, President.
CYRUS CURTISS.
JOHN P. CUMMING.
WILSON G. HUNT.
A. A. LOW.
ELIJAH F. PURDY.
PHILIP BISSINGER, Pres't German Society.
ANDREW CARRIGAN, President Irish Em. Society.
C. GODFREY GUNTHER, Mayor City of New York.
ALFRED M. WOOD, Mayor City of Brooklyn.

1866.

GULIAN C. VERPLANCK, President.
WILSON G. HUNT, Vice-President.
F. S. WINSTON, vice Cyrus Curtiss, resigned April, 1866.
CYRUS H. LOUTREL, vice A. A. Low, resigned April, 1866.
ISAAC T. SMITH, vice Elijah F. Purdy, died January, 1866.
JOHN P. CUMMING.
PHILIP BISSINGER, Pres't German Society.
RICHARD O'GORMAN, President Irish Em. Society.
JOHN T. HOFFMAN, Mayor City of New York.
WILLIAM BOOTH, Mayor City of Brooklyn.

1867.

GULIAN C. VERPLANCK, President.
F. S. WINSTON, Vice-President.
CYRUS H. LOUTREL.
ISAAC T. SMITH.
FRIEDRICH KAPP, vice John P. Cumming, resigned Jan., 1867.
P. McELROY, vice Wilson G. Hunt, term expired June, 1867.
PHILIP BISSINGER, Pres't German Society.
RICHARD O'GORMAN, President Irish Em. Society.
JOHN T. HOFFMAN, Mayor City of New York.
WILLIAM BOOTH, Mayor City of Brooklyn.

1868.

GULIAN C. VERPLANCK, President.
F. S. WINSTON, Vice-President.
CYRUS H. LOUTREL.
ISAAC T. SMITH
FRIEDRICH KAPP.
P. McELROY.
PHILIP BISSINGER, Pres't German Society.
RICHARD O'GORMAN, President Irish Em. Society.
JOHN T. HOFFMAN, Mayor City of New York.
MARTIN KALBFLEISCH, Mayor City of Brooklyn.

1869.

GULIAN C. VERPLANCK, President.
F. S. WINSTON, Vice-President.
CYRUS H. LOUTREL.
ISAAC T. SMITH.
FRIEDRICH KAPP.
P. McELROY.
PHILIP BISSINGER, Pres't German Society.
RICHARD O'GORMAN, President Irish Em. Society.
A. OAKEY HALL, Mayor City of New York.
MARTIN KALBFLEISCH, Mayor City of Brooklyn.

1870.

GULIAN C. VERPLANCK, President.
F. S. WINSTON, Vice-President.
CYRUS H. LOUTREL.
ISAAC T. SMITH.
FRIEDRICH KAPP.
P. McELROY.
PHILIP BISSINGER, Pres't German Society.
JAMES LYNCH, President Irish Em. Society.
A. OAKEY HALL, Mayor City of New York.
MARTIN KALBFLEISCH, Mayor City of Brooklyn.

VII. Statistical Tables.

Statement of the number of Alien Passengers arriving in the United States by sea from foreign countries, from September 30, 1819, to December 31, 1860.

Year.	Males.	Females.	Sex not stated.	Total.
Year ending Sept. 30, 1820,	4,871	2,393	1,121	8,385
1821,	4,651	1,636	2,840	9,127
1822,	3,816	1,013	2,082	6,911
1823,	3,598	848	1,908	6,354
1824,	4,706	1,393	1,813	7,912
1825,	6,917	2,959	323	10,199
1826,	7,702	3,078	57	10,837
1827,	11,803	5,939	1,133	18,875
1828,	17,261	10,060	61	27,382
1829,	11,303	5,112	6,105	22,520
1830,	6,439	3,135	13,748	23,322
1831,	14,909	7,724	..	22,633
1832,	34,596	18,583	..	53,179
Quarter ending Dec. 31, 1832,	4,691	2,512	100	7,303
Year ending Dec. 31, 1833,	41,546	17,094	..	58,640
1834,	38,796	22,540	4,029	65,365
1835,	28,196	17,027	151	45,374
1836,	47,865	27,553	824	76,242
1837,	48,837	27,653	2,850	79,340
1838,	23,474	13,685	1,755	38,914
1839,	42,932	25,125	12	68,069
1840,	52,883	31,132	51	84,066
1841,	48,082	32,031	176	80,289
1842,	62,277	41,907	381	104,565
First three quarters of 1843,	30,069	22,424	3	52,496
Year ending Sept. 30, 1844,	44,431	34,184	..	78,615
1845,	65,015	48,115	1,241	114,371
1846,	87,777	65,742	897	154,416
1847,	136,086	97,917	965	234,968
1848,	133,906	92,149	472	226,527
1849,	177,232	119,280	512	297,024
Year ending Sept. 30, 1850,	196,331	112,635	1,038	310,004
Quarter ending Dec. 31, 1850,	32,990	26,805	181	59,976
Year ending Dec. 31, 1851,	217,181	162,219	66	379,466
1852,	212,469	157,696	1,438	371,603
1853,	207,958	160,615	72	368,645
1854,	256,177	171,656	..	427,833
1855,	115,307	85,567	3	200,877
1856,	115,846	84,590	..	200,436
1857,	146,215	105,091	..	251,306
1858,	72,824	50,002	300	123,126
1859,	69,161	51,640	481	121,282
1860,	88,477	65,077	86	153,640
Total, . .	2,977,603	2,035,536	49,275	5,062,414

The following aggregates also exhibit the number of arrivals of passengers from foreign countries during periods of nearly ten years each, and thus indicate the accelerated progress of immigration:

Periods.	Passengers of Foreign Birth.	American and Foreign.
In the 10 years ending September 30, 1829, . .	128,502	151,636
In the 10¼ years ending December 31, 1839, . .	538,381	572,716
In the 9¾ years ending September 30, 1849, . .	1,427,337	1,479,478
In the 11¼ years ending December 31, 1860, . .	2,968,194	3,255,591
In the 41¼ years ending December 31, 1860, . .	5,062,414	5,459,421

Adjusting the returns to the periods of the decennial census, by the aid of the quarterly reports, we find very nearly the following numbers:

Three Census Periods.	Passengers of Foreign Birth.
In the 10 years previous to June 1, 1840, ...	552,000
Do. do. do. 1850, ...	1,558,300
Do. do. do. 1860, ...	2,707,624

Distribution of Ages on Arrival.

Ages.	Number of Ages stated from 1820 to 1860.			Proportions.		
	Males.	Females.	Total.	Males.	Females.	Total.
Under 5, . .	218,417	200,676	419,093	4·143	3·806	7·949
5 and under 10,	199,704	180,606	380,310	3·788	3·425	7·213
10 and under 15,	194,580	166,833	361,413	3·691	3·164	6·855
15 and under 20,	404,338	349,755	754,093	7·669	6·633	14·302
20 and under 25,	669,853	428,974	1,098,827	12·706	8·136	20·842
25 and under 30,	576,822	269,554	846,376	10·940	5·112	16·052
30 and under 35,	352,619	163,778	516,397	6·688	3·106	9·794
35 and under 40,	239,468	114,165	353,633	4·542	2·165	6·707
40 and upwards,	342,022	200,322	542,344	6·487	3·799	10·286
Total, .	3,197,823	2,074,663	5,272,486	60·654	39·346	100·000

Total Proportions for Different Periods.

Ages.	1820 to 1830.	1830 to 1840.	1840 to 1850.	1850 to 1860.	1820 to 1860.
Under 5,	6·904	8·511	8·284	7·674	7·949
5 and under 10,	5·763	7·552	7·434	7·077	7·213
10 and under 15,	4·568	7·817	7·564	6·328	6·855
15 and under 20,	11·052	11·830	13·059	15·762	14·302
20 and under 25,	22·070	19·705	21·518	20·617	20·842
25 and under 30,	19·574	16·661	15·722	15·944	16·052
30 and under 35,	10·194	10·215	9·914	9·609	9·794
35 and under 40,	8·171	7·875	6·563	6·466	6·707
40 and upwards,	11·704	9·834	9·942	10·523	10·286
Total,	100·000	100·000	100·000	100·000	100·000

Occupation of Passengers arriving in the United States from foreign countries during the forty-one years ending with 1860.

Occupation.	1820 to 1830.	1831 to 1840.	1841 to 1850.	1851 to 1860.	1820 to 1860.
Merchants,	19,434	41,881	46,388	124,149	231,852
Farmers,	15,005	88,240	256,880	404,712	764,837
Mechanics,	6,805	56,582	164,411	179,726	407,524
Mariners,	4,995	8,004	6,398	10,087	29,484
Miners,	341	368	1,735	37,523	39,967
Laborers,	10,280	53,169	281,229	527,639	872,317
Shoemakers,	1,109	1,966	63	336	3,474
Tailors,	983	2,252	65	334	3,634
Seamstresses and Milliners,	413	1,672	2,096	1,065	5,246
Actors,	183	87	233	85	588
Weavers and Spinners,	2,937	6,600	1,303	717	11,557
Clergymen,	415	932	1,559	1,420	4,326
Clerks,	882	1,143	1,065	792	3,882
Lawyers,	244	461	831	1,140	2,676
Physicians,	805	1,959	2,116	2,229	7,109
Engineers,	226	311	654	825	2,016
Artists,	139	513	1,223	615	2,490
Teachers,	275	267	832	154	1,528
Musicians,	140	165	236	188	729
Printers,	179	472	14	40	705
Painters,	232	369	8	38	647
Masons,	793	1,435	24	58	2,310
Hatters,	137	114	1	4	256
Manufacturers,	175	107	1,833	1,005	3,120
Millers,	199	189	33	210	631
Butchers,	329	432	76	108	945
Bakers,	583	569	28	92	1,272
Servants,	1,327	2,571	24,538	21,058	49,494
Other Occupations,	5,466	4,004	2,892	13,844	26,206
Not stated,	101,442	363,252	969,411	1,544,494	2,978,599
Total,	176,473	640,086	1,768,175	2,874,687	5,459,421

Country where born.

Countries.	1820 to 1830.	1831 to 1840.	1841 to 1850.	1851 to 1860.	1820 to 1860.
England,	15,837	7,611	32,092	247,125	302,665
Ireland,	27,106	29,188	162,332	748,740	967,366
Scotland,	3,180	2,667	3,712	38,331	47,890
Wales,	170	185	1,261	6,319	7,935
Gt. Britain and Irel'd,	35,534	243,540	848,366	297,578	1,425,018
Total U. Kingdom,	81,827	283,191	1,047,763	1,338,093	2,750,874
France,	8,868	45,575	77,262	76,358	208,063
Spain,	2,616	2,125	2,209	9,298	16,248
Portugal,	180	829	550	1,055	2,614
Belgium,	28	22	5,074	4,738	9,862
Prussia,	146	4,250	12,149	43,887	60,432
Germany	7,583	148,204	422,477	907,780	1,486,044
Holland,	1,127	1,412	8,251	10,789	21,579
Denmark,	189	1,063	539	3,749	5,540
Norway and Sweden,	94	1,201	13,903	20,931	36,129
Poland,	21	369	105	1,164	1,659
Russia,	89	277	551	457	1,374
Turkey,	21	7	59	83	170
Switzerland,	3,257	4,821	4,644	25,011	37,733
Italy,	389	2,211	1,590	7,012	11,202
Greece,	20	49	16	31	116
Sicily,	17	35	79	429	560
Sardinia,	32	7	201	1,790	2,030
Corsica,	2	5	2	..	9
Malta,	1	35	78	5	119
Iceland,	..	..	..	10	10
Europe,	2	..	51	473	526
British America,	2,486	13,624	41,723	59,309	117,142
South America,	542	856	3,579	1,224	6,201
Central America,	107	44	368	449	968
Mexico,	4,818	6,599	3,271	3,078	17,766
West Indies,	3,998	12,301	13,528	10,660	40,487
China,	3	8	35	41,397	41,443
East Indies,	9	39	36	43	127
Persia,	..	..	7	15	22
Asia,	3	1	4	19	27
Liberia,	1	8	5	5	19
Egypt,	..	4	..	..	4
Morocco,	..	4	1	..	5
Algiers,	..	..	2	..	2
Barbary States,	4	..	..	..	4
Cape of Good Hope,	2	..	..	..	2
Africa,	10	36	47	186	279
Azores,	13	29	327	2,873	3,242
Canary Islands,	271	6	1	8	286
Madeira Islands,	70	52	3	189	314
Cape Verd Islands,	4	15	3	7	29
Sandwich Islands,	1	6	28	44	79
Society Islands,	..	..	1	6	7
Australia,	2	3	..	104	109
St. Helena,	..	1	3	13	17
Isle of France,	..	2	1	..	3
South Sea Islands,	79	..	..	..	79
New Zealand,	..	..	..	4	4
Not stated,	32,892	69,799	52,725	25,438	180,854
Total Aliens,	151,824	599,125	1,713,251	2,598,214	5,062,414
United States,	24,649	40,961	54,924	276,473	397,007
Total,	176,473	640,086	1,768,175	2,874,687	5,459,421

STATEMENT, BY OCCUPATIONS, *of the Passengers arrived in the United States during the Thirteen Years, from* 1856 *to* 1868 *inclusive.*

OCCUPATIONS.	1856.	1857.	1858.	1859.	1860.	1861.	1862.	1863.	1864.	1865.	1866.	1867.	1868.	Total.
Laborers . .	37,019	43,249	22,317	21,696	31,268	19,413	17,752	46,198	48,041	45,245	58,629	55,443	68,947	515,217
Farmers . .	24,722	34,702	20,506	16,323	21,742	11,668	9,265	12,349	13,837	20,012	30,302	29,717	19,804	264,949
Mechanics . .	9,805	18,074	11,995	13,092	13,033	7,575	6,934	14,418	14,156	20,218	23,939	25,966	17,298	196,503
Merchants . .	11,101	12,114	10,217	12,495	11,207	7,523	7,763	7,582	9,468	12,676	15,834	11,841	8,393	138,214
Miners . . .	6,136	5,660	4,254	9,510	3,834	2,337	1,732	4,314	6,093	7,631	8,010	7,205	4,698	71,414
Servants . .	1,748	1,322	1,142	1,281	1,415	770	3,704	9,088	15,629	9,236	8,905	6,367	8,021	68,628
Mariners . .	906	990	1,109	826	1,007	734	1,624	2,088	2,106	2,518	2,687	2,501	1,892	20,988
Clerks . . .	135	271	259	194	200	122	658	1,277	1,574	2,775	2,731	2,317	1,351	13,864
Bakers . . .	19	51	74	46	104	28	183	520	647	1,003	966	988	751	5,380
Butchers . .	54	22	38	38	58	27	194	403	545	842	840	974	623	4,658
S'mstr's & mil'nrs	215	258	261	250	273	49	182	347	640	304	373	336	282	3,770
Physicians . .	163	147	178	253	221	216	236	284	315	399	521	438	365	3,736
Artists . . .	37	69	45	97	80	31	88	377	340	606	662	661	468	3,561
Clergymen . .	118	173	132	157	183	213	274	231	258	374	453	454	302	3,322
Weavers & spin'rs	1,255	189	80	114	141	43	57	347	130	143	135	156	76	2,866
Tailors . .	25	108	156	137	204	41	66	75	147	366	322	299	205	2,151
Shoemakers .	22	86	117	141	156	383	85	73	148	209	272	250	186	2,128
Lawyers . .	90	78	113	166	116	106	108	156	132	249	359	252	17	1,942
Manufacturers .	22	187	74	62	50	218	94	66	107	181	254	198	183	1,696
Engineers . .	105	72	165	118	132	98	97	95	86	100	142	111	24	1,345
Teachers . .	35	28	46	86	57	22	19	16	29	59	142	33	237	809
Masons . .	10	16	68	40	59	22	21	31	37	77	132	184	102	799
Millers . .	73	26	39	37	48	29	21	5	24	40	54	65	36	497
Musicians . .	15	31	115	45	108	26	14	7	12	10	21	32	14	450
Actors . . .	4	44	33	54	27	5	17	15	20	18	47	94	..	378
Painters . .	1	31	31	15	29	11	3	27	29	43	65	60	18	363
Printers . .	12	21	19	8	14	12	22	15	19	20	44	22	19	247
Hatters . .	2	..	3	..	..	1	1	..	1	1	12	4	1	26
All other occup'ns	602	246	451	609	835	218	389	360	308	455	648	437	426	5,984
Occup's not spec.	130,045	153,717	70,869	77,619	93,090	60,761	62,860	99,047	106,657	161,589	202,442	192,222	191,493	1,602,411
Aggregate . .	224,496	271,982	144,906	155,509	179,691	112,702	114,463	199,811	221,535	287,399	359,943	339,627	326,232	2,938,296

TABLE *showing the Numbers and Nativities of Alien Emigrants who arrived at the Port of New York from May* 5, 1847, *to January* 1, 1870.

NATIONALITY.	1847.	1848.	1849.	1850.	1851.	1852.	1853.	1854.	1855.	1856.	1857.	1858.
Ireland	52,946	98,061	112,591	117,038	163,306	118,131	113,164	82,302	43,043	44,276	57,119	25.075
Germany	53,180	51,973	55,705	45,535	69,919	118,611	119,644	176,986	52,892	56,113	80,974	31,874
England	8,864	23,062	28,321	28,163	28,553	31,551	27,126	30,578	22,938	23,787	28,622	12,324
Scotland	2,354	6,415	8,840	6,772	7,302	7,694	6,456	4,909	4,240	4,723	5,170	2,718
France	3,330	2,734	2,683	3,462	5,964	8,868	7,470	7,986	4,174	2,984	3,069	1,786
Switzerland	1,947	1,622	1,405	2,380	4,499	6,471	4,604	8,883	3,273	2,559	2,454	1,315
Holland	3,611	1,560	2,447	1,174	1,798	1,223	1,085	1,466	822	1,666	1,734	348
Wales	472	1,054	1,782	1,520	2,189	2,531	1,182	1,288	1,118	1,376	887	566
Norway	882	1,207	3,300	3,150	2,112	1,889	377	81	203	438	62	3
Sweden	139	165	1,007	1,110	872	2,008	1,630	1,859	304	918	619	237
Italy	197	321	602	476	618	359	553	785	667	690	596	669
Belgium	551	..	118	230	475	82	34	398	1,201	850	444	253
Spain	101	253	214	257	278	471	659	646	457	330	263	146
West Indies	299	392	449	554	575	265	..	11	19	225	330	344
Denmark	95	52	159	90	229	157	94	102	174	469	453	284
Poland	26	79	133	188	422	188	186	169	346	142	245	88
Sardinia	..	..	172	165	98	69	72	148	67	426	405	324
South America	..	31	33	104	121	120	175	111	112	163	66	92
Portugal	34	57	287	65	26	37	237	205	24	30	93	27
Nova Scotia	..	..	151	164	81	73	6	128	9	30	40	18
Russia	10	28	38	18	23	33	39	55	20	56	42	19
Canada	..	..	59	61	50	48	..	2	64	57	30	17
Mexico	..	12	23	41	42	23	51	34	20	19	11	13
Sicily	..	..	21	28	12	42	37	58	18	10	26	19
China	..	2	9	11	22	14	53	20	18	8	11	15
East Indies	23	..	34	32	10	18	..	..	5	..	..	7
Greece	..	1	6	4	1	11	1	7	3	3	8	2
Turkey	1	..	6	4	4	5	10	6	2	4	..	6
Arabia	..	..	8	..	..	..	..	..	..	..	..	..
Africa	..	..	..	..	..	..	..	..	..	..	..	..
Australia	..	..	..	..	..	..	..	..	..	..	..	..
Japan	..	..	..	..	..	..	..	..	..	..	..	..
Central America	..	..	..	..	..	..	..	..	..	..	..	..
Unknown	..	95	..	..	..	..	..	..	..	..	..	..
Annual Totals	129,062	189,176	220,603	212,796	289,601	300,992	284,945	319,223	136,233	142,342	183,773	78,589

TABLE *showing the Numbers and Nativities of Alien Emigrants, etc.—continued.*

NATIONALITY.	1859.	1860.	1861.	1862.	1863.	1864.	1865.	1866.	1867.	1868.	1869.	Total.
Ireland	32,652	47,330	25,784	32,217	91,157	89,399	70,462	68,047	65,134	47,571	66,204	1,664,009
Germany	28,270	37,899	27,139	27,740	35,002	57,446	83,451	106,716	117,591	101,989	99,605	1,636,254
England	10,375	11,361	5,632	7,975	18,757	23,710	27,286	36,186	33,712	29,695	41,090	539,668
Scotland	2,325	1,617	659	692	1,937	1,126	3,962	4,979	6,315	7,390	10,643	111,238
France	1,532	1,549	1,200	1,187	1,303	1,804	2,059	3,246	3,204	2,811	2,795	77,200
Switzerland	791	1,422	1,398	1,254	1,194	1,652	2,513	3,685	3,985	3,302	2,999	65,607
Holland	261	440	331	456	407	615	729	1,506	2,156	1,265	1,247	28,347
Wales	500	811	697	1,062	1,143	659	505	540	142	699	1,111	23,834
Norway	36	53	93	22	238	88	158	583	309	1,008	3,465	19,757
Sweden	318	361	382	663	1,370	1,516	2,337	3,907	4,843	14,529	23,453	64,538
Italy	399	542	750	487	444	475	591	918	1,032	993	1,548	14,712
Belgium	57	76	165	195	456	186	97	157	1,623	149	146	7,943
Spain	234	228	190	124	202	196	224	315	203	210	210	6,411
West Indies	416	523	165	156	256	236	283	246	214	171	378	6,507
Denmark	493	495	612	1,689	1,580	565	727	1,526	1,372	1,087	2,600	15,104
Poland	114	80	43	50	137	198	423	231	268	268	598	4,622
Sardinia	164	89	67	39	..	..	..	..	..	1	..	2,306
South America	138	110	88	92	60	124	109	155	97	134	102	2,337
Portugal	45	19	14	13	3	34	42	96	79	13	60	1,530
Nova Scotia	81	23	11	67	77	40	77	40	22	52	119	1,309
Russia	69	61	36	46	47	37	93	154	185	145	376	1,630
Canada	25	25	19	33	17	35	43	28	42	33	27	715
Mexico	13	22	45	13	38	92	70	56	28	34	90	790
Sicily	1	4	1	9	1	3	3	1	..	3	..	297
China	4	13	10	15	5	41	36	26	17	49	15	414
East Indies	..	4	2	1	3	1	7	15	4	2	25	193
Greece	6	2	1	6	2	13	5	5	8	10	7	112
Turkey	3	3	5	3	2	5	5	8	6	22	5	115
Arabia	..	..	..	..	..	..	..	..	..	..	..	8
Africa	..	..	..	..	6	..	37	15	2	10	17	87
Australia	..	..	..	..	..	..	..	..	44	26	12	112
Japan	..	..	..	..	..	..	18	12	87	3	4	101
Central America	..	..	..	..	..	..	..	7	7	21	38	78
Unknown	..	..	..	..	..	..	..	12	..	..	..	107
Annual Totals	79,322	105,162	65,539	76,306	156,844	182,296	196,352	233,418	242,731	213,686	258,989	4,297,980

Avowed Destination of Passengers landed at Castle Garden, from August 1st, 1855, to January 1st, 1870.

DESTINATION.	1855.	1856.	1857.	1858.	1859.	1860.	1861.	1862.	1863.	1864.	1865.	1866.	1867.	1868.	1869.	Total.
New York	19,489	55,055	78,585	34,296	40,923	56,131	32,783	38,312	84,105	92,409	99,438	97,607	91,610	65,714	85,810	972,267
Pennsylvania	4,469	11,749	16,600	6,708	7,370	9,512	5,114	6,116	15,395	18,212	22,276	24,874	27,424	16,926	32,135	224,880
Illinois	3,444	11,064	15,750	6,690	3,940	4,077	4,010	5,009	8,435	11,531	17,177	22,386	26,964	34,625	38,213	213,315
Wisconsin	4,667	13,327	12,704	4,953	2,441	2,589	3,217	4,574	5,075	4,365	6,127	9,160	14,921	16,537	17,003	121,660
Ohio	3,250	7,085	10,054	6,176	4,668	5,195	3,863	3,942	6,574	9,257	10,316	12,923	13,812	11,133	12,180	120,428
Massachusetts	2,037	6,494	6,904	3,212	5,119	6,371	3,433	4,453	11,734	14,129	8,957	11,874	10,424	7,604	8,384	111,129
Canada	3,346	8,526	9,673	4,218	2,212	1,877	1,554	2,830	3,089	2,644	1,367	1,741	2,333	2,723	2,695	50,828
New Jersey	1,119	3,242	3 806	1,922	2,621	3,414	1,892	1,483	3,744	5,306	5,395	7,877	7,271	5,916	8,101	63,109
Unknown	1,354	6,300	6,469	1,967	2,029	3,542	....	2,457	....	....	11	96	10	....	....	22,035
Michigan	1,648	3,296	4,108	1,697	1,305	1,478	1,520	1,900	3,062	3,167	3,178	4,185	7,119	7,324	7,218	52,205
Connecticut	829	2,292	2,974	1,227	1,929	2,579	1,416	1,248	3,339	3,603	2,323	3,711	4,209	3,458	4,032	39,169
Iowa	795	2,380	3,775	1,724	664	776	1,289	1,082	1,094	1,948	3,400	4,493	5,610	7,040	8,216	44,286
Missouri	434	1,064	2,366	1,690	1,598	1,614	900	850	2,188	3,379	5,016	4,918	7,361	6,517	4,414	44,309
Indiana	881	1,388	2,474	1,271	1,122	1,206	906	938	1,357	1,826	2,730	3,201	3,240	3,852	3,184	29,576
Rhode Island	551	1,354	1,389	510	1,001	1,291	530	481	1,696	1,848	1,353	2,392	2,470	2,279	2,285	21,430
Maryland	485	1,164	1,535	907	902	1,014	434	401	1,012	1,580	1,888	1,818	1,704	1,604	1,585	18,033
California	447	778	877	1,084	1,108	1,141	1,028	1,423	1,149	1,459	877	1,678	1,979	3,989	3,806	22,823
Minnesota	127	427	1,253	828	542	466	760	942	1,433	1,109	1,514	3,459	3,783	5,891	6,826	29,360
Utah	250	1,579	14	3	740	905	1,441	3,418	3,561	1,694	1,092	3,082	514	3,115	2,327	23,735
Virginia	292	567	702	548	575	452	481	102	187	334	560	1,006	913	731	785	8,235
Kentucky	183	460	660	520	546	650	301	215	593	910	1,060	1,636	1,670	1,392	881	11,657
District of Columbia	202	407	232	336	308	301	168	585	1,054	1,026	1,229	890	817	873	401	9,129
Vermont	168	250	297	172	198	270	135	153	297	362	263	238	559	533	510	4,405
Louisiana	60	171	206	240	255	321	180	50	240	327	268	550	669	567	249	4,353
South Carolina	80	178	157	168	185	296	45	2	...	6	77	171	192	148	149	1,854
Maine	143	148	186	210	122	142	176	121	340	609	413	330	550	293	230	4,013
Tennessee	72	178	127	165	147	269	62	56	190	398	393	566	489	549	510	4,171
Georgia	70	147	167	162	193	178	35	2	4	...	22	225	264	127	127	1,623
New Hampshire	71	177	179	69	131	123	89	63	110	562	202	189	311	411	172	2,859
Delaware	40	81	113	65	117	42	16	55	110	143	149	238	281	409	152	2,011
New Brunswick	2	...	97	75	82	63	98	43	99	89	50	60	98	113	59	1,028
Texas	5	76	55	43	52	92	38	3	6	2	41	124	427	266	292	1,522

Avowed Destination of Passengers landed at Castle Garden, &c.—Continued.

DESTINATION.	1855.	1856.	1857.	1858.	1859.	1860.	1861.	1862.	1863.	1864.	1865.	1866.	1867.	1868.	1869.	Total.
Kansas	1	11	25	88	77	43	25	63	122	281	388	468	706	1,085	1,669	5.052
North Carolina	11	66	41	52	48	15	52	.....	.....	7	37	140	83	114	118	784
Mississippi	6	14	62	21	50	45	12	.....	.....	1	52	65	73	84	118	603
Alabama	7	30	21	24	39	21	11	.....	7	.....	27	96	75	114	105	577
New Dominion	30	2	42	56	17	47	22	149	65	43	45	57	77	150	49	816
Nebraska	.....	2	27	42	31	18	3	.....	89	13	116	119	640	1,410	1,653	4,198
South America	25	30	18	14	36	29	13	7	28	15	34	27	32	185	91	556
Cuba	.....	.....	25	32	46	21	20	17	29	29	50	11	21	14	6	349
Arkansas	8	30	9	10	16	17	3	6	.....	.....	4	32	71	78	18	302
Florida	13	12	5	11	32	9	6	6	1	4	5	10	29	34	22	199
Mexico	.....	12	1	5	7	13	4	3	18	10	71	19	26	14	7	210
Oregon	1	.....	7	6	6	9	6	.....	2	23	18	38	19	30	24	189
West Indies	2	11	.....	6	5	1	4	7	.....	17	15	15	18	14	26	141
New Mexico	.....	.....	5	.....	23	8	3	.....	.....	.....	.....	.....	.....	5	6	50
Central America	.....	.....	.....	3	9	23	10	5	5	.....	.....	7	28	21	2	113
Vancouver's Isle	.....	.....	.....	.....	1	3	1	.....	.....	.....	.....	.....	.....	.....	1	6
Washington Territory	.....	.....	.....	.....	3	.....	.....	.....	.....	.....	.....	.....	.....	.....	3	6
Australia	.....	1	.....	.....	.....	1	1	1	2	1	.....	3	2	.....	1	13
Bermuda	.....	.....	.....	.....	1	1	.....	.....	.....	.....	.....	.....	.....	.....	.....	2
Sandwich Isles	.....	.....	.....	.....	.....	1	.....	.....	.....	.....	.....	.....	.....	.....	.....	1
Russian America	.....	.....	.....	.....	.....	.....	1	.....	.....	.....	.....	.....	.....	.....	.....	1
British Columbia	.....	.....	.....	.....	.....	.....	.....	295	8	22	7	11	39	66	18	466
Nevada	.....	.....	.....	.....	.....	.....	.....	.....	.....	.....	.....	4	17	18	41	80
Colorado	.....	.....	.....	.....	.....	.....	.....	.....	.....	.....	.....	30	22	38	80	170
Idaho	.....	.....	.....	.....	.....	.....	.....	.....	.....	.....	.....	1	7	15	9	32
Dakotah	.....	.....	.....	.....	.....	.....	.....	.....	.....	.....	.....	.....	2	38	9	49
West Virginia	.....	.....	.....	.....	.....	.....	.....	.....	.....	.....	.....	.....	.....	22	150	172
Montana	.....	.....	.....	.....	.....	.....	.....	.....	.....	.....	.....	.....	.....	14	19	33
Japan	.....	.....	.....	.....	.....	.....	.....	.....	.....	.....	.....	.....	.....	.....	1	1
Wyoming Territory	.....	.....	.....	.....	.....	.....	.....	.....	.....	.....	.....	.....	.....	.....	5	5
China	.....	.....	.....	.....	.....	.....	.....	.....	.....	.....	.....	.....	.....	.....	6	6
Totals	51,114	141,525	185,076	84,226	85,602	108,682	68,311	81,458	161,648	184,700	200,031	228,851	241,985	216,222	257,188	2,296,619

GENERAL TABLE,

Showing the number of Aliens arrived and landed at the Port of New York for whom bonds were demanded or Commutation and Hospital moneys were paid, as also the total number treated, cared for, forwarded, &c., classified under the different heads, together with the total amount of Receipts from all sources, and the whole amount of expenditures, from the organization of the Commissioners of Emigration, May 5, 1847, to December 31st, 1869.

YEAR.	Number of Aliens arrived for whom Commutation and Hospital moneys were paid and bonds demanded.	Number treated and cared for in Ward's Island Institutions.	Number treated in Marine Hospital, Staten Island, until transferred from control of Commissioners of Emigration.	Number supplied temporarily with board and lodging and money relief in the City.	Number supplied temporarily with food at Castle Garden Landing Depot.	Number provided with employment through the Labor Exchange.	Number forwarded to destination in U. S. and Europe, &c.	Number treated in other Institutions in this City at expense of this Commission.	Number relieved and provided for in various Counties of this State at expense of this Commission.	Grand total of persons treated, cared for, relieved, forwarded, &c., by and at expense of the Commissioners of Emigration.	Total Receipts of Commutation and Hospital Moneys, and from all sources.	Total Expenditures.
1847....	129,062	1,629	6,474	503	......	....	798	1,190	....	10,594	$193,292 10	$148,147 31
1848....	189,176	4,057	8,661	6,640	......	....	2,102	694	5,369	27,523	301,901 99	274,833 49
1849....	220,603	8,320	6,159	16,854	......	....	2,999	1,360	5,566	41,258	318,608 29	378,817 34
1850....	212,796	10,156	3,411	27,314	......	8,000	2,301	267	5,937	57,386	358,010 36	369,461 39
1851....	289,601	14,939	6,343	23,941	......	18,204	7,391	1,658	12,550	85,026	469,538 27	463,654 00
1852....	300,992	15,182	8,887	117,568	......	14,971	4,601	1,364	18,432	181,005	572,329 26	569,516 74
1853....	284,945	14,365	4,796	44,514	......	14,334	3,262	1,152	9,351	91,774	591,651 92	586,859 19
1854....	319,223	15,950	4,762	69,085	......	13,964	4,608	2,021	10,504	120,894	688,802 98	635,215 77
1855....	136,233	12,901	2,402	93,925	......	15,151	4,996	807	12,175	142,357	365,966 24	490,189 77
1856....	142,342	7,610	1,648	11,172	......	9,378	589	1,081	5,346	36,824	311,244 34	257,416 02
1857....	183,773	8,539	1,856	5,411	......	10,933	529	864	4,253	32,385	392,270 43	350,911 79
1858....	78,589	6,906	1,204	6,144	......	9,346	515	245	4,200	26,560	191,368 64	217,868 25
1859....	79,322	4,361	274	4,582	......	7,150	176	485	2,407	19,435	182,566 34	199,875 78
1860....	105,162	4,729	......	5,237	......	7,717	401	527	2,104	20,715	289,467 92	210,359 66
1861....	65,539	5,079	......	3,186	1,389	4,807	950	340	5,123	20,874	175,434 56	178,401 77
1862....	76,306	3,247	......	835	1,098	5,261	278	132	5,707	16,558	174,454 29	138,524 56
1863....	156,844	4,911	......	1,743	3,019	11,817	365	138	8,563	30,556	341,027 00	333,105 71
1864....	182,296	7,363	......	1,737	2,904	9,993	266	287	6,407	28,957	420,366 17	373,763 39
1865....	196,352	7,425	......	975	4,243	8,681	361	379	7,516	29,580	471,034 85	447,580 20
1866....	233,418	10,306	......	3,158	3,343	8,494	521	203	12,943	38,968	544,056 16	545,983 21
1867....	242,731	13,237	......	1,905	7,284	10,325	613	235	11,367	44,966	583,154 40	534,362 22
1868....	213,686	14,250	......	2,396	14,569	31,143	902	277	8,394	71,931	577,349 36	662,958 12
1869....	258,989	13,911	......	1,103	13,799	34,955	917	1,801	6,701	73,187	695,499 59	606,158 58
Total,	4,297,980	201,373	56,877	447,928	51,648	254,624	40,441	17,507	170,915	1,249,333	$9,209,395 46	$8,973,964 26

STATEMENT

Showing Amount Reimbursed by the Commissioners of Emigration to the City and County of New York, and the several other Cities and Counties in the State of New York, and to various Charitable Institutions and Hospitals in the State, for Care and Support of Emigrants, from May 5, 1847, *to December* 31, 1869, *inclusive.*

Year.	City of New York.	Institutions.	Counties.	Total.
1847	$2,333 36	$280 00	$2,270 68	$4,884 04
1848	2,540 00	1,487 93	18,421 95	22,449 88
1849	6,306 98	1,857 59	37,400 95	45,565 52
1850	10,832 75	2,650 71	26,736 40	40,219 86
1851	13,042 94	8,784 40	67,781 17	89,608 51
1852	10,912 97	12,755 08	64,763 90	88,431 95
1853	20,000 00	9,737 01	122,135 16	151,872 17
1854	27,525 36	9,117 50	78,532 85	115,175 71
1855	..	8,645 56	43,181 17	51,826 73
1856	..	10,528 07	13,439 97	23,968 04
1857	..	6,680 16	85,563 85	92,244 01
1858	..	8,002 73	16,893 16	24,895 89
1859	206 29	6,173 92	23,555 75	29,935 96
1860	753 81	7,001 68	51,113 59	58,869 08
1861	2,237 94	6,373 36	11,244 63	19,855 93
1862	1,051 11	4,545 83	10,419 12	16,016 06
1863	810 76	5,402 96	9,578 50	15,792 22
1864	2,453 62	5,207 09	11,689 00	19,349 71
1865	5,370 36	8,950 38	17,944 05	32,264 79
1866	2,814 10	9,201 70	22,980 39	34,996 19
1867	1,689 59	10,095 99	22,160 29	33,945 87
1868	63,976 08	12,920 72	24,840 40	101,737 20
1869	18,986 76	11,971 59	17,788 31	48,746 66
	$193,844 78	$168,371 96	$800,435 24	$1,162,651 98

WAGES.*

I.—*The Average Wages paid at the Labor Exchange for Unskilled Labor during the Years* 1868 *and* 1869.

	Males, per Month.		Females, per Month.	
	1868.	1869.	1868.	1869.
January	$10 00	$9 00	$8 00	$9 00
February	10 50	11 50	8 50	9 25
March	12 50	11 50	8 50	10 00
April	15 00	18 50	9 00	10 00
May	18 00	19 25	9 00	10 00
June	20 00	23 75	9 00	10 00
July	24 00	24 00	9 50	10 00
August	16 00	17 25	9 00	10 00
September	14 00	14 25	9 00	10 00
October	12 00	14 50	9 50	10 00
November	12 00	13 25	9 00	9 50
December	10 00	10 00	8 50	9 00

The wages for common laborers varied from $1 75 to $2 per day, without board.

* The following circular letter is from time to time published by the Chief Clerk of the Labor Exchange, for the information of all employers who would avail themselves of the advantages of this institution:

"1. The 'Labor Exchange,' lately organized by the Commissioners of Emigration of the State of New York, is a free market for emigrant labor, open to all employers from all parts of the United States. While prcouring prompt and remunerative employment to emigrants, it offers to employers superior opportunities to choose suitable employees out of the large and varied supply of applicants for work daily resorting to this office.

"2. This office charges no fees, commissions, nor any other remuneration from employer or employee.

"It furnishes to employers not only domestic help, agricultural or unskilled labor, but also all kind of skilled laborers, mechanics, artisans, etc.

"3. Land speculators are excluded from the privileges of this office; and all propositions contemplating the sale or leasing of land to emigrants will be rejected.

"4. Employers applying at this office must be either known to the Superintendent, or produce satisfactory references.

"Agents must be duly authorized by their principals, and well recommended.

"5. This office does not make contracts for emigrants with the employer; it does not fix the amount of wages nor the term of service, nor prescribe any other condition of the contract; it leaves all these matters to be settled by the voluntary agreement of the parties immediately interested, and assists them only by giving all needful information and advice.

"6. Employers must provide for and take care of the transportation for their employees to the respective places of destination. If means sufficient to cover travelling expenses are remitted to this office, with the request to send hired help to the applicant, we shall see to it that the employee is properly started on his voyage. The expenses and risk of transportation to distant places will be greatly reduced, if employers residing in the country, and desiring emigrant help, would club together, and appoint one of their number employing and forwarding agent for all the members of the club."

II.—*Wages paid for Skilled Labor in New York City during the Year* 1869.

Apprentices	$4 to $5 per week ; no board.
Bakers	$6 to $14 per month, and board.
Barbers	$9 to $15 per week ; no board.
Brushmakers	$2 to $2 50 per day ; no board.
Barkeepers	$10 to $30 per month, and board.
Basketmakers	$8 to $15 per week ; no board.
Blacksmiths	$2 to $3 50 per day ; no board.
Bookbinders	$7 to $18 per week ; no board.
Bricklayers	$5 per day ; no board.
Brewers	$15 to $25 per month, and board.
Brassfinishers	$10 to $20 per week ; no board.
Butchers	$10 to $20 per month, and board.
Cabinetmakers	$1 50 to $3 per day ; no board.
Cooks	$25 to $100 per month, and board.
Capmakers	$8 to $12 per week, and board.
Chemists	$10 to $12 per week ; no board.
Carpenters	$3 to $3 50 per day ; no board.
Carriagemakers	$2 50 to $3 per day ; no board.
Cheesemakers	$20 per month, and board.
Cigarmakers	$8 to $15 per week ; no board.
Confectioners	$30 to $50 per month, and board.
Cutlers	$12 to $15 per week ; no board.
Coopers	$18 to $20 per week ; no board.
Dyers	$20 to $25 per month, and board.
Deckhands	$25 to $30 per month, and board
Druggists	$18 to $25 per month, and board
Engravers	$15 to $35 per week ; no board.
Engineers	$15 to $18 per week ; no board.
Florists	$15 to $25 per month, and board
Filecutters	$12 to $18 per week ; no board.
Furriers	$9 to $14 per week ; no board.
Frescoe-painters	$15 to $35 per week ; no board.
Gilders	$10 to $18 per week ; no board.
Gardeners	$15 to $25 per month, and board.
Glaziers	$8 to $12 per week ; no board.
Gasfitters	$12 to $18 per week ; no board.
Goldsmiths	$10 to $30 per week ; no board.
Gunsmiths	$10 to $18 per week ; no board.
Hatters	$15 to $20 per week ; no board.
Heaters	$25 to $30 per month, and board.
Harnessmakers	$10 to $15 per week ; no board.
Ironmoulders	$15 to $18 per week ; no board.
Locksmiths	$8 to $15 per week ; no board.
Lithographers	$12 to $25 per week ; no board.
Machinists	$15 to $18 per week ; no board.

Masons	$5 per day; no board.
Miners	90 cents and $1 per ton; no board.
Millers	$12 to $18 per month, and board.
Polishers	$10 to $15 per week; no board.
Paperhangers	$10 to $15 per week; no board.
Puddlers	$2 per day; no board.
Plasterers	$5 per day; no board.
Plumbers	$2 50 to $3 per day; no board.
Printers	$12 to $18 per week; no board.
Porters	$8 to $15 per week; no board.
Painters	$10 to $15 per week; no board.
Ropemakers	$12 per week; no board.
Slate-roofers	$2 50 to $3 per day; no board.
Saddlers	$12 to $15 per week; no board.
Shoemakers	$9 to $15 per week; no board.
Soapmakers	$10 to $12 per week; no board.
Spinners	$9 to $12 per week; no board.
Stonecutters	$5 per day; no board.
Tailors	$10 to $30 per week; no board.
Tanners	$15 per month, and board.
Tinsmiths	$10 to $15 per week; no board.
Turners	$10 to $18 per week; no board.
Upholsterers	$12 to $18 per week; no board.
Varnishers	$9 to $12 per week; no board.
Waiters	$30 per month, and board.
Watchmakers	$15 to $20 per week; no board.
Weavers	$9 to $12 per week; no board.
Wheelwrights	$10 to $12 per week; no board.
Woodcarvers	$12 to $18 per week; no board.
Winecoopers	$30 per month, and board.
Wagonsmiths	$10 to $18 per week; no board.

TABLE

Showing the Number of Passengers brought to New York by Sailing and Steam Vessels, and the Comparative Mortality and Births on the Voyage, from the Years 1864 *to* 1869 *inclusive.*

	STEAMSHIPS.						SAILING-VESSELS.						TOTAL.					
Years.	Number of Vessels.	Cabin Passengers.	Steerage Passengers.	Births.	Deaths.	Percentage of Deaths of all Passeng's.	Number of Vessels.	Cabin Passengers.	Steerage Passengers.	Births.	Deaths.	Percentage of Deaths of St'rage Pass.	Number of Vessels.	Cabin Passengers.	Steerage Passengers	Births.	Deaths.	Percentage of Deaths of St'rage Pass.
1864	196	9,729	78,200	46	74	0·0946	349	773	102,070	186	750	0·7348	546	10,502	180,270	232	824	0·4571
1865	220	14,621	112,701	52	118	0·1047	302	661	83,770	186	581	0·6943	522	15,282	196,471	238	699	0·3558
1866	401	27,507	156,931	83	816	0·5200	349	636	74,898	162	851	1·1363	750	28,143	231,829	245	1,667	0·7190
1867	464	29,187	193,445	99	255	0·1318	282	543	48,495	127	494	1·0186	746	29,730	241,940	226	749	0·3096
1868	451	27,937	180,449	96	200	0·1108	200	241	31,953	102	393	1·2299	651	28,178	212,402	198	593	0·2792
1869	504	29,471	229,190	110	210	0·0913	209	273	28,333	76	138	0·4871	713	29,744	257,523	186	348	0·1351

Made in the USA
Monee, IL
20 October 2026

66035304R00148